Deep Learning Essentials

Your hands-on guide to the fundamentals of deep learning
and neural network modeling

Wei Di
Anurag Bhardwaj
Jianing Wei

BIRMINGHAM - MUMBAI

Deep Learning Essentials

Commissioning Editor: Veena Pagare
Acquisition Editor: Aman Singh
Content Development Editor: Snehal Kolte
Technical Editor: Sayli Nikalje
Copy Editor: Safis Editing
Project Coordinator: Manthan Patel
Proofreader: Safis Editing
Indexer: Francy Puthiry
Graphics: Tania Datta
Production Coordinator: Arvindkumar Gupta

First published: January 2018

Production reference: 1250118

Published by Packt Publishing Ltd.
Livery Place
35 Livery Street
Birmingham
B3 2PB, UK.

ISBN 978-1-78588-036-0

www.packtpub.com

`mapt.io`

Mapt is an online digital library that gives you full access to over 5,000 books and videos, as well as industry leading tools to help you plan your personal development and advance your career. For more information, please visit our website.

Why subscribe?

- Spend less time learning and more time coding with practical eBooks and Videos from over 4,000 industry professionals

- Improve your learning with Skill Plans built especially for you

- Get a free eBook or video every month

- Mapt is fully searchable

- Copy and paste, print, and bookmark content

PacktPub.com

Did you know that Packt offers eBook versions of every book published, with PDF and ePub files available? You can upgrade to the eBook version at `www.PacktPub.com` and as a print book customer, you are entitled to a discount on the eBook copy. Get in touch with us at `service@packtpub.com` for more details.

At `www.PacktPub.com`, you can also read a collection of free technical articles, sign up for a range of free newsletters, and receive exclusive discounts and offers on Packt books and eBooks.

Contributors

About the authors

Wei Di is a data scientist with many years, experience in machine learning and artificial intelligence. She is passionate about creating smart and scalable intelligent solutions that can impact millions of individuals and empower successful businesses. Currently, she works as a staff data scientist at LinkedIn. She was previously associated with the eBay Human Language Technology team and eBay Research Labs. Prior to that, she was with Ancestry.com, working on large-scale data mining in the area of record linkage. She received her PhD from Purdue University in 2011.

I'd like to thank my family for their support of my work. Also, thanks to my two little kids, Ivan and Elena, in their young and curious hearts, I see the pursuit of new challenges every day, which encouraged me to take this opportunity to write this book.

Anurag Bhardwaj currently leads the data science efforts at Wiser Solutions, where he focuses on structuring a large scale e-commerce inventory. He is particularly interested in using machine learning to solve problems in product category classification and product matching, as well as various related problems in e-commerce. Previously, he worked on image understanding at eBay Research Labs. Anurag received his PhD and master's from the State University of New York at Buffalo and holds a BTech in computer engineering from the National Institute of Technology, Kurukshetra, India.

Jianing Wei is a senior software engineer at Google Research. He works in the area of computer vision and computational imaging. Prior to joining Google in 2013, he worked at Sony US Research Center for 4 years in the field of 3D computer vision and image processing. Jianing obtained his PhD in electrical and computer engineering from Purdue University in 2010.

I would like to thank my co-authors, Wei Di and Anurag Bhardwaj, for their help and collaboration in completing this book. I have learned a lot in this process. I am also really grateful to my family for their support.

About the reviewer

Amita Kapoor is Associate Professor in the Department of Electronics, SRCASW, University of Delhi. She did both her master's and PhD in electronics. During her PhD, she was awarded the prestigious DAAD fellowship to pursue a part of her research work in the Karlsruhe Institute of Technology, Germany. She won the Best Presentation Award at the 2008 International Conference on Photonics for her paper. She is a member of professional bodies including the Optical Society of America, the International Neural Network Society, the Indian Society for Buddhist Studies, and the IEEE.

Packt is searching for authors like you

If you're interested in becoming an author for Packt, please visit `authors.packtpub.com` and apply today. We have worked with thousands of developers and tech professionals, just like you, to help them share their insight with the global tech community. You can make a general application, apply for a specific hot topic that we are recruiting an author for, or submit your own idea.

Table of Contents

Preface

Deep learning is the most disruptive trend in the tech world, having jumped out of research laboratories right into production environments. It is the science and art of working through hidden layers of data to get deep insights. Deep learning is currently one of the best providers of solutions to problems in image recognition, speech recognition, object recognition, and **natural language processing** (**NLP**).

We'll start off by brushing up on machine learning and quickly get into the fundamentals of deep learning and its implementation. Moving on, we'll teach you about the different types of neural networks and their applications in the real world. With the help of insightful examples, you'll learn to recognize patterns using a deep neural network and get to know other important concepts such as data manipulation and classification.

Using the reinforcement learning technique with deep learning, you'll build AI that can outperform any human and also work with the LSTM network. During the course of this book, you will come across a wide range of different frameworks and libraries, such as TensorFlow, Python, Nvidia, and others. By the end of the book, you'll be able to deploy a production-ready deep learning framework for your own applications.

Who this book is for

If you are an aspiring data scientist, deep learning enthusiast, or AI researcher looking to build the power of deep learning to your business applications, then this book is the perfect resource for you to start addressing AI challenges.

To get the most out of this book, you must have intermediate Python skills and be familiar with machine learning concepts well in advance.

What this book covers

Chapter 1, *Why Deep Learning?*, provides an overview of deep learning. We begin with the history of deep learning, its rise, and its recent advances in certain fields. We will also describe some of its challenges, as well as its future potential.

Chapter 2, *Getting Yourself Ready for Deep Learning*, is a starting point to set oneself up for experimenting with and applying deep learning techniques in the real world. We will answer the key questions as to what skills and concepts are needed to get started with deep learning. We will cover some basic concepts of linear algebra, the hardware requirements for deep learning implementation, as well as some of its popular software frameworks. We will also take a look at setting up a deep learning system from scratch on a cloud-based GPU instance.

Chapter 3, *Getting Started with Neural Networks*, focuses on the basics of neural networks, including input/output layers, hidden layers, and how networks learn through forward and backpropagation. We will start with the standard multilayer perceptron networks and their building blocks, and illustrate how they learn step by step. We will also introduce a few popular standard models, such as **Convolutional Neural Networks (CNNs)**, **Restricted Boltzmann Machines (RBM)**, **recurrent neural networks (RNNs)**, as well as a variation of them is called **Long Short-Term Memory (LSTM)**.

Chapter 4, *Deep Learning in Computer Vision*, explains CNNs in more detail. We will go over the core concepts that are essential to the workings of CNNs and how they can be used to solve real-world computer vision problems. We will also look at some of the popular CNN architectures and implement a basic CNN using TensorFlow.

Chapter 5, *NLP – Vector Representation*, covers the basics of NLP for deep learning. This chapter will describe the popular word embedding techniques used for feature representation in NLP. It will also cover popular models such as Word2Vec, Glove, and FastText. This chapter also includes an example of embedding training using TensorFlow.

Chapter 6, *Advanced Natural Language Processing*, takes a more model-centric approach to text processing. We will go over some of the core models, such as RNNs and LSTM networks. We will implement a sample LSTM using TensorFlow and describe the foundational architecture behind commonly used text processing applications of LSTM.

Chapter 7, *Multimodality*, introduces some fundamental progress in the multimodality of using deep learning. This chapter also shares some novel, advanced multimodal applications of deep learning.

Chapter 8, *Deep Reinforcement Learning*, covers the basics of reinforcement learning. It illustrates how deep learning can be applied to improve reinforcement learning in general. This chapter goes through the basic implementation of a basic deep reinforcement learning using TensorFlow and will also discuss some of its popular applications.

Chapter 9, *Deep Learning Hacks*, empowers readers by providing many practical tips that can be applied when using deep learning, such as the best practices for network weight initialization, learning parameter tuning, how to prevent overfitting, and how to prepare your data for better learning when facing data challenges.

Chapter 10, *Deep Learning Trends*, summarizes some of the upcoming ideas in deep learning. It looks at some of the upcoming trends in newly developed algorithms, as well as some of the new applications of deep learning.

To get the most out of this book

There are a couple of things you can do to get the most out of this book. Firstly, it is recommended to at least have some basic knowledge of Python programming and machine learning.

Secondly, before proceeding to Chapter 3, *Getting Started with Neural Networks* and others, be sure to follow the setup instructions in Chapter 2, *Getting Yourself Ready for Deep Learning*. You will also be able to set up your own environment as long as you can practice the given examples.

Thirdly, familiarized yourself with TensorFlow and read its documentation. The TensorFlow documentation (https://www.tensorflow.org/api_docs/) is a great source of information and also contains a lot of great examples and important examples. You can also look around online, as there are various open source examples and deep-learning-related resources.

Fourthly, make sure you explore on your own. Try different settings or configurations for simple problems that don't require much computational time; this can help you to quickly get some ideas of how the model works and how to tune parameters.

Lastly, dive deeper into each type of model. This book explains the gist of various deep learning models in plain words while avoiding too much math; the goal is to help you understand the mechanisms of neural networks under the hood. While there are currently many different tools publicly available that provide high-level APIs, a good understanding of deep leaning will greatly help you to debug and improve model performance.

Download the example code files

You can download the example code files for this book from your account at www.packtpub.com. If you purchased this book elsewhere, you can visit www.packtpub.com/support and register to have the files emailed directly to you.

You can download the code files by following these steps:

1. Log in or register at www.packtpub.com.
2. Select the **SUPPORT** tab.
3. Click on **Code Downloads & Errata**.
4. Enter the name of the book in the **Search** box and follow the onscreen instructions.

Once the file is downloaded, please make sure that you unzip or extract the folder using the latest version of:

- WinRAR/7-Zip for Windows
- Zipeg/iZip/UnRarX for Mac
- 7-Zip/PeaZip for Linux

The code bundle for the book is also hosted on GitHub at https://github.com/ PacktPublishing/Deep-Learning-Essentials. We also have other code bundles from our rich catalog of books and videos available at https://github.com/PacktPublishing/. Check them out!

Download the color images

We also provide a PDF file that has color images of the screenshots/diagrams used in this book. You can download it here: https://www.packtpub.com/sites/default/files/ downloads/DeepLearningEssentials_ColorImages.pdf.

Conventions used

There are a number of text conventions used throughout this book.

`CodeInText`: Indicates code words in text, database table names, folder names, filenames, file extensions, pathnames, dummy URLs, user input, and Twitter handles. Here is an example: "In addition, `alpha` is the learning rate, `vb` is the bias of the visible layer, `hb` is the bias of the hidden layer, and `W` is the weight matrix. The sampling function `sample_prob` is the Gibbs-Sampling function and it decides which node to turn on."

A block of code is set as follows:

```
import mxnet as mx
tensor_cpu = mx.nd.zeros((100,), ctx=mx.cpu())
tensor_gpu = mx.nd.zeros((100,), ctx=mx.gpu(0))
```

Any command-line input or output is written as follows:

```
$ sudo add-apt-repository ppa:graphics-drivers/ppa -y
$ sudo apt-get update
$ sudo apt-get install -y nvidia-375 nvidia-settings
```

Bold: Indicates a new term, an important word, or words that you see onscreen.

 Warnings or important notes appear like this.

 Tips and tricks appear like this.

Get in touch

Feedback from our readers is always welcome.

General feedback: Email `feedback@packtpub.com` and mention the book title in the subject of your message. If you have questions about any aspect of this book, please email us at `questions@packtpub.com`.

Errata: Although we have taken every care to ensure the accuracy of our content, mistakes do happen. If you have found a mistake in this book, we would be grateful if you would report this to us. Please visit `www.packtpub.com/submit-errata`, selecting your book, clicking on the Errata Submission Form link, and entering the details.

Piracy: If you come across any illegal copies of our works in any form on the Internet, we would be grateful if you would provide us with the location address or website name. Please contact us at `copyright@packtpub.com` with a link to the material.

If you are interested in becoming an author: If there is a topic that you have expertise in and you are interested in either writing or contributing to a book, please visit `authors.packtpub.com`.

Reviews

Please leave a review. Once you have read and used this book, why not leave a review on the site that you purchased it from? Potential readers can then see and use your unbiased opinion to make purchase decisions, we at Packt can understand what you think about our products, and our authors can see your feedback on their book. Thank you!

For more information about Packt, please visit `packtpub.com`.

1

Why Deep Learning?

This chapter will give an overview of deep learning, the history of deep learning, the rise of deep learning, and its recent advances in certain fields. Also, we will talk about challenges, as well as its future potential.

We will answer a few key questions often raised by a practical user of deep learning who may not possess a machine learning background. These questions include:

- What is **artificial intelligence** (**AI**) and deep learning?
- What's the history of deep learning or AI?
    - What are the major breakthroughs of deep learning?
    - What is the main reason for its recent rise?
- What's the motivation of deep architecture?
    - Why should we resort to deep learning and why can't the existing machine learning algorithms solve the problem at hand?
    - In which fields can it be applied?
    - Successful stories of deep learning

- What's the potential future of deep learning and what are the current challenges?

What is AI and deep learning?

The dream of creating certain forms of intelligence that mimic ourselves has long existed. While most of them appear in science fiction, over recent decades we have gradually been making progress in actually building intelligent machines that can perform certain tasks just like a human. This is an area called **artificial intelligence**. The beginning of AI can perhaps be traced back to Pamela McCorduck's book, *Machines Who Think*, where she described AI as an *ancient wish to forge the gods*.

Deep learning is a branch of AI, with the aim specified as moving machine learning closer to its original goals: AI.

The path it pursues is an attempt to mimic the activity in layers of neurons in the neocortex, which is the wrinkly 80% of the brain where thinking occurs. In a human brain, there are around 100 billion neurons and 100 ~ 1000 trillion synapses.

It learns hierarchical structures and levels of representation and abstraction to understand the patterns of data that come from various source types, such as images, videos, sound, and text.

Higher level abstractions are defined as the composition of lower-level abstraction. It is called **deep** because it has more than one state of nonlinear feature transformation. One of the biggest advantages of deep learning is its ability to automatically learn feature representation at multiple levels of abstraction. This allows a system to learn complex functions mapped from the input space to the output space without many dependencies on human-crafted features. Also, it provides the potential for pre-training, which is learning the representation on a set of available datasets, then applying the learned representations to other domains. This may have some limitations, such as being able to acquire good enough quality data for learning. Also, deep learning performs well when learning from a large amount of unsupervised data in a greedy fashion.

The following figure shows a simplified **Convolutional Neural Network (CNN)**:

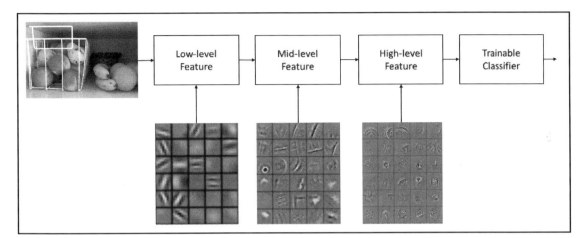

Illustration of a simplified convolutional neural network with an illustration of the hierarchical features learnt

The deep learning model, that is, the learned deep neural network often consists of multiple layers. Together they work hierarchically to build an improved feature space. The first layer learns the first order features, such as color and edges. The second layer learns higher-order features, such as corners. The third layer learns about small patches or texture. Layers often learn in an unsupervised mode and discover general features of the input space. Then the final layer features are fed into a supervised layer to complete the task, such as classification or regression.

Between layers, nodes are connected through weighted edges. Each node, which can be seen as a simulated neocortex, is associated with an activation function, where its inputs are from the lower layer nodes. Building such large, multi-layer arrays of neuron-like information flow is, however, a decade-old idea. From its creation to its recent successes, it has experienced both breakthroughs and setbacks.

With the newest improvements in mathematical formulas, increasingly powerful computers, and large-scale datasets, finally, spring is around the corner. Deep learning has become a pillar of today's tech world and has been applied in a wide range of fields. In the next section, we will trace its history and discuss the ups and downs of its incredible journey.

The history and rise of deep learning

The earliest neural network was developed in the 1940s, not long after the dawn of AI research. In 1943, a seminal paper called *A Logical Calculus of Ideas Immanent in Nervous Activity* was published, which proposed the first mathematical model of a neural network . The unit of this model is a simple formalized neuron, often referred to as a McCulloch–Pitts neuron. It is a mathematical function conceived as a model of biological neurons, a neural network. They are elementary units in an artificial neural network. An illustration of an artificial neuron can be seen from the following figure. Such an idea looks very promising indeed, as they attempted to simulate how a human brain works, but in a greatly simplified way:

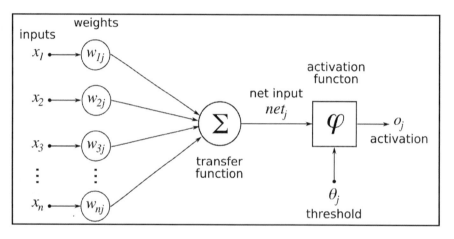

An illustration of an artificial neuron model (source: https://commons.wikimedia.org/wiki/File:ArtificialNeuronModel_english.png)

These early models consist of only a very small set of virtual neurons and a random number called **weights** are used to connect them. These weights determine how each simulated neuron transfers information between them, that is, how each neuron responds, with a value between 0 and 1. With this mathematical representation, the neural output can feature an edge or a shape from the image, or a particular energy level at one frequency in a phoneme. The previous figure, *An illustration of an artificial neuron model*, illustrates a mathematically formulated artificial neuron, where the input corresponds to the dendrites, an activation function controls whether the neuron fires if a threshold is reached, and the output corresponds to the axon. However, early neural networks could only simulate a very limited number of neurons at once, so not many patterns can be recognized by using such a simple architecture. These models languished through the 1970s.

The concept of backpropagation, the use of errors in training deep learning models, was first proposed in the 1960s. This was followed by models with polynomial activation functions. Using a slow and manual process, the best statistically chosen features from each layer were then forwarded on to the next layer. Unfortunately, then the first AI winter kicked in, which lasted about 10 years. At this early stage, although the idea of mimicking the human brain sounded very fancy, the actual capabilities of AI programs were very limited. Even the most impressive one could only deal with some toy problems. Not to mention that they had a very limited computing power and only small size datasets available. The hard winter occurred mainly because the expectations were raised so high, then when the results failed to materialize AI received criticism and funding disappeared:

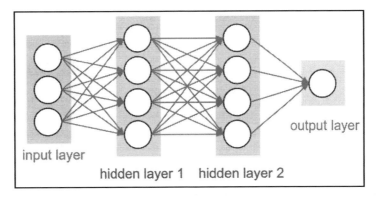

Illustration of an artificial neuron in a multi-layer perceptron neural network (source: https://github.com/cs231n/cs231n.github.io/blob/master/assets/nn1/neural_net2.jpeg)

Slowly, backpropagation evolved significantly in the 1970s but was not applied to neural networks until 1985. In the mid-1980s, Hinton and others helped spark a revival of interest in neural networks with so-called **deep models** that made better use of many layers of neurons, that is, with more than two hidden layers. An illustration of a multi-layer perceptron neural network can be seen in the previous figure, *Illustration of an artificial neuron in a multi-layer perceptron neural network*. By then, Hinton and their co-authors (https://www.iro.umontreal.ca/~vincentp/ift3395/lectures/backprop_old.pdf) demonstrated that backpropagation in a neural network could result in interesting representative distribution. In 1989, Yann LeCun (http://yann.lecun.com/exdb/publis/pdf/lecun-89e.pdf) demonstrated the first practical use of backpropagation at Bell Labs. He brought backpropagation to convolutional neural networks to understand handwritten digits, and his idea eventually evolved into a system that reads the numbers of handwritten checks.

This is also the time of the 2nd AI winter (1985-1990). In 1984, two leading AI researchers Roger Schank and Marvin Minsky warned the business community that the enthusiasm for AI had spiraled out of control. Although multi-layer networks could learn complicated tasks, their speed was very slow and results were not that impressive. Therefore, when another simpler but more effective methods, such as support vector machines were invented, government and venture capitalists dropped their support for neural networks. Just three years later, the billion dollar AI industry fell apart.

However, it wasn't really the failure of AI but more the end of the hype, which is common in many emerging technologies. Despite the ups and downs in its reputation, funding, and interests, some researchers continued their beliefs. Unfortunately, they didn't really look into the actual reason for why the learning of multi-layer networks was so difficult and why the performance was not amazing. In 2000, the vanishing gradient problem was discovered, which finally drew people's attention to the real key question: Why don't multi-layer networks learn? The reason is that for certain activation functions, the input is condensed, meaning large areas of input mapped over an extremely small region. With large changes or errors computed from the last layer, only a small amount will be reflected back to front/lower layers. This means little or no learning signal reaches these layers and the learned features at these layers are weak.

Note that many upper layers are fundamental to the problem as they carry the most basic representative pattern of the data. This gets worse because the optimal configuration of an upper layer may also depend on the configuration of the following layers, which means the optimization of an upper layer is based on a non-optimal configuration of a lower layer. All of this means it is difficult to train the lower layers and produce good results.

Two approaches were proposed to solve this problem: layer-by-layer pre-training and the **Long Short-Term Memory (LSTM)** model. LSTM for recurrent neural networks was first proposed by Sepp Hochreiter and Juergen Schmidhuber in 1997.

In the last decade, many researchers made some fundamental conceptual breakthroughs, and there was a sudden burst of interest in deep learning, not only from the academic side but also from the industry. In 2006, Professor Hinton at Toronto University in Canada and others developed a more efficient way to teach individual layers of neurons, called *A fast learning algorithm for deep belief nets* (https://www.cs.toronto.edu/~hinton/absps/fastnc. pdf.). This sparked the second revival of the neural network. In his paper, he introduced **Deep Belief Networks (DBNs)**, with a learning algorithm that greedily trains one layer at a time by exploiting an unsupervised learning algorithm for each layer, a **Restricted Boltzmann Machine (RBM)**. The following figure, *The layer-wise pre-training that Hinton introduced* shows the concept of layer-by-layer training for this deep belief networks.

The proposed DBN was tested using the MNIST database, the standard database for comparing the precision and accuracy of each image recognition method. This database includes 70,000, 28 x 28 pixel, hand-written character images of numbers from 0 to 9 (60,000 is for training and 10,000 is for testing). The goal is to correctly answer which number from 0 to 9 is written in the test case. Although the paper did not attract much attention at the time, results from DBM had considerably higher precision than a conventional machine learning approach:

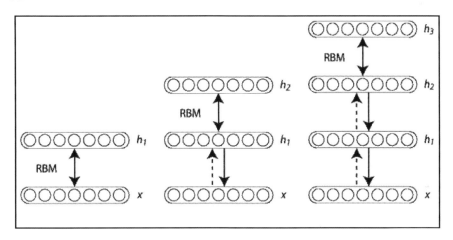

The layer-wise pre-training that Hinton introduced

Fast-forward to 2012 and the entire AI research world was shocked by one method. At the world competition of image recognition, **ImageNet Large Scale Visual Recognition Challenge (ILSVRC)**, a team called **SuperVision** (http://image-net.org/challenges/LSVRC/2012/supervision.pdf) achieved a winning top five- test error rate of 15.3%, compared to 26.2% achieved by the second-best entry. The ImageNet has around 1.2 million high-resolution images belonging to 1000 different classes. There are 10 million images provided as learning data, and 150,000 images are used for testing. The authors, Alex Krizhevsky, Ilya Sutskever, and Geoffrey E. Hinton from Toronto University, built a deep convolutional network with 60 million parameters, 650,000 neurons, and 630 million connections, consisting of seven hidden layers and five convolutional layers, some of which were followed by max-pooling layers and three fully-connected layers with a final 1000-way softmax. To increase the training data, the authors randomly sampled 224 x 224 patches from available images. To speed up the training, they used non-saturating neurons and a very efficient GPU implementation of the convolution operation. They also used *dropout* to reduce overfitting in the fully connected layers that proved to be very effective.

Since then deep learning has taken off, and today we see many successful applications not only in image classification, but also in regression, dimensionality reduction, texture modeling, action recognition, motion modeling, object segmentation, information retrieval, robotics, natural language processing, speech recognition, biomedical fields, music generation, art, collaborative filtering, and so on:

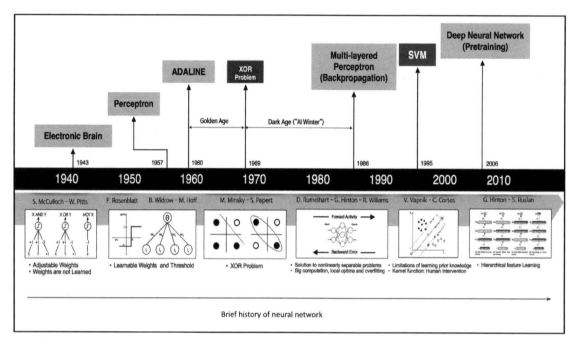

Illustration of the history of deep learning/AI

It's interesting that when we look back, it seems that most theoretical breakthroughs had already been made by the 1980s-1990s, so what else has changed in the past decade? A not-too-controversial theory is that *the success of deep learning is largely a success of engineering.* Andrew Ng once said:

> *If you treat the theoretical development of deep learning as the engine, fast computer, the development of graphics processing units (GPU) and the occurrence of massive labeled datasets are the fuels.*

Indeed, faster processing, with GPUs processing pictures, increased computational speeds by 1000 times over a 10-year span.

Almost at the same time, the big data era arrived. Millions, billions, or even trillions of bytes of data are collected every day. Industry leaders are also making an effort in deep learning to leverage the massive amounts of data they have collected. For example, Baidu has 50,000 hours of training data for speech recognition and is expected to train about another 100,000 hours of data. For facial recognition, 200 million images were trained. The involvement of large companies greatly boosted the potential of deep learning and AI overall by providing data at a scale that could hardly have been imagined in the past.

With enough training data and faster computational speed, neural networks can now extend to deep architecture, which has never been realized before. On the one hand, the occurrence of new theoretical approaches, massive data, and fast computation have boosted progress in deep learning. On the other hand, the creation of new tools, platforms, and applications boosted academic development, the use of faster and more powerful GPUs, and the collection of big data. This loop continues and deep learning has become a revolution built on top of the following pillars:

- Massive, high-quality, labeled datasets in various formats, such as images, videos, text, speech, audio, and so on.
- Powerful GPU units and networks that are capable of doing fast floating-point calculations in parallel or in distributed ways.
- Creation of new, deep architectures: AlexNet (*Krizhevsky and others, ImageNet Classification with Deep Convolutional Neural Networks, 2012*), Zeiler Fergus Net (*Zeiler and others, Visualizing and Understanding Convolutional Networks, 2013*), GoogleLeNet (*Szegedy and others, Going Deeper with Convolutions, 2015*), Network in Network (*Lin and others, Network In Network, 2013*), VGG (*Simonyan and others, Very deep convolutional networks for large-scale image recognition, 2015*) for *Very Deep CNN*, ResNets (*He and others, Deep Residual Learning for Image Recognition, 2015*), inception modules, and Highway networks, MXNet, Region-Based CNNs (R-CNN, *Girshick and others, Rich feature hierarchies for accurate object detection and semantic segmentation; Girshick, Fast R-CNN, 2015; Ren and others Faster R-CNN: Towards Real-Time Object Detection with Region Proposal Networks, 2016*), Generative Adversarial Networks (*Goodfellow and others 2014*).
- Open source software platforms, such as TensorFlow, Theano, and MXNet provide easy-to-use, low level or high-level APIs for developers or academics so they are able to quickly implement and iterate their ideas and applications.
- Approaches to improve the vanishing gradient problem, such as using non-saturating activation functions like ReLU rather than tanh and the logistic functions.

- Approaches help to avoid overfitting:
    - New regularizer, such as Dropout which keeps the network sparse, maxout, batch normalization.
    - Data-augmentation that allows training larger and larger networks without (or with less) overfitting.
- Robust optimizers—modifications of the SGD procedure including momentum, RMSprop, and ADAM have helped eke out every last percentage of your loss function.

Why deep learning?

So far we discussed what is deep learning and the history of deep learning. But why is it so popular now? In this section, we talk about advantages of deep learning over traditional shallow methods and its significant impact in a couple of technical fields.

Advantages over traditional shallow methods

Traditional approaches are often considered *shallow* machine learning and often require the developer to have some prior knowledge regarding the specific features of input that might be helpful, or how to design effective features. Also, *shallow* learning often uses only one hidden layer, for example, a single layer feed-forward network. In contrast, deep learning is known as representation learning, which has been shown to perform better at extracting non-local and global relationships or structures in the data. One can supply fairly raw formats of data into the learning system, for example, raw image and text, rather than extracted features on top of images (for example, SIFT by David Lowe's *Object Recognition from Local Scale-Invariant Features* and HOG by Dalal and their co-authors, *Histograms of oriented gradients for human detection*), or IF-IDF vectors for text. Because of the depth of the architecture, the learned representations form a hierarchical structure with knowledge learned at various levels. This parameterized, multi-level, computational graph provides a high degree of the representation. The emphasis on shallow and deep algorithms are significantly different in that shallow algorithms are more about feature engineering and selection, while deep learning puts its emphasis on defining the most useful computational graph topology (architecture) and the ways of optimizing parameters/hyperparameters efficiently and correctly for good generalization ability of the learned representations:

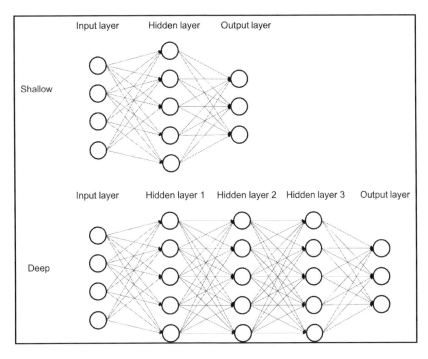

Comparing deep and shallow architecture. It can be seen deep architecture has many layers of hierarchical topology

Deep learning algorithms are shown to perform better at extracting non-local and global relationships and patterns in the data, compared to relatively shallow learning architectures. Other useful characteristics of learnt abstract representations by deep learning include:

- It tries to explore most of the abundant huge volume of the dataset, even when the data is unlabeled.
- The advantage of continuing to improve as more training data is added.
- Automatic data representation extraction, from unsupervised data or supervised data, distributed and hierarchical, usually best when input space is locally structured; spatial or temporal—for example, images, language, and speech.
- Representation extraction from unsupervised data enables its broad application to different data types, such as image, textural, audio, and so on.
- Relatively simple linear models can work effectively with the knowledge obtained from the more complex and more abstract data representations. This means with the advanced feature extracted, the following learning model can be relatively simple, which may help reduce computational complexity, for example, in the case of linear modeling.

- Relational and semantic knowledge can be obtained at higher levels of abstraction and representation of the raw data (*Yoshua Bengio and Yann LeCun, Scaling Learning Algorithms towards AI, 2007,* source: `https://journalofbigdata.springeropen.com/articles/10.1186/s40537-014-0007-7`).
- Deep architectures can be representationally efficient. This sounds contradictory, but its a great benefit because of the distributed representation power by deep learning.
- The learning capacity of deep learning algorithms is proportional to the size of data, that is, performance increases as the input data increases, whereas, for shallow or traditional learning algorithms, the performance reaches a plateau after a certain amount of data is provided as shown in the following figure, *Learning capability of deep learning versus traditional machine learning:*

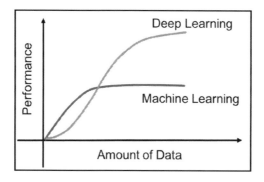

Learning capability of deep learning versus traditional machine learning

Impact of deep learning

To show you some of the impacts of deep learning, let's take a look at two specific areas: image recognition and speed recognition.

The following figure, *Performance on ImageNet classification over time,* shows the top five error rate trends for ILSVRC contest winners over the past several years. Traditional image recognition approaches employ hand-crafted computer vision classifiers trained on a number of instances of each object class, for example, SIFT + Fisher vector. In 2012, deep learning entered this competition. Alex Krizhevsky and Professor Hinton from Toronto university stunned the field with around 10% drop in the error rate by their deep convolutional neural network (AlexNet). Since then, the leaderboard has been occupied by this type of method and its variations. By 2015, the error rate had dropped below human testers:

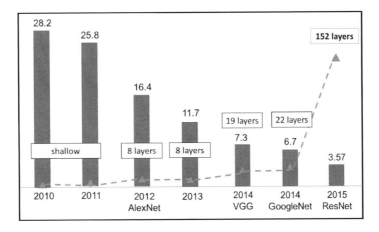

Performance on ImageNet classification over time

The following figure, *Speech recognition progress* depicts recent progress in the area of speech recognition. From 2000-2009, there was very little progress. Since 2009, the involvement of deep learning, large datasets, and fast computing has significantly boosted development. In 2016, a major breakthrough was made by a team of researchers and engineers in **Microsoft Research AI (MSR AI)**. They reported a speech recognition system that made the same or fewer errors than professional transcriptionists, with a **word error rate (WER)** of 5.9%. In other words, the technology could recognize words in a conversation as well as a person does:

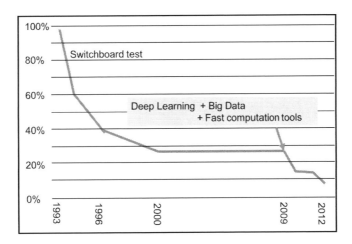

Speech recognition progress

A natural question to ask is, what are the advantages of deep learning over traditional approaches? Topology defines functionality. But why do we need expensive deep architecture? Is this really necessary? What are we trying to achieve here? It turns out that there are both theoretical and empirical pieces of evidence in favor of multiple levels of representation. In the next section, let's dive into more details about the deep architecture of deep learning.

The motivation of deep architecture

The depth of the architecture refers to the number of levels of the composition of non-linear operations in the function learned. These operations include weighted sum, product, a single neuron, kernel, and so on. Most current learning algorithms correspond to shallow architectures that have only 1, 2, or 3 levels. The following table shows some examples of both shallow and deep algorithms:

Levels	Example	Group
1-layer	Logistic regression, Maximum Entropy Classifier Perceptron, Linear SVM	Linear classifier
2-layers	Multi-layer Perceptron, SVMs with kernels Decision trees	Universal approximator
3 or more layers	Deep learning Boosted decision trees	Compact universal approximator

There are mainly two viewpoints of understanding the deep architecture of deep learning algorithms: the neural point view and the feature representation view. We will talk about each of them. Both of them may come from different origins, but together they can help us to better understand the mechanisms and advantages deep learning has.

The neural viewpoint

From a neural viewpoint, an architecture for learning is biologically inspired. The human brain has deep architecture, in which the cortex seems to have a generic learning approach. A given input is perceived at multiple levels of abstraction. Each level corresponds to a different area of the cortex. We process information in hierarchical ways, with multi-level transformation and representation. Therefore, we learn simple concepts first then compose them together. This structure of understanding can be seen clearly in a human's vision system. As shown in the following figure, *Signal path from the retina to human lateral occipital cortex (LOC), which finally recognizes the object*, the ventral visual cortex comprises a set of areas that process images in increasingly more abstract ways, from edges, corners and contours, shapes, object parts to object, allowing us to learn, recognize, and categorize three-dimensional objects from arbitrary two-dimensional views:

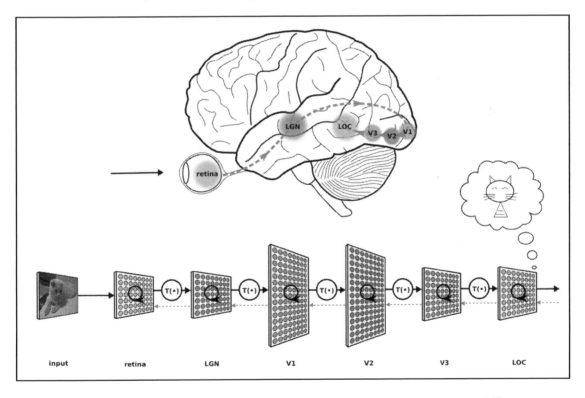

The signal path from the retina to human lateral occipital cortex (LOC), which finally recognizes the object. Figure credit to Jonas Kubilius (https://neuwritesd.files.wordpress.com/2015/10/visual_stream_small.png)

The representation viewpoint

For most traditional machine learning algorithms, their performance depends heavily on the representation of the data they are given. Therefore, domain prior knowledge, feature engineering, and feature selection are critical to the performance of the output. But hand-crafted features lack the flexibility of applying to different scenarios or application areas. Also, they are not data-driven and cannot adapt to new data or information comes in. In the past, it has been noticed that a lot of AI tasks could be solved by using a simple machine learning algorithm on the condition that the right set of features for the task are extracted or designed. For example, an estimate of the size of a speaker's vocal tract is considered a useful feature, as it's a strong clue as to whether the speaker is a man, woman, or child. Unfortunately, for many tasks, and for various input formats, for example, image, video, audio, and text, it is very difficult to know what kind of features should be extracted, let alone their generalization ability for other tasks that are beyond the current application. Manually designing features for a complex task requires a great deal of domain understanding, time, and effort. Sometimes, it can take decades for an entire community of researchers to make progress in this area. If one looks back at the area of computer vision, for over a decade researchers have been stuck because of the limitations of the available feature extraction approaches (SIFT, HOG, and so on). A lot of work back then involved trying to design complicated machine learning schema given such base features, and the progress was very slow, especially for large-scale complicated problems, such as recognizing 1000 objects from images. This is a strong motivation for designing flexible and automated feature representation approaches.

One solution to this problem is to use the data driven type of approach, such as machine learning to discover the representation. Such representation can represent the mapping from representation to output (supervised), or simply representation itself (unsupervised). This approach is known as representation learning. Learned representations often result in much better performance as compared to what can be obtained with hand-designed representations. This also allows AI systems to rapidly adapt to new areas, without much human intervention. Also, it may take more time and effort from a whole community to hand-craft and design features. While with a representation learning algorithm, we can discover a good set of features for a simple task in minutes or a complex task in hours to months.

This is where deep learning comes to the rescue. Deep learning can be thought of as representation learning, whereas feature extraction happens automatically when the deep architecture is trying to process the data, learning, and understanding the mapping between the input and the output. This brings significant improvements in accuracy and flexibility since human designed feature/feature extraction lacks accuracy and generalization ability.

In addition to this automated feature learning, the learned representations are both distributed and with a hierarchical structure. Such successful training of intermediate representations helps feature sharing and abstraction across different tasks.

The following figure shows its relationship as compared to other types of machine learning algorithms. In the next section, we will explain why these characteristics (distributed and hierarchical) are important:

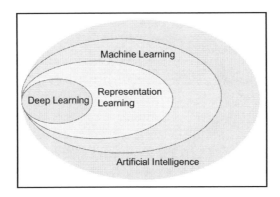

A Venn diagram showing how deep learning is a kind of representation learning

Distributed feature representation

A distributed representation is dense, whereas each of the learned concepts is represented by multiple neurons simultaneously, and each neuron represents more than one concept. In other words, input data is represented on multiple, interdependent layers, each describing data at different levels of scale or abstraction. Therefore, the representation is distributed across various layers and multiple neurons. In this way, two types of information are captured by the network topology. On the one hand, for each neuron, it must represent something, so this becomes a local representation. On the other hand, so-called distribution means a map of the graph is built through the topology, and there exists a many-to-many relationship between these local representations. Such connections capture the interaction and mutual relationship when using local concepts and neurons to represent the whole. Such representation has the potential to capture exponentially more variations than local ones with the same number of free parameters. In other words, they can generalize non-locally to unseen regions. They hence offer the potential for better generalization because learning theory shows that the number of examples needed (to achieve the desired degree of generalization performance) to tune $O(B)$ effective degrees of freedom is $O(B)$. This is referred to as the power of distributed representation as compared to local representation (http://www.iro.umontreal.ca/~pift6266/H10/notes/mlintro.html).

An easy way to understand the example is as follows. Suppose we need to represent three words, one can use the traditional one-hot encoding (length N), which is commonly used in NLP. Then at most, we can represent N words. The localist models are very inefficient whenever the data has componential structure:

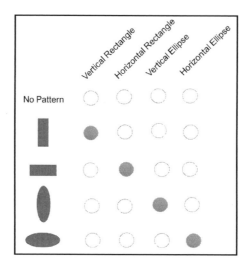

One-hot encoding

A distributed representation of a set of shapes would look like this:

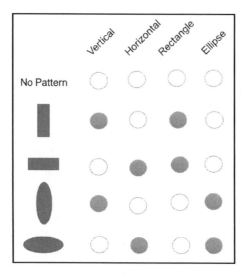

Distributed representation

If we wanted to represent a new shape with a sparse representation, such as one-hot-encoding, we would have to increase the dimensionality. But what's nice about a distributed representation is we may be able to represent a new shape with the existing dimensionality. An example using the previous example is as follows:

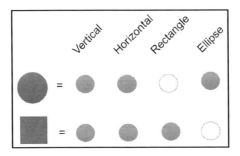

Representing new concepts using distributed representation

Therefore, non-mutually exclusive features/attributes create a combinatorially large set of distinguishable configurations and the number of distinguishable regions grows almost exponentially with the number of parameters.

One more concept we need to clarify is the difference between distributed and distributional. Distributed is represented as continuous activation levels in a number of elements, for example, a dense word embedding, as opposed to one-hot encoding vectors.

On the other hand, distributional is represented by contexts of use. For example, Word2Vec is distributional, but so are count-based word vectors, as we use the contexts of the word to model the meaning.

Hierarchical feature representation

The learnt features capture both local and inter-relationships for the data as a whole, it is not only the learnt features that are distributed, the representations also come hierarchically structured. The previous figure, *Comparing deep and shallow architecture. It can be seen that shallow architecture has a more flat topology, while deep architecture has many layers of hierarchical topology* compares the typical structure of shallow versus deep architectures, where we can see that the shallow architecture often has a flat structure with one layer at most, whereas the deep architecture structures have multiple layers, and lower layers are composited that serve as input to the higher layer. The following figure uses a more concrete example to show what information has been learned through layers of the hierarchy.

As shown in the image, the lower layer focuses on edges or colors, while higher layers often focus more on patches, curves, and shapes. Such representation effectively captures part-and-whole relationships from various granularity and naturally addresses multi-task problems, for example, edge detection or part recognition. The lower layer often represents the basic and fundamental information that can be used for many distinct tasks in a wide variety of domains. For example, Deep Belief networks have been successfully used to learn high-level structures in a wide variety of domains, including handwritten digits and human motion capture data. The hierarchical structure of representation mimics the human understanding of concepts, that is, learning simple concepts first and then successfully building up more complex concepts by composing the simpler ones together. It is also easier to monitor what is being learnt and to guide the machine to better subspaces. If one treats each neuron as a feature detector, then deep architectures can be seen as consisting of feature detector units arranged in layers. Lower layers detect simple features and feed into higher layers, which in turn detect more complex features. If the feature is detected, the responsible unit or units generate large activations, which can be picked up by the later classifier stages as a good indicator that the class is present:

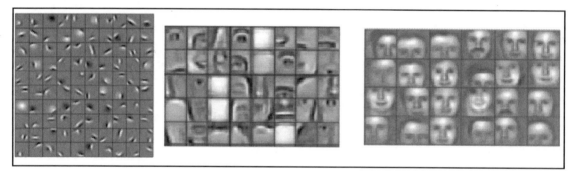

Illustration of hierarchical features learned from a deep learning algorithm. Image by Honglak Lee and colleagues *as published in Convolutional Deep Belief Networks for Scalable Unsupervised Learning of Hierarchical Representations, 2009*

The above figure illustrates that each feature can be thought of as a detector, which tries to the detector a particular feature (blob, edges, nose, or eye) on the input image.

Applications

Now we have a general understanding of deep learning and its technical advantages over traditional methods. But how do we benefit from it in reality? In this section, we will introduce how deep learning makes tremendous impact in some practical applications across a variety of fields.

Lucrative applications

In the past few years, the number of researchers and engineers in deep learning has grown at an exponential rate. Deep learning breaks new ground in almost every domain it touches using novel neural networks architectures and advanced machine learning frameworks. With significant hardware and algorithmic developments, deep learning has revolutionized the industry and has been highly successful in tackling many real-world AI and data mining problems.

We have seen an explosion in new and lucrative applications using deep learning frameworks in areas as diverse as image recognition, image search, object detection, computer vision, optical character recognition, video parsing, face recognition, pose estimation (*Cao and others, Realtime Multi-Person 2D Pose Estimation using Part Affinity Fields, 2016*), speech recognition, spam detection, text to speech or image caption, translation, natural language processing, chatbots, targeted online advertising serving, click-through optimization, robotics, computer vision, energy optimization, medicine, art, music, physics, autonomous car driving, data mining of biological data, bioinformatics (protein sequence prediction, phylogenetic inferences, multiple sequence alignment) big data analytics, semantic indexing, sentiment analysis, web search/information retrieval, games (*Atari* (`http://karpathy.github.io/2016/05/31/rl/`) and *AlphaGo* (`https://deepmind.com/research/alphago/`)), and beyond.

Success stories

In this section, we will enumerate a few major application areas and their success stories.

In the area of computer vision, image recognition/object recognition refers to the task of using an image or a patch of an image as input and predicting what the image or patch contains. For example, an image can be labeled dog, cat, house, bicycle, and so on. In the past, researchers were stuck at how to design good features to tackle challenging problems such as scale-invariant, orientation invariant, and so on. Some of the well-known feature descriptors are Haar-like, **Histogram of Oriented Gradient (HOG)**, **Scale-Invariant Feature Transform (SIFT)**, and **Speeded-Up Robust Feature (SURF)**. While human designed features are good at certain tasks, such as HOG for human detection, it is far from ideal.

Until 2012, deep learning stunned the field with its resounding success at the **ImageNet Large Scale Visual Recognition Challenge (ILSVRC)**. In that competition, a convolutional neural network (often called AlexNet, see the following figure), developed by Alex Krizhevsky, Ilya Sutskever, and Geoffrey Hinton won 1st place with an astounding 85% accuracy—11% better than the algorithm that won the second place! In 2013, all winning entries were based on deep learning, and by 2015 multiple CNN-based algorithms had surpassed the human recognition rate of 95%. Details can be found at their publication *Delving Deep into Rectifiers: Surpassing Human-Level Performance on ImageNet Classification*:

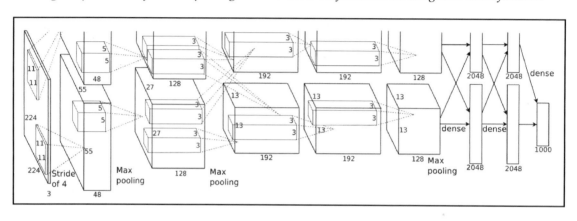

Illustration of AlexNet architecture. It has two streams because the training process is so computationally expensive that they had to split the training into two GPUs

In other areas of computer vision, deep learning also shows surprising and interesting power in mimicking human intelligence. For example, deep learning cannot only identify various elements in the picture accurately (and locate them), it can also understand interesting areas such as humans and organize words/phrases into sentences to describe what's happening in the picture. For more details, one can refer to the work presented by Andrej Karpathy and Fei-Fei Li at http://cs.stanford.edu/people/karpathy/deepimagesent/. They trained a deep learning network to identify dozens of interesting areas and objects, and described the subjects and movements in the picture with correct English grammar. This involves training on both image information and language information to make the right connection between them.

As a further progress, Justin Johnson, Andrej Karpathy and Feifei Li published a new work in 2016 called *DenseCap: Fully Convolutional Localization Networks for Dense Captioning*. Their proposed **fully Convolutional Localization Network (FCLN)** architecture can localize and describe salient regions in images in natural language. Some examples are shown in the following figure:

arched doorway in front of building. arched doorway with arched doorway. people walking on the sidewalk. a large stone archway. a tree with green leaves. an old stone building. a building with a clock. an arched doorway. a tree with no leaves. clock on the building. a bush in the background. a man walking down the sidewalk. a woman walking on the sidewalk. brick building with brick.

trees behind the zebra. head of a zebra. a side view mirror. two zebras standing in a field. a tree with no leaves. the zebras ears are black. a tree with a zebra. a tree with no leaves. a car in the mirror. side view mirror on a car. black and white mane of zebra. a zebra is outside.

a man on a skateboard. man riding a bicycle. orange cone on the ground. man riding a bicycle. two people riding a skateboard. red helmet on the man. skateboard on the ground. white shirt with red and white stripes. orange and white cone. trees are behind the people.

yellow and black train. train on the tracks. a tall light pole. a clear blue sky. train on the tracks. a tall light pole. a blue sky with no clouds. people walking on the sidewalk. a building with a lot of windows. grass growing on the ground.

Deep learning networks generate natural language descriptions for salient objects in the picture. More examples can be found from project page: https://cs.stanford.edu/people/karpathy/densecap/

Recently, attention-based neural encoder-decoder frameworks have been widely adopted for image captioning, where novel adaptive attention models with a visual sentinel have been incorporated and better performance has been achieved. Details can be found at their work of *Knowing When to Look: Adaptive Attention via A Visual Sentinel for Image Captioning.*

Early in 2017, Ryan Dahl and others from the Google Brain team proposed a deep learning network called **Pixel Recursive Super Resolution** to take very low-resolution images of faces and enhance their resolution significantly. It can predict what each face most likely looks like. For example, in the following figure, in the left-hand column, you can see the original 8 x 8 photos, the prediction results in the middle can be found fairly close to the ground truth (in the very right column):

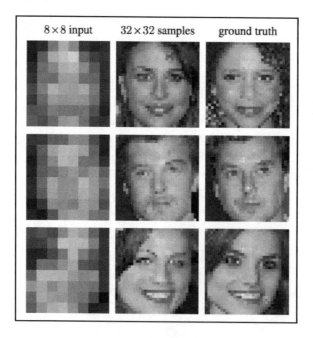

Illustration of super-resolution using deep learning algorithm. Left column: the input low-resolution image, the right-column: system estimation, middle-column: the ground truth. From Ryan Dahl, Mohammad Norouzi, Jonathon Shlens, Pixel Recursive Super Resolution, ICCV 2017

In the area of semantic indexing for search engines, given the advantages of automated feature representation by deep learning, data in various formats can now be represented in a more efficient and useful manner. This provides a powerful source of knowledge discovery and comprehension in addition to increased speed and efficiency. **Microsoft Audio Video Indexing Service (MAVIS)** is an example that uses deep learning (ANN)-based speech recognition to enable searching for audio and video files with speech.

In the area of **natural language processing (NLP)**, word/character representation learning (such as Word2Vec) and machine translation are great practical examples. In fact, in the past two or three years, deep learning has almost replaced traditional machine translation.

Machine translation is automated translation, which typically refers to statistical inference-based systems that deliver more fluent-sounding but less consistent translations for speech or text between various languages. In the past, popular methods have been statistical techniques that learn the translation rules from a large corpus, as a replacement for a language expert. While cases like this overcome the bottleneck of data acquisition, many challenges exist. For example, hand-crafted features may not be ideal as they cannot cover all possible linguistic variations. It is difficult to use global features, the translation module heavily relies on pre-processing steps including word alignment, word segmentation, tokenization, rule-extraction, syntactic parsing, and so on. The recent development of deep learning provides solutions to these challenges. A machine translator that translates through one large neural network is often called **Neural Machine Translation (NMT)**. Essentially, it's a sequence to sequence learning problem, where the goal of the neural networks is to learn a parameterized function of $P(y_T \mid x_{1..N}, y_{1..T-1})$ that maps from the input sequence/source sentence to the output sequence/target sentence. The mapping function often contains two stages: encoding and decoding. The encoder maps a source sequence $x_{1..N}$ to one or more vectors to produce hidden state representations. The decoder predicts a target sequence $y_{1..M}$ symbol by symbol using the source sequence vector representations and previously predicted symbols.

As illustrated by the the following figure, this vase-like shape produces good representation/embeddings at the middle hidden layer:

An example of translating from Chinese to English

However, NMT systems are known to be computationally expensive both in training and in translation inference. Also, most NMT systems have difficulty with rare words. Some recent improvements include the attention mechanism (*Bahdanau and others, Neural Machine Translation by Jointly Learning to Align and Translate, 2014*), Subword level modelling (*Sennrich and others, Neural Machine Translation of Rare Words with Subword Units, 2015*) and character level translation, and the improvements of loss function (Chung and others, *A Character-Level Decoder without Explicit Segmentation for Neural Machine Translation 2016*). In 2016, Google launched their own NMT system to work on a notoriously difficult language pair, Chinese to English and tried to overcome these disadvantages.

Google's NMT system (GNMT) conducts about 18 million translations per day from Chinese to English. The production deployment is built on top of the publicly available machine learning toolkit TensorFlow (`https://www.tensorflow.org/`) and Google's **Tensor Processing Units** (**TPUs**), which provide sufficient computational power to deploy these powerful GNMT models while meeting the stringent latency requirements. The model itself is a deep LSTM model with eight encoder and eight decoder layers using attention and residual connections. On the WMT'14 English-to-French and English-to-German benchmarks, GNMT achieves competitive results. Using a human side-by-side evaluation on a set of isolated simple sentences, it reduces translation errors by an average of 60% compared to Google's phrase-based production system. For more details, one can refer to their tech blog (`https://research.googleblog.com/2016/09/a-neural-network-for-machine.html`) or paper (*Wu and others, Google's Neural Machine Translation System: Bridging the Gap between Human and Machine Translation, 2016*). The following figure shows the improvements per language pairs by the deep learning system. One can see that for **French -> English**, it is almost as good as a human translator:

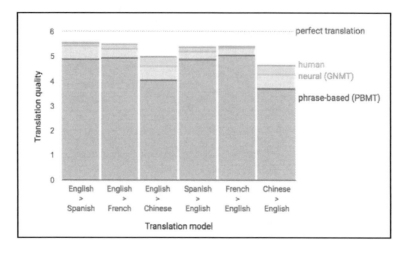

NMT translation performance from Google. Credit to Google blog: https://research.googleblog.com/2016/09/a-neural-network-for-machine.html

In 2016, Google released **WaveNet** (`https://deepmind.com/blog/wavenet-generative-model-raw-audio/`) and Baidu released deep speech, both are deep learning networks that generated voice automatically. The systems learn to mimic human voices by themselves and improve over time, and it is getting harder and harder for an audience to differentiate them from a real human speaking. Why is this important? Although Siri (`https://www.wikiwand.com/en/Siri`) and Alexa (`https://www.wikiwand.com/en/Amazon_Alexa`) can talk well, in the past, text2voice systems were mostly manually trained, which was not in a completely autonomous way to create new voices.

While there is still some gap before computers can speak like humans, we are definitely a step closer to realizing automatic voice generation. In addition, deep learning has shown its impressive abilities in music composition and sound generation from videos, for example Owens and their co-authors work *Visually Indicated Sounds, 2015.*

Deep learning has been applied extensively in self-driving cars, from perception to localization, to path planning. In perception, deep learning is often used to detect cars and pedestrians, for example using the Single Shot MultiBox Detector (*Liu and others, SSD: Single Shot MultiBox Detector, 2015*) or YOLO Real-Time Object Detection (*Redmon and others, You Only Look Once: Unified, Real-Time Object Detection, 2015*). People can also use deep learning to understand the scene the car is seeing, for example, the SegNet (*Badrinarayanan, SegNet: A Deep Convolutional Encoder-Decoder Architecture for Image Segmentation, 2015*), segmenting the scene into pieces with semantic meaning (sky, building, pole, road, fence, vehicle, bike, pedestrian, and so on). In localization, deep learning can be used to perform odometry, for example, VINet (*Clark and others, VINet: Visual-Inertial Odometry as a Sequence-to-Sequence Learning Problem, 2017*), which estimates the exact location of the car and its pose (yaw, pitch, roll). In path planning where it is often formulated as an optimization problem, deep learning, specifically reinforcement learning, can also be applied, for example, the work by Shalev-Shwartz, and its co-authors (*Safe, Multi-Agent, Reinforcement Learning for Autonomous Driving, 2016*). In addition to its applications in different stages of the self-driving pipeline, deep learning has also been used to perform end-to-end learning, mapping raw pixels from the camera to steering commands (*Bojarski and others, End to End Learning for Self-Driving Cars, 2016*).

Deep learning for business

To leverage the power of deep learning for business, the first question would be how to choose the problems to solve? In an interview with Andrew Ng, he talked about his opinion, the rule of thumb is:

> *Anything a typical human can do with up to 1 second of thought, we can probably now or soon automate with AI.*

If we look around, we can easily find that companies today, large or small, have already applied deep learning to production with impressive performance and speed. Think about Google, Microsoft, Facebook, Apple, Amazon, IBM, and Baidu. It turns out we are using deep learning based applications and services on a daily basis.

Nowadays, Google can caption your uploaded images with multiple tags and descriptions. Its translation system is almost as good as a human translator. Its image search engine can return related images by either image queries or language-based semantic queries. Project Sunroof (`https://www.google.com/get/sunroof`) has been helping homeowners explore whether they should go solar - offering solar estimates for over 43 million houses across 42 states.

Apple is working hard to invest in machine learning and computer vision technologies, including the CoreML framework on iOS, Siri, and ARKit (augmented reality platform) on iOS, and their autonomous solutions including self-driving car applications.

Facebook can now automatically tag your friends. Researchers from Microsoft have won the ImageNet competition with better performance than a human annotator and improved their speech recognition system, which has now surpassed humans.

Industry leading companies have also contributed their large-scale deep learning platforms or tools in some way. For example, TensorFlow from Google, MXNet from Amazon, PaddlePaddle from Baidu, and Torch from Facebook. Just recently, Facebook and Microsoft introduced a new open ecosystem for interchangeable AI frameworks. All these toolkits provide useful abstractions for neural networks: routines for n-dimensional arrays (Tensors), simple use of different linear algebra backends (CPU/GPU), and automatic differentiation.

With so many resources and good business models available, it can be foreseen that the process from theoretical development to practical industry realization will be shortened over time.

Future potential and challenges

Despite the exciting past and promising prospects, challenges are still there. As we open this Pandora's box of AI, one of the key questions is, where are we going? What can it do? This question has been addressed by people from various backgrounds. In one of the interviews with Andrew Ng, he posed his point of view that while today's AI is making rapid progress, such momentum will slow down up until AI reaches a human level of performance. There are mainly three reasons for this, the feasibility of the things a human can do, the massive size of data, and the distinctive human ability called **insight**. Still, it sounds very impressive, and might be a bit scary, that one day AI will surpass humans and perhaps replace humans in many areas:

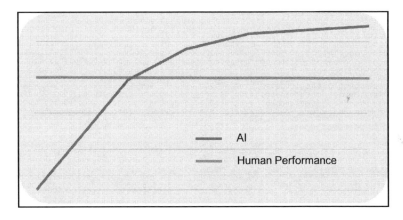

When AI surpasses human performance, the progress slows down

There are basically two main streams of AI, the positive ones, and the passive ones. As the creator of Paypal, SpaceX, and Tesla Elon Musk commented one-day:

Robots will do everything better than us, and people should be really concerned by it.

But right now, most AI technology can only do limited work in certain domains. In the area of deep learning, there are perhaps more challenges than the successful adoptions in people's life. Until now, most of the progress in deep learning has been made by exploring various architectures, but we still lack the fundamental understanding of why and how deep learning has achieved such success. Additionally, there are limited studies on why and how to choose structural features and how to efficiently tune hyper-parameters. Most of the current approaches are still based on validation or cross-validation, which is far from being theoretically grounded and is more on the side of experimental and ad hoc (*Plamen Angelov and Alessandro Sperduti, Challenges in Deep Learning, 2016*). From a data source perspective, how to deal with fast moving and streamed data, high dimensional data, structured data in the form of sequences (time series, audio and video signals, DNA, and so on), trees (XML documents, parse trees, RNA, and so on), graphs (chemical compounds, social networks, parts of an image, and so on) is still in development, especially when concerning their computational efficiency.

Additionally, there is a need for multi-task unified modeling. As the Google DeepMind's research scientist Raia Hadsell summed it up:

> *There is no neural network in the world, and no method right now that can be trained to identify objects and images, play Space Invaders, and listen to music.*

Until now, many trained models have specialized in just one or two areas, such as recognizing faces, cars, human actions, or understanding speech, which is far from true AI. Whereas a truly intelligent module would not only be able to process and understand multi-source inputs, but also make decisions for various tasks or sequences of tasks. The question of how to best apply the knowledge learned from one domain to other domains and adapt quickly remains unanswered.

While many optimization approaches have been proposed in the past, such as Gradient Descent or Stochastic Gradient Descent, Adagrad, AdaDelta, or Adma (Adaptive Moment Estimation), some known weaknesses, such as trap at local minima, lower performance, and high computational time still occur in deep learning. New research in this direction would yield fundamental impacts on deep learning performance and efficiency. It would be interesting to see whether global optimization techniques can be used to assist deep learning regarding the aforementioned problems.

Last but not least, there are perhaps more opportunities than challenges to be faced when applying deep learning or even developing new types of deep learning algorithms to fields that so far have not yet been benefited from. From finance to e-commerce, social networks to bioinformatics, we have seen tremendous growth in the interest of leveraging deep learning. Powered by deep learning, we are seeing applications, startups, and services which are changing our life at a much faster pace.

Summary

In this chapter, we have introduced the high-level concept of deep learning and AI in general. We talked about the history of deep learning, the up and downs, and its recent rise. From there, we dived deeper to discuss the differences between shallow algorithms and deep algorithms. We specifically discussed the two aspects of understanding deep learning: the neural point view and feature representation learning point of view. We then gave several successful applications across various fields. In the end, we talked about challenges that deep learning still faces and the potential future for machine-based AI.

In the next chapter, we will help you set up the development environment and get our hands dirty.

2

Getting Yourself Ready for Deep Learning

Due to recent achievements of **Artificial Neural Networks** (**ANNs**) in different applications of **artificial intelligence** (**AI**), such as computer vision, **natural language processing** (**NLP**) and speech recognition, deep learning has emerged as the prominent technology fundamental to most real-world implementations. This chapter aims to be a starting point on how to set oneself up for experimenting with and applying deep learning techniques in the real world.

We will answer the key question as to what skills and concepts are needed to get started with deep learning. We will specifically answer following questions:

- What skills are needed to understand and get started with deep learning?
- What are the core concepts from linear algebra that are required for deep learning?
- What hardware requirements exist for practical implementations of deep learning systems?
- What software frameworks exist today that allow developers easy development of their deep learning applications?
- How do you set up a deep learning system over a cloud-based **graphics processing unit** (**GPU**) instance such as AWS?

Basics of linear algebra

One of the most fundamental skills required to get oneself setup with deep learning is a foundational understanding of linear algebra. Though linear algebra itself is a vast subject, and covering it in full is outside the scope of this book, we will go through some important aspects of linear algebra in this chapter. Hopefully, this will give you a sufficient understanding of some core concepts and how they interplay with deep learning methodologies.

Data representation

In this section, we will look at core data structures and representations used most commonly across different linear algebra tasks. This is not meant to be a comprehensive list at all but only serves to highlight some of the prominent representations useful for understanding deep learning concepts:

- **Vectors**: One of the most fundamental representations in linear algebra is a vector. A vector can be defined as an array of objects, or more specifically an array of numbers that preserves the ordering of the numbers. Each number can be accessed in a vector based on its indexed location. For example, consider a vector x containing seven days a week encoded from 1 to 7, where 1 represents Sunday and 7 represents Saturday. Using this notation, a particular day of the week, say Wednesday, can be directly accessed from the vector as x [4]:

$$x = \begin{bmatrix} x_1 \\ x_2 \\ . \\ . \\ . \\ x_n \end{bmatrix}$$

- **Matrices**: These are a two-dimensional representation of numbers, or basically a vector of vectors. Each matrix, m, is composed of a certain number of rows, r, and a specified number of columns, c. Each of i rows, where $1 <= i <= r$, is a vector of c numbers. Each of the j columns, where $1 <= j <= c$, is also a vector of r numbers. Matrices are a particularly useful representation when we are working with images. Though real-world images are three-dimensional in nature, most of the computer vision problems are focused on the two-dimensional presentation of images. As such, a matrix representation is an intuitive representation of images:

$$\begin{bmatrix} A_{1,1} & A_{1,2} \\ A_{2,1} & A_{2,2} \end{bmatrix}$$

- **Identity matrices**: An identity matrix is defined as a matrix which, when multiplied with a vector, does not change the vector. Typically, an identity matrix has all elements as 0 except on its main diagonal, which is all 1s:

$$\begin{bmatrix} 1 & 0 & 0 \\ 0 & 1 & 0 \\ 0 & 0 & 1 \end{bmatrix}$$

Data operations

In this section, we will look at some of the most common transformations applied on matrices.

- **Matrix transpose**: Matrix transpose is a matrix transform that simply mirrors the matrix along its main diagonal. Mathematically it is defined as follows:

$$(A^T)_{i,j} = A_{j,i}$$

$$A = \begin{bmatrix} A_{1,1} & A_{1,2} \\ A_{2,1} & A_{2,2} \\ A_{3,1} & A_{3,2} \end{bmatrix} \implies A^T = \begin{bmatrix} A_{1,1} & A_{2,1} & A_{3,1} \\ A_{1,2} & A_{2,2} & A_{3,2} \end{bmatrix}$$

- **Matrix multiplication**: Matrix multiplication is one of the most fundamental operations that can be applied to any two matrices. A matrix, A, of shape A_r x A_c can be multiplied by another matrix, B, of shape B_r x B_c if and only if $A_c = B_r$. The resultant matrix, C, is the shape A_r x B_c. The multiplication operation is defined as follows:

$$C_{i,j} = \sum_k A_{i,k} B_{k,j}$$

Matrix multiplication generally has very useful properties. For example, matrix multiplication is distributive:

$$A(B + C) = AB + AC$$

Matrix multiplication is also associative:

$$A(BC) = (AB)C$$

Matrix multiplication also has a very simple form for its transpose:

$$(AB)^T = B^T A^T$$

Matrix multiplication is not commutative, which means $A \times B \neq B \times A$. However, the dot products between two vectors is commutative:

$$x^T y = y^T x$$

Matrix properties

In this section, we will look at some of the important properties matrices which are very useful for deep learning applications.

- **Norm**: Norm is an important property of a vector or a matrix that measures the size of the vector or the matrix. Geometrically it can also be interpreted as the distance of a point, x, from an origin. A L_p norm is therefore defined as follows:

$$\|x\|_p = \left(\sum_i |x_i|^p \right)^{\frac{1}{p}}$$

Though a norm can be computed for various orders of p, most popularly known norms are L1 and L_2 norm. L_1 norm is usually considered a good choice for sparse models:

$$\|x\|_1 = \sum_i |x_i|$$

Another norm popular in the deep learning community is the max norm, also referred to as L^∞. This is simply equivalent to the value of the largest element in the vector:

$$||x||_\infty = \max_i |x_i|$$

So far, all the previously mentioned norms are applicable to vectors. When we want to compute the size of a matrix, we use **Frobenius norm**, defined as follows:

$$||A||_F = \sqrt{\sum_{i,j} A_{i,j}^2}$$

Norms are usually used as they can be used to compute the dot product of two vectors directly:

$$x^T y = ||x||_2 ||y||_2 \cos(\theta)$$

- **Trace**: Trace is an operator that is defined as the sum of all the diagonal elements of a matrix:

$$Tr(A) = \sum_i A_{i,i}$$

Trace operators are quite useful in computing the **Frobenius norm** of the matrix, as follows:

$$||A||_F = \sqrt{Tr(AA^T)}$$

Another interesting property of trace operator is that it is invariant to matrix transpose operations. Hence, it is often used to manipulate matrix expressions to yield meaningful identities:

$$Tr(A) = Tr(A^T)$$

- **Determinant**: A determinant of a matrix is defined as a scalar value which is simply a product of all the eigenvalues of a matrix. They are generally very useful in the analysis and solution of systems of linear equations. For instance, according to Cramer's rule, a system of linear equations has a unique solution, if and only if, the determinant of the matrix composed of the system of linear equations is non-zero.

Deep learning with GPU

As the name suggests, deep learning involves learning a deeper representation of data, which requires large amounts of computational power. Such massive computational power is usually not possible with modern day CPUs. GPUs, on the other hand, lend themselves very nicely to this task. GPUs were originally designed for rendering graphics in real time. The design of a typical GPU allows for the disproportionately larger number of **arithmetic logical unit** (**ALU**), which allows them to crunch a large number of calculations in real time.

GPUs used for general purpose computation have a high data parallel architecture, which means they can process a large number of data points in parallel, leading to higher computational throughput. Each GPU is composed of thousands of cores. Each of such cores consists of a number of functional units which contain cache and ALU among other modules. Each of these functional units executes exactly the same instruction set thereby allowing for massive data parallelism in GPUs. In the next section, we compare and contrast the design of a GPU with CPU.

The following table illustrates the differences between the design of CPU with a GPU. As shown, GPUs are designed to execute a large number of threads optimized to execute an identical control logic. Hence, each of the GPU cores is rather simple in design. CPUs, on the other hand, are designed to operate with fewer cores but are the more general purpose. Their basic core design can handle highly complex control logic, which is usually not possible in GPUs. Hence CPUs can be thought of like a commodity processing unit as opposed to GPUs which are specialized units:

GPU	CPU
Large number of simpler cores	Fewer number of complex cores
Higher level of multi-threaded optimization	Single-threaded optimization
Good for specialized computing	Good for general purpose computing

In terms of relative performance comparison, GPU's have a much lower latency than CPUs for performing high data parallel operations. This is also especially true if the GPU has enough device memory to load all the required data needed for peak load computation. However, for a head to head the number of core comparison, CPU's have a much lower latency as each CPU core is much more complex and has an advanced state control logic as opposed to a GPU.

As such, the design of the algorithm has a great bearing on potential benefits of using GPU versus CPU. The following table outlines what algorithms are a good choice for a GPU implementation. Erik Smistad and their co-authors outline five different factors that determine the suitability of the algorithm towards using a GPU–data parallelism, thread count, branch divergence, memory usage, and synchronization.

The table *Factors affecting GPU Computing* by Dutta-Roy illustrates the impact of all of these factors on the suitability of using a GPU. As shown following, any algorithm which fares under the **High** column is more suited to using a GPU than others:

	High	Medium	Low
Data parallelism	Almost entire method is data parallel* (75–100%).	More than half of the method is data parallel (50–75%).	None or up to half of the method is data parallel (0–50%).
Thread count	The thread count is equal to or more than the number of pixels/voxels in the image.	The thread count is in the thousands.	The thread count is less than a thousand.
Branch divergence	More than 10% of the AUEs** have branch divergence and the code complexity in the branch is substantial.	Less than 10% of the AUEs have branch divergence, but the code complexity is substantial.	The code complexity in the branches is low.
Memory usage	More than 5N***	From 2N to 5N.	2N or less.
Synchronization	Global synchronization is performed more than hundred times. This is usually true for iterative methods.	Global synchronization is performed between 10 and 100 times.	Only a few global or local synchronizations.

* Data Parallel : An algorithm that can perform the same instructions on multiple data elements in parallel is said to be data parallel.

** AUE: An AUE is thus a group of threads that are all executed atomically on thread processors in the same core. Nvidia calls them wraps while AMD calls them wavefronts.

*** N is the total number of pixels/voxels in the image

Factors affecting GPU Computing (Source: Dutta Roy et al. https://medium.com/@taposhdr/gpu-s-have-become-the-new-core-for-image-analytics-b8ba8bd8d8f3)

Deep learning hardware guide

There are few other important things to note while setting up your own hardware for deep learning application development. In this section, we will outline some of the most important aspects of GPU computing.

CPU cores

Most deep learning applications and libraries use a single core CPU unless they are used within a parallelization framework like **Message-Passing Interface** (**MPI**), MapReduce, or Spark. For example, **CaffeOnSpark** (`https://github.com/yahoo/CaffeOnSpark`) by the team at Yahoo! uses Spark with Caffe for parallelizing network training across multiple GPUs and CPUs. In most normal settings in a single box, one CPU core is enough for deep learning application development.

CPU cache size

CPU cache size is an important CPU component that is used for high-speed computations. A CPU cache is often organized as a hierarchy of cache layers, from L1 to L4—L1, and L2 being smaller and faster cache layers as opposed to the larger and slower layers L3 and L4. In an ideal setting, every data needed by the application resides in caches and hence no read is required from RAM, thereby making the overall operation faster.

However, this is hardly the scenario for most of the deep learning applications. For example, for a typical ImageNet experiment with a batch size of 128, we need more than 85MB of CPU cache to store all information for one mini batch [13]. Since such datasets are not small enough to be cache-only, a RAM read cannot be avoided. Hence modern day CPU cache sizes have little to no impact on the performance of deep learning applications.

RAM size

As we saw previously in this section, most of the deep learning applications read directly from RAM instead of CPU caches. Hence, it is often advisable to keep the CPU RAM almost as large, if not larger, than GPU RAM.

The size of the GPU RAM depends on the size of your deep learning model. For example, ImageNet based deep learnings models have a large number of parameters taking 4 GB to 5 GB of space, hence a GPU with at least 6 GB of RAM would be an ideal fit for such applications. Paired with a CPU with at least 8 GB or preferably more CPU RAM will allow application developers to focus on key aspects of their application instead of debugging RAM performance issues.

Hard drive

Typical deep learning applications required large sets of data that is in 100s of GB. Since this data cannot be set in any RAM, there is an ongoing data pipeline is constructed. A deep learning application loads the mini-batch data from GPU RAM, which in turns keeps on reading data from CPU RAM, which loads data directly from the hard drive. Since GPU's have a larger number of cores and each of these cores have a mini-batch of their data, they constantly need to be reading large volumes of data from the disk to allow for high data parallelism.

For example, in AlexNet's **Convolutional Neural Network (CNN)** based model, roughly 300 MB of data needs to be read every second. This can often cripple the overall application performance. Hence, a **solid state driver** (SSD) is often the right choice for most deep learning application developers.

Cooling systems

Modern-day GPU's are energy efficient and have in-built mechanisms to prevent them from overheating. For instance, when a GPU increases their speed and power consumption, their temperature rises as well. Typically at around 80°C, their inbuilt temperature control kicks in, which reduces their speed thereby automatically cooling the GPUs. The real bottleneck in this process is the poor design of pre-programmed schedules for fan speeds.

In a typical deep learning application, an 80°C temperature is reached within the first few seconds of the application, thereby lowering the GPU performance from the start and providing a poor GPU throughput. To complicate matters, most of the existing fan scheduling options are not available in Linux where most of the current day deep learning applications work.

A number of options exist today to alleviate this problem. First, a **Basic Input/Output System (BIOS)** upgrade with a modified fan schedule can provide the optimal balance between overheating and performance. Another option to use for an external cooling system, such as a water cooling system. However, this option is mostly applicable to GPU farms where multiple GPU servers are running. External cooling systems are also a bit expensive so cost also becomes an important factor in selecting the right cooling system for your application.

Deep learning software frameworks

Every good deep learning application needs to have several components to be able to function correctly. These include:

- A model layer which allows a developer to design his or her own model with more flexibility
- A GPU layer that makes it seamless for application developers to choose between GPU/CPU for its application
- A parallelization layer that can allow the developer to scale his or her application to run on multiple devices or instances

As you can imagine, implementing these modules is not easy. Often a developer needs to spend more time on debugging implementation issues rather than the legitimate model issues. Thankfully, a number of software frameworks exist in the industry today which make deep learning application development practically the first class of its programming language.

These frameworks vary in architecture, design, and feature but almost all of them provide immense value to developers by providing them easy and fast implementation framework for their applications. In this section, we will take a look at some popular deep learning software frameworks and how they compare with each other.

TensorFlow – a deep learning library

TensorFlow is an open source software library for numerical computation using data flow graphs. Designed and developed by Google, TensorFlow represents the complete data computation as a flow graph. Each node in this graph can be represented as a mathematical operator. An edge connecting two nodes represents the multi-dimensional data that flows between the two nodes.

One of the primary advantages of TensorFlow is that it supports CPU and GPU as well as mobile devices, thereby making it almost seamless for developers to write code against any device architecture. TensorFlow also has a very big community of developers leading to a huge momentum behind this framework.

Caffe

Caffe was designed and developed at **Berkeley Artificial Intelligence Research (BAIR)** Lab. It was designed with expression, speed, and modularity in mind. It has an expressive architecture as it allows for a very configurable way to define models and optimization parameters without necessitating any additional code. This configuration also allows an easy switch from CPU to GPU mode and vice-versa with but a single flag change.

Caffe also boasts good performance benchmark numbers when it comes to speed. For instance, on a single NVIDIA K40 GPU, Caffe can process over 60 million images per day. Caffe also has a strong community, ranging from academic researchers as well as industrial research labs using Caffe across a heterogeneous application stack.

MXNet

MXNet is a multi-language machine learning library. It offers two modes of computation:

- **Imperative mode**: This mode exposes an interface much like regular NumPy like API. For example, to construct a tensor of zeros on both CPU and GPU using MXNet, you use the following code block:

```
import mxnet as mx
tensor_cpu = mx.nd.zeros((100,), ctx=mx.cpu())
tensor_gpu = mx.nd.zeros((100,), ctx=mx.gpu(0))
```

In the example earlier, MXNet specifies the location where to hold the tensor either in CPU or in a GPU device at location 0. One important distinction with MXNet is that all computations happen lazily instead of instantaneously. This allows MXNet to achieve incredible utilization of the device, unlike any other framework.

- **Symbolic mode**: This mode exposes a computation graph like TensorFlow. Though the imperative API is quite useful, one of its drawbacks is its rigidity. All computations need to be known beforehand along with pre-defined data structures. Symbolic API aims to remove this limitation by allowing MXNet to work with symbols or variables instead of fixed data types. These symbols can then be compiled or interpreted to be executed as a set of operations as shown follows:

```
import mxnet as mx
x = mx.sym.Variable("X") # represent a symbol.
y = mx.sym.Variable("Y")
z = (x + y)
m = z / 100
```

Torch

Torch is a Lua based deep learning framework developed by Ronan Collobert, Clement Farabet, and Koray Kavukcuoglu. It was initially used by the CILVR Lab at New York University. The Torch is powered by C/C++ libraries under its hood and also uses **Compute Unified Device Architecture (CUDA)** for its GPU interactions. It aims to be the fastest deep learning framework while also providing a simple C-like interface for rapid application development.

Theano

Theano is a Python library that allows you to define, optimize, and evaluate mathematical expressions involving multi-dimensional arrays efficiently. Some of the key features of Theano is its very tight integration with NumPy, making it almost native to a large number of Python developers. It also provides a very intuitive interface to using GPU or CPU. It has an *efficient symbolic differentiation*, allowing it to provide derivatives for functions with one or many inputs. It is also numerically stable and has a dynamic code generation capability leading to faster expression evaluations. Theano is a good framework choice if you have advanced machine learning expertise and are looking for a low-level API for a fine-grained control of your deep learning application.

Microsoft Cognitive Toolkit

Microsoft Cognitive Toolkit is also known as **CNTK**; it is the latest entry to the increasing set of deep learning frameworks. CNTK has two major functionalities that it supports:

- Support for multiple features such as:
    - CPU/GPU for training and prediction
    - Both Windows and Linux operating systems
    - Efficient recurrent network training through batching techniques
    - Data parallelization using one-bit quantized **singular value decomposition** (**SVD**)
- Efficient modularization that separates:
    - Compute network
    - Execution engine
    - Learning algorithms
    - Model configuration

Keras

Keras is a deep learning framework that is probably the most different from every other framework described previously. Most of the described frameworks are low-level modules that directly interact with GPU using CUDA.

Keras, on the other hand, could be understood as a meta-framework that interacts with other frameworks such as Theano or TensorFlow to handle its GPU interactions or other system-level access management. As such, it is highly flexible and very user-friendly, allowing developers to choose from a variety of underlying model implementations. Keras community support is also gaining good momentum and, as of September 2017, TensorFlow team plans to integrate Keras as a subset of the TensorFlow project.

Framework comparison

Though a number of deep learning software frameworks exist, it is hard to understand their feature parity. The table *Feature parity of DL frameworks* outlines each of these frameworks with their feature parity:

	Languages	Community Support	Modeling Flexibility	Easy configuration	Speed	GPU Parallelization	Tutorials
TensorFlow	Python	Excellent	Excellent	Excellent	Strong	Strong	Excellent
Caffe	C++	Excellent	Strong	Strong	Strong	Good	Strong
MXNet	R, Python, Julia, Scala	Excellent	Strong	Strong	Strong	Excellent	Excellent
Torch	Lua, Python	Strong	Excellent	Excellent	Excellent	Strong	Strong
Theano	Python, C++	Strong	Strong	Good	Strong	Good	Excellent
CNTK	C++	Excellent	Strong	Good	Strong	Good	Strong
Keras	Python	Excellent	Excellent	Excellent	Strong	Strong	Strong

Feature parity of DL frameworks

Recently, Shaohuai Shi and their co-authors in their paper (https://arxiv.org/pdf/1608.07249.pdf) also presented a comprehensive performance benchmarking of four popular frameworks from as preceding: Caffe, CNTK, TensorFlow and Torch. They first benchmark the performance of these frameworks on three most popular types of neural networks—**fully connected neural network (FCN)**, CNN, and recurrent neural network (RNN). They also benchmark performance of these systems when they use multiple GPUs as well as CPUs.

In their paper, they outline the comparative performance of all the systems. Their experimental results demonstrate that all the frameworks can utilize GPUs very efficiently and show performance gains over CPUs. However, there is still no clear winner among all of them, which suggests there are still improvements to be made across all of these frameworks.

Setting up deep learning on AWS

In this section, we will show two different ways of setting up a deep learning system using **Amazon Web Services (AWS)**.

Setup from scratch

In this section, we will illustrate how to set up a deep learning environment on an AWS EC2 GPU instance g2.2xlarge running Ubuntu Server 16.04 LTS. For this example, we will use a pre-baked **Amazon Machine Image (AMI)** which already has a number of software packages installed—making it easier to set up an end-end deep learning system. We will use a publicly available AMI Image ami-b03ffedf, which has following pre-installed packages:

- CUDA 8.0
- Anaconda 4.20 with Python 3.0
- Keras / Theano

1. The first step to setting up the system is to set up an AWS account and spin a new EC2 GPU instance using the AWS web console as (`http://console.aws.amazon.com/`) shown in figure *Choose EC2 AMI*:

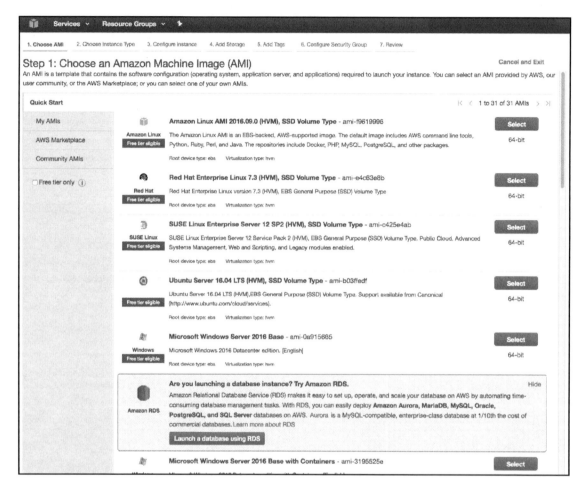

Choose EC2 AMI

2. We pick a **g2.2xlarge** instance type from the next page as shown in figure *Choose instance type*:

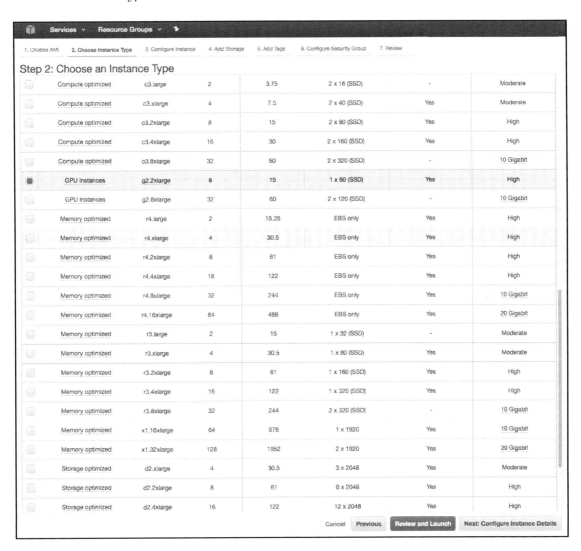

Choose instance type

3. After adding a 30 GB of storage as shown in figure *Choose storage*, we now launch a cluster and assign an EC2 key pair that can allow us to `ssh` and log in to the box using the provided key pair file:

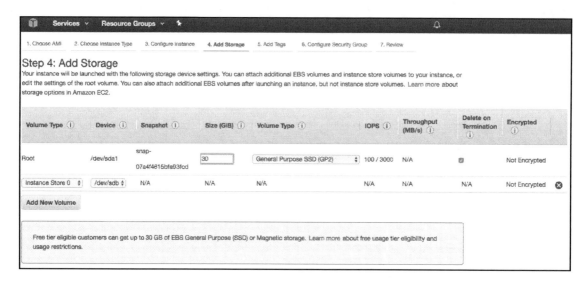

Choose storage

4. Once the EC2 box is launched, next step is to install relevant software packages. To ensure proper GPU utilization, it is important to ensure graphics drivers are installed first. We will upgrade and install NVIDIA drivers as follows:

```
$ sudo add-apt-repository ppa:graphics-drivers/ppa -y
$ sudo apt-get update
$ sudo apt-get install -y nvidia-375 nvidia-settings
```

While NVIDIA drivers ensure that host GPU can now be utilized by any deep learning application, it does not provide an easy interface to application developers for easy programming on the device.

Various different software libraries exist today that help achieve this task reliably. **Open Computing Language (OpenCL)** and CUDA are more commonly used in industry. In this book, we use CUDA as an application programming interface for accessing NVIDIA graphics drivers. To install CUDA driver, we first SSH into the EC2 instance and download CUDA 8.0 to our $HOME folder and install from there:

```
$ wget
https://developer.nvidia.com/compute/cuda/8.0/Prod2/local_installers/cuda-r
epo-ubuntu1604-8-0-local-ga2_8.0.61-1_amd64-deb
$ sudo dpkg -i cuda-repo-ubuntu1604-8-0-local_8.0.44-1_amd64-deb
$ sudo apt-get update
$ sudo apt-get install -y cuda nvidia-cuda-toolkit
```

Once the installation is finished, you can run the following command to validate the installation:

```
$ nvidia-smi
```

Now your EC2 box is fully configured to be used for a deep learning development. However, for someone who is not very familiar with deep learning implementation details, building a deep learning system from scratch can be a daunting task.

To ease this development, a number of advanced deep learning software frameworks exist, such as Keras and Theano. Both of these frameworks are based on a Python development environment, hence we first install a Python distribution on the box, such as Anaconda:

```
$ wget https://repo.continuum.io/archive/Anaconda3-4.2.0-Linux-x86_64.sh
$ bash Anaconda3-4.2.0-Linux-x86_64.sh
```

Finally, Keras and Theanos are installed using Python's package manager `pip`:

```
$ pip install --upgrade --no-deps git+git://github.com/Theano/Theano.git
$ pip install keras
```

Once the `pip` installation is completed successfully, the box is now fully set up for a deep learning development.

Setup using Docker

The previous section describes getting started from scratch which can be tricky sometimes given continuous changes to software packages and changing links on the web. One way to avoid dependence on links is to use container technology like Docker.

In this chapter, we will use the official NVIDIA-Docker image that comes pre-packaged with all the necessary packages and deep learning framework to get you quickly started with deep learning application development:

```
$ sudo add-apt-repository ppa:graphics-drivers/ppa -y
$ sudo apt-get update
$ sudo apt-get install -y nvidia-375 nvidia-settings nvidia-modprobe
```

1. We now install Docker Community Edition as follows:

```
$ curl -fsSL https://download.docker.com/linux/ubuntu/gpg | sudo
apt-key add -
# Verify that the key fingerprint is 9DC8 5822 9FC7 DD38 854A E2D8
8D81 803C 0EBF CD88
$ sudo apt-key fingerprint 0EBFCD88
$ sudo add-apt-repository \
  "deb [arch=amd64] https://download.docker.com/linux/ubuntu \
  $(lsb_release -cs) \
  stable"
$ sudo apt-get update
$ sudo apt-get install -y docker-ce
```

2. We then install NVIDIA-Docker and its plugin:

```
$ wget -P /tmp
https://github.com/NVIDIA/nvidia-docker/releases/download/v1.0.1/nv
idia-docker_1.0.1-1_amd64.deb
$ sudo dpkg -i /tmp/nvidia-docker_1.0.1-1_amd64.deb && rm
/tmp/nvidia-docker_1.0.1-1_amd64.deb
```

3. To validate if the installation happened correctly, we use the following command:

```
$ sudo nvidia-docker run --rm nvidia/cuda nvidia-smi
```

4. Once it's setup correctly, we can use the official TensorFlow or Theano Docker image:

```
$ sudo nvidia-docker run -it tensorflow/tensorflow:latest-gpu bash
```

5. We can run a simple Python program to check if TensorFlow works properly:

```
import tensorflow as tf
a = tf.constant(5, tf.float32)
b = tf.constant(5, tf.float32)
with tf.Session() as sess:
    sess.run(tf.add(a, b)) # output is 10.0
    print("Output of graph computation is = ",output)
```

You should see the TensorFlow output on the screen now as shown in figure *Tensorflow sample output:*

```
Last login: Tue Jan 16 17:20:00 on ttys001
Anurag:~ anuragbhardwaj$ python tensor-toy.py
dyld: warning, LC_RPATH $ORIGIN/../../_solib_darwin_x86_64/_U_S_Stensorflow_Spyt
hon_C_Upywrap_Utensorflow_Uinternal.so___Utensorflow in /Library/Python/2.7/site
-packages/tensorflow/python/_pywrap_tensorflow_internal.so being ignored in rest
ricted program because it is a relative path
Couldn't import dot_parser, loading of dot files will not be possible.
2018-01-16 17:39:57.587007: I tensorflow/core/platform/cpu_feature_guard.cc:137]
 Your CPU supports instructions that this TensorFlow binary was not compiled to
use: SSE4.2 AVX AVX2 FMA
('Value after running graph:', 10.0)
Anurag:~ anuragbhardwaj$ █
```

Tensorflow sample output

Summary

In this chapter, we have summarized key concepts required to get started with the real-world implementation of deep learning systems. We described core concepts from linear algebra that are central to understanding the foundations of deep learning technology. We provide a hardware guide to deep learning by covering various aspects of GPU-based implementation and what is a right hardware choice for application developers. We outline a list of most popular deep learning software frameworks that exist today and provide a feature-level parity as well as a performance benchmark for them. Finally, we demonstrate how to set up a cloud-based deep learning application on AWS.

In the next chapter, we will introduce neural networks and outline a self-start module to understanding them in greater details.

3
Getting Started with Neural Networks

In this chapter, we will be focusing on the basics of neural networks, including input/output layers, hidden layers, and how the networks learn through forward and backpropagation. We will start with the standard multilayer perceptron networks, talk about their building blocks, and illustrate how they learn step-by-step. We will also introduce a few, popular standard models such as **Convolutional Neural Networks (CNN)**, **Restricted Boltzmann Machines (RBM)**, and **recurrent neural network (RNN)** as well as its variation **Long Short-Term Memory (LSTM)**. We will outline the key, critical components for the successful application of the models, and explain some important concepts to help you gain a better understanding of why these networks work so well in certain areas. In addition to a theoretical introduction, we will also show example code snippets using TensorFlow on how to construct layers and activation functions, and how to connect different layers. In the end, we will demonstrate an end-to-end example of MNIST classification using TensorFlow. With the setup you learned from `Chapter 2`, *Getting Yourself Ready for Deep Learning* it's time we jump into some real examples to get our hands dirty.

The outline of this chapter is as follows:

- Multilayer perceptrons:
    - The input layers
    - The output layers
    - Hidden layers
    - Activation functions

- How a network learns
- Deep learning models:
  - Convolutional Neural Networks
  - Restricted Boltzmann Machines
  - RNN/LSTM
- MNIST hands-on classification example

Multilayer perceptrons

The multilayer perceptron is one of the simplest networks. Essentially, it is defined as having one input layer, one output layer, and a few hidden layers (more than one). Each layer has multiple neurons and the adjacent layers are fully connected. Each neuron can be thought of as a cell in these huge networks. It determines the flow and transformation of the incoming signals. Signals from the previous layers are pushed forward to the neuron of the next layer through the connected weights. For each artificial neuron, it calculates a weighted sum of all incoming inputs by multiplying the signal with the weights and adding a bias. The weighted sum will then go through a function called an **activation function** to decide whether it should be fired or not, which results in output signals for the next level.

For example, a fully-connected, feed-forward neural network is pictured in the following diagram. As you may notice, there is an intercept node on each layer (x_0 and a_0). The non-linearity of the network is mainly contributed by the shape of the activation function.

The architecture of this fully connected, the feed-forward neural network looks essentially like the following:

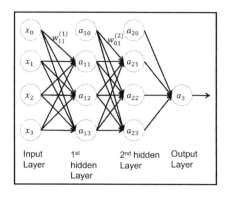

Fully connected, feed-forward neural network with two hidden layers

The input layer

The input layer is often defined as your raw input data. For text data, this can be words or characters. For an image, this can be raw pixel values from different color channels. Also, with varying dimensions of input data, it forms different structures, such as a one-dimensional vector or a tensor-like structure.

The output layer

The output layer is basically the output value of the network and is formed depending on the problem setting. In unsupervised learning, such as encoding or decoding, the output can be the same as the input. For classification problems, the output layer can have n neurons for n-way classification and utilize a softmax function to output the probability of being each class. Overall, the output layer maps to your target space and the perceptron in it would change accordingly, based on your problem setting.

Hidden layers

Hidden layers are layers between the input and output layers. Neurons on hidden layers can take various forms, such as a max pooling layer, convolutional layer, and so on, all be performing different mathematical functionalities. If you think of the entire network as a pipe of mathematical transformations, the hidden layers are each transformed and then composed together to map your input data to the output space. We will introduce more variations of the hidden layer when we talk about convolutional neural networks and RNN in later sections of this chapter.

Activation functions

The activation function in each artificial neuron decides whether the incoming signals have reached the threshold and should output signals for the next level. It is crucial to set up the right activation function because of the gradient vanishing issue, which we will talk about later.

Another important feature of an activation function is that it should be differentiable. The network learns from the errors that are calculated at the output layer. A differentiable activation function is needed to perform backpropagation optimization while propagating backwards in the network to compute gradients of error (loss) with respect to weights, and then optimize weights accordingly, using gradient descent or any other optimization technique to reduce the error.

The following table lists a few common activation functions. We will dive into them a bit deeper, talk about the differences between them, and explain how to choose the right activation function:

Name	Equation	Derivative	1-D Graph	1-D Graph(derivative)
Binary Step	$\sigma(x) = \begin{cases} 1, & x > 0 \\ 0.5, & x = 0 \\ 0, & x < 0 \end{cases}$	$\sigma'(x) = \begin{cases} 0, & x \neq 0 \\ ?, & x = 0 \end{cases}$		
Identity	$\sigma(x) = x$	$\sigma'(x) = 1$		
Sigmoid	$\sigma(x) = \dfrac{1}{1 + e^{-x}}$	$\sigma'(x)\\ = \sigma(x)(1 - \sigma(x))$		
Tanh	$\sigma(x) = \dfrac{e^x - e^{-x}}{e^x + e^{-x}}$	$\sigma'(x) = 1 - \sigma(x)^2$		
Rectified Linear (ReLU)	$\sigma(x) = \max(0, x)$	$\sigma'(x) = \begin{cases} 1, & x \geq 0 \\ 0, & x < 0 \end{cases}$		
Leaky ReLU	$\sigma(x) = \begin{cases} x, & x \geq 0 \\ \alpha x, & x < 0 \end{cases}$	$\sigma'(x) = \begin{cases} 1, & x \geq 0 \\ \alpha, & x < 0 \end{cases}$		

Sigmoid or logistic function

A sigmoid function has a distinctive S shape and it is a differentiable real function for any real input value. Its range is between 0 and 1. It is an activation function in the following form:

$$\sigma(x) = \frac{1}{1 + e^{-x}}$$

Its first derivative, which is used during backpropagation of the training step, has the following form:

$$\frac{d\sigma(x)}{d(x)} = \sigma(x) \cdot (1 - \sigma(x))$$

The implementation is as follows:

```
def sigmoid(x):
    return tf.div(tf.constant(1.0),
               tf.add(tf.constant(1.0), tf.exp(tf.neg(x))))
```

The derivative of a `sigmoid` function is as follows:

```
def sigmoidprime(x):
    return tf.multiply(sigmoid(x), tf.subtract(tf.constant(1.0),
sigmoid(x)))
```

However, a `sigmoid` function can cause the gradient vanishing problem or saturation of the gradient. It is also known to have a slow convergence. Therefore, in practical use, it is not recommended to use a `sigmoid` as the activation function, ReLU has become more popular.

Tanh or hyperbolic tangent function

The mathematical formula of tanh is as follows:

$$f(x) = \frac{1 - e^{-2x}}{1 + e^{-2x}}$$

Its output is centered at zero with a range of -1 to 1. Therefore, optimization is easier and thus in practice, it is preferred over a sigmoid activation function. However, it still suffers from the vanishing gradient problem.

ReLU

The Rectified Linear Unit (ReLU) has become quite popular in recent years. Its mathematical formula is as follows:

$$\sigma(x) = \begin{cases} max(0, x) & , x >= 0 \\ 0 & , x < 0 \end{cases}$$

Compared to sigmoid and tanh, its computation is much simpler and more efficient. It was proved that it improves convergence by six times (for example, a factor of 6 in Krizhevsky and it's co-authors in their work of *ImageNet Classification with Deep Convolutional Neural Networks*, 2012), possibly due to the fact that it has a linear and non-saturating form. Also, unlike tanh or sigmoid functions which involve the expensive exponential operation, ReLU can be achieved by simply thresholding activation at zero. Therefore, it has become very popular over the last couple of years. Almost all deep learning models use ReLU nowadays. Another important advantage of ReLU is that it avoids or rectifies the vanishing gradient problem.

Its limitation resides in the fact that its direct output is not in the probability space. It cannot be used in the output layer, but only in the hidden layers. Therefore, for classification problems, one needs to use the softmax function on the last layer to compute the probabilities for classes. For a regression problem, one should simply use a linear function. Another problem with ReLU is that it can cause dead neuron problems. For example, if large gradients flow through ReLU, it may cause the weights to be updated such that a neuron will never be active on any other future data points.

To fix this problem, another modification was introduced called **Leaky ReLU**. To fix the problem of dying neurons it introduces a small slope to keep the updates alive.

Leaky ReLU and maxout

A Leaky ReLU will have a small slope α on the negative side, such as 0.01. The slope α can also be made into a parameter of each neuron, such as in PReLU neurons (P stands for parametric). The problem with this activation function is the inconsistency of the effectiveness of such modifications to various problems.

Maxout is another attempt to solve the dead neuron problem in ReLU. It takes the form $max(w_1^T x + b_1, w_2^T x + b_2)$. From this form, we can see that both ReLU and leaky ReLU are just special cases of this form, that is, for ReLU, it's $w_1 = 0, b_1 = 0$. Although it benefits from linearity and having no saturation, it has doubled the number of parameters for every single neuron.

Softmax

When using ReLU as the activation function for classification problems a softmax function is used on the last layer. It helps to generate the probability such as scores similar to ($0 < p(y = j|z_j) < 1, sum(p(y = j|z_j)) = 1$) for each of the classes:

$$p(y = j|z_j) = \phi(z_j) = \frac{e^{z_j}}{\sum_j^K z_j}$$

Choosing the right activation function

In most cases, we should always consider ReLU first. But keep in mind that ReLU should only be applied to hidden layers. If your model suffers from dead neurons, then think about adjusting your learning rate, or try Leaky ReLU or maxout.

It is not recommended to use either sigmoid or tanh as they suffer from the vanishing gradient problem and also converge very slowly. Take sigmoid for example. Its derivative is greater than 0.25 everywhere, making terms during backpropagating even smaller. While for ReLU, its derivative is one at every point above zero, thus creating a more stable network.

Now you have gained a basic knowledge of the key components in neural networks, let's move on to understanding how the networks learn from data.

How a network learns

Suppose we have a two-layer network. Let's represent inputs/outputs with (a_0, y), and the two layers by states, that is, the connection weights with bias value: (w_1, b_1) and (w_2, b_2). We will also use σ as the activation function.

Weight initialization

After the configuration of the network, training starts with initializing the weights' values. A proper weight initialization is important in the sense that all the training does is to adjust the coefficients to best capture the patterns from data in order to successfully output the approximation of the target value. In most cases, weights are initialized randomly. In some finely-tuned settings, weights are initialized using a pre-trained model.

Forward propagation

Forward propagation is basically calculating the input data multiplied by the networks' weight plus the offset, and then going through the activation function to the next layer:

$$z_1 = a_0 * w_1 + b_1$$
$$a_1 = \sigma(z_1)$$
$$z_2 = a_1 * w_2 + b_2$$
$$a_2 = \sigma(z_2)$$

An example code block using TensorFlow can be written as follows:

```
# dimension variables
dim_in = 2
dim_middle = 5
dim_out = 1

# declare network variables
a_0 = tf.placeholder(tf.float32, [None, dim_in])
y = tf.placeholder(tf.float32, [None, dim_out])

w_1 = tf.Variable(tf.random_normal([dim_in, dim_middle]))
b_1 = tf.Variable(tf.random_normal([dim_middle]))
w_2 = tf.Variable(tf.random_normal([dim_middle, dim_out]))
b_2 = tf.Variable(tf.random_normal([dim_out]))

# build the network structure
z_1 = tf.add(tf.matmul(a_0, w_1), b_1)
a_1 = sigmoid(z_1)
z_2 = tf.add(tf.matmul(a_1, w_2), b_2)
a_2 = sigmoid(z_2)
```

Backpropagation

All the networks learn from the error and then update the network weights/parameters to reflect the errors based on a given cost function. The gradient is the slope representing the relationship between a network's weights and its error.

Calculating errors

The first thing in backpropagation is to calculate the errors from forward propagation for your target value. The input provides y as a test for the accuracy of the network's output, so we compute the following vector:

$$\nabla a = a_2 - y$$

This is written in code as follows:

```
# define error, which is the difference between the activation function
output from the last layer and the label
error = tf.sub(a_2, y)
```

Backpropagation

With the errors, backpropagation works backwards to update the network weights on the direction of gradients of the error. First, we need to compute the deltas of the weights and biases. Note that ∇z_2 is used to update b_2 and w_2, and ∇z_1 is used to update b_1 and w_1:

$$\nabla z_2 = \nabla a \cdot \sigma'(z_2)$$

$$\nabla b_2 = \nabla z_2$$

$$\nabla w_2 = a_1^T \cdot \nabla z_2$$

$$\nabla z_1 = \nabla a_1 \cdot \sigma'(z_1)$$

$$\nabla b_1 = \nabla z_1$$

$$\nabla w_1 = a_0^T \cdot \nabla z_1$$

This is written in TensorFlow code as follows:

```
d_z_2 = tf.multiply(error, sigmoidprime(z_2))
d_b_2 = d_z_2
d_w_2 = tf.matmul(tf.transpose(a_1), d_z_2)

d_a_1 = tf.matmul(d_z_2, tf.transpose(w_2))
d_z_1 = tf.multiply(d_a_1, sigmoidprime(z_1))
d_b_1 = d_z_1
d_w_1 = tf.matmul(tf.transpose(a_0), d_z_1)
```

Updating the network

Now the deltas have been computed, it's time to update the network's parameters. In most cases, we use a type of gradient descent. Let η represent the learning rate, the parameter update formula is:

$$w_1 \leftarrow w_1 - \eta \cdot \nabla w_1$$

$$b_1 \leftarrow b_1 - \eta \cdot \nabla b_1$$

$$w_2 \leftarrow w_2 - \eta \cdot \nabla w_2$$

$$b_2 \leftarrow b_2 - \eta \cdot \nabla b_2$$

This is written in TensorFlow code as follows:

```
eta = tf.constant(0.01)
step = [
    tf.assign(w_1,
            tf.subtract(w_1, tf.multiply(eta, d_w_1)))
  , tf.assign(b_1,
            tf.subtract(b_1, tf.multiply(eta,
                            tf.reduce_mean(d_b_1, axis=[0]))))
  , tf.assign(w_2,
            tf.subtract(w_2, tf.multiply(eta, d_w_2)))
  , tf.assign(b_2,
            tf.subtract(b_2, tf.multiply(eta,
                            tf.reduce_mean(d_b_2, axis=[0]))))
]
```

Automatic differentiation

TensorFlow provides a very convenient API that can help us to directly derive the deltas and update the network parameters:

```
# Define the cost as the square of the errors
cost = tf.square(error)

# The Gradient Descent Optimizer will do the heavy lifting
learning_rate = 0.01
optimizer = tf.train.GradientDescentOptimizer(learning_rate).minimize(cost)

# Define the function we want to approximate
def linear_fun(x):
    y = x[:,0] * 2 + x[:,1] * 4 + 1
    return y.reshape(y.shape[0],1)
```

```
# Other variables during learning
train_batch_size = 100
test_batch_size = 50

# Normal TensorFlow - initialize values, create a session and run the model
sess = tf.Session()
#sess.run(tf.global_variables_initializer())
sess.run(tf.initialize_all_variables())

for i in range(1000):
    x_value = np.random.rand(train_batch_size,2)
    y_value = linear_fun(x_value)
    sess.run(optimizer, feed_dict={a_0:x_value, y: y_value})
    if i % 100 == 0:
        test_x = np.random.rand(test_batch_size,2)
        res_val = sess.run(res, feed_dict =
                        {a_0: test_x,
                         y : linear_fun(test_x)})
        print res_val
```

In addition to this basic setting, let's now talk about a few important concepts you might encounter in practice.

Vanishing and exploding gradients

These are very important issues in many deep neural networks. The deeper the architecture, the more likely it suffers from these issues. What is happening is that during the backpropagation stage, weights are adjusted in proportion to the gradient value. So we may have two different scenarios:

- If the gradients are too small, then this is called the *vanishing gradients* problem. It makes the learning process very slow or even stops updating entirely. For example, using sigmoid as the activation function, where its derivatives are always smaller than 0.25, after a few layers of backpropagation, the lower layers will hardly receive any useful signals from the errors, thus the network is not updated properly.
- If the gradients get too large then it can cause the learning to diverge, this is called *exploding gradients*. This often happens when the activation function is not bounded or the learning rate is too big.

Optimization algorithms

Optimization is the key to how a network learns. Learning is basically an optimization process. It refers to the process that minimizes the error, cost, or finds the locus of least errors. It then adjusts the network coefficients step by step. A very basic optimization approach is the one we used in the previous section on *gradient descents*. However, there are multiple variations that do a similar job but with a bit of improvement added. TensorFlow provides multiple options for you to choose as the optimizer, for example, *GradientDescentOptimizer, AdagradOptimizer, MomentumOptimizer, AdamOptimizer, FtrlOptimizer*, and *RMSPropOptimizer*. For the API and how to use them, please see this page:

```
https://www.tensorflow.org/versions/master/api_docs/python/tf/train#optimizers.
```

These optimizers should be sufficient for most deep learning techniques. If you aren't sure which one to use, use *GradientDescentOptimizer* as a starting point.

Regularization

Like all other machine learning approaches, overfitting is something that needs to be controlled all the time, especially given that networks have so many parameters to learn. One of the methods to deal with overfitting is called **regularization**. Typical regularization is done by adding some constraints on the parameters, such as L1 or L2 regularization, which prevent the weights or coefficients of the networks growing too big. Take L2 regularization as an example. It is achieved by augmenting the cost function with the squared magnitude of all weights in the neural network. What it does is to heavily penalize the peaky weight vectors and diffuse the weight vectors.

That is, we encourage the network to use all of its input rather than only a part of it by diffusing the weight vectors more evenly. Overly large weights mean the network depends too much on a few heavily weighted inputs, which can make it difficult to generalize to new data. During the gradient descent stage, L2 regularization is essentially causing every weight to decay to zero, and this is called **weight decay**.

Another common type of regularization is L1 regularization, which often leads to the weight vectors becoming too sparse. It helps to understand which features are more useful for predictions by changing many others to zero. It may help the network to be more resistant to noise in the inputs, but empirically L2 regularization performs better.

Max-norm is another way of enforcing an absolute upper-bound on the magnitude of the incoming weight vector for every neuron. That is, during the gradient descent step, we normalize the vector back with radius c if $||w||_2 > c$. This is called a **projected gradient descent**. This sometimes stabilizes the learning of the networks as the coefficients never grow too big (always bounded) even if the learning rate is too high.

Dropout is a very different kind of method for preventing overfitting and is often used together with the techniques we previously mentioned. During training, dropout is achieved by only keeping a certain percentage of neurons active while setting others to zero. A pre-set hyperparameter p is used to generate a random sampling for which neurons should be set to zero (dropped out). $p = 0.5$ is often used in practice. Intuitively, dropout makes the different parts of the network learn from different information as only part of the network is updating during each batch. Overall, it prevents overfitting by providing a way of approximately combining many different neural network architectures exponentially and efficiently. For more details, one can refer to Hinton's dropout paper (*Srivastava and others, Dropout: A Simple Way to Prevent Neural Networks from Overfitting, 2013*).

Deep learning models

In this section, we will dive into three popular deep learning models one by one: CNNs, **Restricted Boltzmann Machines (RBM)**, and the **recurrent neural network (RNN)**.

Convolutional Neural Networks

Convolutional Neural Networks are biologically-inspired variants of the multilayer perceptron and have been proven to be very effective in areas such as image recognition and classification. ConvNets have been successfully applied when identifying faces, objects, and traffic signs as well as powering vision in robots and self-driving cars. CNNs exploit spatially-local correlation by enforcing a local connectivity pattern between neurons of adjacent layers. In other words, the inputs of hidden units in the layer m are from a subset of units in layer $m - 1$, units that have spatially contiguous receptive fields.

LeNet was one of the very first convolutional neural networks proposed by Yann LeCun in 1988. It was mainly used for character recognition tasks such as reading zip codes, digits, and so on. In 2012, Alex Krizhevsky and Hinton won the ImageNet competition with an astounding improvement, dropping classification error from 26% to 15% using CNN, which started an era of revival for deep learning.

There are a few fundamental building components of CNN:

- Convolutional layer (CONV)
- Activation layer (nonlinearity, for example, ReLU)
- Pooling or sub-sampling layer (POOL)
- Fully Connected layer (FC, using softmax)

The most common form of a ConvNet is to stack on a few pairs of CONV-ReLU layers, each followed by a POOL layer. This pattern repeats till the entire input image has been aggregated and transformed spatially into small patches. Then, at the last layer, it transits into a fully-connected layer, which often utilizes softmax to output probabilities, especially if it's a multi-way classification problem, as shown in the following figure:

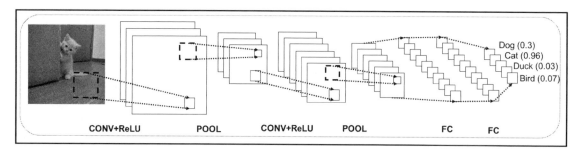

A typical convolutional neural network with CONV-ReLU, POOL layers repeated and followed by the fully-connected layers at the end

Convolution

Convolution involves a few concepts, such as convolve, stride, and padding.

For two-dimensional images, convolve happens for each of the color channels. Suppose you have a weight matrix and the image (shown as values at each pixel) as shown in the following figure.

The weight matrix (often called **kernel** or **filter**) is applied to the image by placing the kernel over the image to be convolved and moving it across the entire image. If the weight matrix moves 1 pixel at a time, it is called a **stride** of 1. At each placement, the numbers (pixel values) from the original image are multiplied by the number of the weight matrix that is currently aligned preceding to it.

The sum of all these products is divided by the kernel's normalizer. The result is placed into the new image at the position where the weight matrix is centered. The kernel is translated to the next pixel position and the process repeats until all image pixels have been processed.

As we can see from the following figure, a stride of 2 would result in the following:

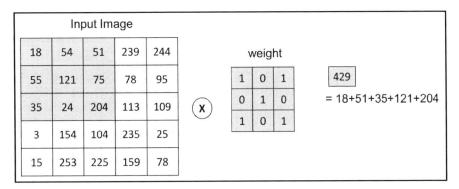

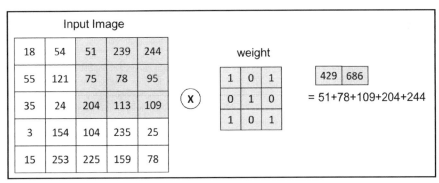

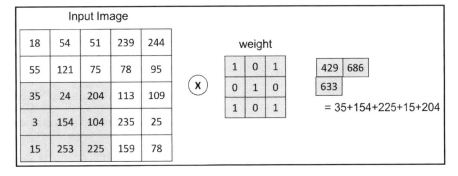

Convolution example of Stride = 2

So with a higher stride number, the images shrink very quickly. To keep the original size of the image, we can add 0s (rows and columns) to the border of the image. This is called the *same padding*. The larger the stride, the larger the padding will have to be:

Input Image						
0	0	0	0	0	0	0
0	18	54	51	239	244	0
0	55	121	75	78	95	0
0	35	24	204	113	109	0
0	3	154	104	235	25	0
0	15	253	225	159	78	0
0	0	0	0	0	0	0

weight

1	0	1
0	1	0
1	0	1

X

139

= 18+121

Zero padding for convolution

Pooling/subsampling

The pooling layer progressively reduces the spatial size of the representation to reduce the number of parameters and computation in the network. For color images, pooling is done independently on each color channel. The most common form of pooling layer generally applied is *max pooling*. There are also other types of pooling units, such as average pooling or L2-norm pooling. You may find some early networks are using average pooling. As *Max Pooling* typically shows better performance in practice, average pooling has recently fallen out of favor. It should be noted that there are only two variations of max pooling commonly seen in practice: 3 x 3 with stride = 2 (also called **overlapping pooling**), and even more commonly, 2 x 2 pooling with stride = 2. Pooling sizes with larger receptive fields are too destructive.

The following figure illustrates the max pooling process:

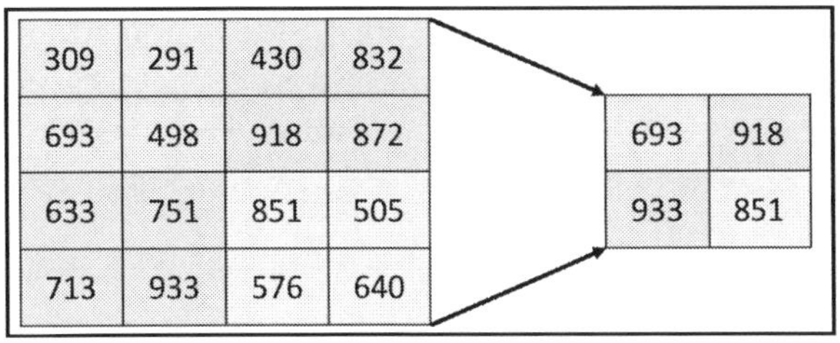

Max pooling

Fully connected layer

Neurons in a fully connected layer have full connections to all activations in the previous layer, which is different to CONV layers. In CONV layers, neurons are connected only to a local region in the input, and many of the neurons in a CONV volume share parameters. Fully connected layer is often used in the last two layers with a softmax function to replace the other activation functions to output probabilities.

Overall

A circle of training includes a forward pass and backpropagation:

- For each input image, we first pass it through the convolutional layer. The convolved results are fed into the activation function (that is, CONV + ReLU).
- The obtained activation map is then aggregated by the max pooling function, that is, POOL. The pooling will result in a smaller size of the patch and help to reduce the number of features.
- CONV (+ReLU) and POOL layers will be repeated a few times before they are connected to the fully connected layers. This increases the depth of the network which increases its capability of modeling complex data. Also, different levels of filters learn the data's hierarchical representation at different levels. Please refer to Chapter 1, *Why Deep Learning?* for more details about deep network representation learning.
- The output layer is often fully connected, but with softmax functions that help to compute the probability-like output.

- The output is then compared with the ground truth to generate error values which are then used to compute the cost. Usually, the loss function is defined as the mean squared error and used in the optimization stage.
- Errors are then backpropagated to update coefficients and bias values.

To take a deep-dive into CovNet applications for computer vision, please refer to `Chapter 4`, *Deep learning in Computer Vision* for details.

Restricted Boltzmann Machines

A RBM is a neural network with only two layers: the visible layer and the hidden layer. Each visible node/neuron is connected to each hidden node. Restriction means there is no intra-layer communication, that is, there are no connections between the visible-visible nodes or the hidden-hidden nodes. It was one of the earliest models to be introduced in the area of artificial intelligence and has been applied successfully in many areas such as dimensionality reduction, classification, feature learning, and anomaly detection.

The following figure shows its basic structure:

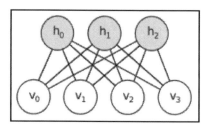

The basic structure of RBM, which only have one visible layer and one hidden layer

It's relatively easy to express RBM in a mathematical format as there are just a few parameters:

- The weight matrix $W(n_v \times n_h)$ describes the connection strength between the visible and the hidden nodes. Each entry W_{ij} is the weight of the connection between visible node i and hidden node j.
- Two bias vectors for the visible layer and the hidden layer respectively a ($1 \times n_v$), element a_i corresponds to the bias value for the ith visible node. Similarly, vector b corresponds to the bias value for the hidden layer, with each element b_j corresponding to the jth node.

Compared to common neural networks, there are some noticeable differences:

- RBM is a generative, stochastic neural network. The parameters are adjusted to learn a probability distribution over the set of inputs.
- RBM is an energy-based model. The energy function produces a scalar value which basically corresponds to the configuration indicating the probability of the model being in that configuration.
- It encodes output in binary mode, not as probabilities.
- Neural networks usually perform weight updates by gradient descent, but RBMs use **contrastive divergence** (**CD**). We will talk about CD in more detail in the following sections.

Energy function

RBM is an energy-based model. The energy function produces a scalar value indicating the probability of the model is in that configuration.

From Geoffrey Hinton's tutorial (*Geoffrey Hinton, A Practical Guide to Training Restricted Boltzmann Machines, 2010*), the energy function is written as follows:

$$E(v, h) = - \sum_{i \in visible} a_i v_i - \sum_{j \in hidden} b_j h_j - \sum_{i \in visible, j \in hidden} v_i h_j w_{ij}$$

The calculation is simple. Basically, you do the dot product between biases and the corresponding units (visible or hidden) to calculate their contribution to the energy function. The third item is the energy representation for connections between the visible nodes and the hidden nodes.

During the model learning stage this energy is being minimized, that is, model parameters (W and a_v, b_h) being updated in the direction of the lower energy configuration.

Encoding and decoding

The training of RBM can be thought of as two passes, the forward encoding path (construction) and the backward decoding (reconstruction). In an unsupervised setting, where we like to train the networks to model the distribution of input data, the forward and backward passes are done as follows.

In a forward pass, the raw input value from the data (for example, pixel values from an image) are represented by the visible nodes. Then they are multiplied with the weights W_{ij} and added with the hidden bias value (note, the visible bias value is not used in the forward pass). The resulting values are passed through an activation function to obtain the final output. If there are following layers connected, this activation result will be used as input to move forward:

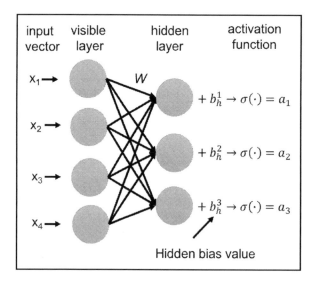

Example of forwarding pass of RBM

In our simple RBM case, which has only one hidden and one visible layer, the activation values of the hidden layer become the input in the backward pass. They are multiplied by the weight matrix, through the edges of the weights, and populated backwards to the visible nodes. At each visible node, all the incoming values are summed up and added to the visible bias value (note, the hidden bias value is not used in the backward pass):

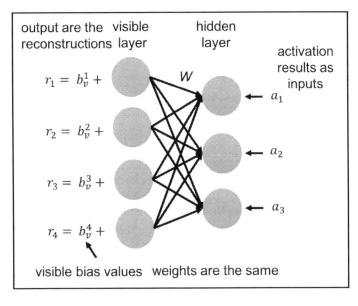

Example of backward pass of RBM

Since the weights of the RBM are randomized at the beginning, in the first few rounds the reconstruction error, which is computed by the reconstruction value versus the actual data value, can be large. So usually, it needs a few iterations to minimize such errors until an error minimum is reached. The forward and the backward pass help the model to learn a joint probability distribution of data inputs x and activation results (as the output of the hidden layer) $p(x, a)$. This is why RBM is thought of as a generative learning algorithm.

The question now is how to update the network parameters.

First, errors are computed using KL-divergence. To learn more about KL-divergence, readers can refer to *page 34* of the book *Information Theory, Inference, and Learning Algorithms* by David MacKay (`http://www.inference.org.uk/itprnn/book.pdf`, link last checked Jan. 2018). Basically, it computes the differences of two distributions by taking the integral of the difference between their distributions. Minimizing KL-divergence means to push the learned model distribution (in the form of activation values of the output from the hidden layer) towards the input data distribution. In many deep learning algorithms, gradient descent is used, such as stochastic gradient descent. However, RBM is using a method of approximated maximum-likelihood learning, called **contrastive divergence**.

Contrastive divergence (CD-k)

Contrastive divergence can be thought of as an *approximate maximum-likelihood* learning algorithm. It computes the divergence/differences between the positive phase (energy of first encoding) and negative phase (energy of the last encoding). It is equivalent to minimizing the KL-divergence between the model distribution and the (empirical) data distribution. The variable *k* is the number of times you run contrastive divergence. In practice, *k = 1* seems to work surprisingly well.

Basically, the gradients are *approximated* using the differences between two parts: positive phase associated gradients, and negative phase associated gradients. The positive and negative terms do not reflect its sign of the term but rather the effect on the model probability distribution it learned. The positive associated gradients increase the probability of training data (by reducing the corresponding free energy), while the second term decreases the probability of samples generated by the model. A pseudo code snippet in TensorFlow can be written as follows:

```
# Define Gibbs-Sampling function
def sample_prob(probs):
    return tf.nn.relu(tf.sign(probs - tf.random_uniform(tf.shape(probs))))

hidden_probs_0 = sample_prob(tf.nn.sigmoid(tf.matmul(X, W) + hidden_bias))
visible_probs = sample_prob(tf.nn.sigmoid( tf.matmul(hidden_0,
tf.transpose(W)) + visible_bias))
hidden_probs_1 = tf.nn.sigmoid(tf.matmul(visible_probs, W) + hidden_bias)
# positive associated gradients increases the probability of training data
w_positive_grad = tf.matmul(tf.transpose(X), hidden_probs_0)
# decreases the probability of samples generated by the model.
w_negative_grad = tf.matmul(tf.transpose(visible_probs), hidden_probs_1)

W = W + alpha * (w_positive_grad - w_negative_grad)
vb = vb + alpha * tf.reduce_mean(X - visible_probs, 0)
hb = hb + alpha * tf.reduce_mean(hidden_probs_0 - hidden_probs_1, 0)
```

In the code snippet above, X is the input data. For example, MNIST images have 784 pixels so the input X is a vector of 784 entries and accordingly, the visible layer has 784 nodes. Also note that in RBM the input data is encoded binary. For MNIST data, one can use one-hot encoding to transfer the input pixel value. In addition, alpha is the learning rate, vb is the bias of the visible layer, hb is the bias of the hidden layer, and W is the weight matrix. The sampling function sample_prob is the Gibbs-Sampling function and it decides which node to turn on.

Stacked/continuous RBM

A deep-belief network (DBN) is simply a few RBMs stacked on top of one another. The output from the previous RBM becomes the input of the following RBM. In 2006, Hinton proposed a fast, greedy algorithm in his paper: *A fast learning algorithm for deep belief nets*, that can learn deep, directed belief networks one layer at a time. DBN learns a hierarchical representation of input and aims to reconstruct the data, therefore it is very useful, especially in an unsupervised setting.

For continuous input, one can refer to another model called continuous restricted Boltzmann machines, which utilize a different type of contrastive divergence sampling. Such models can deal with image pixels or word vectors that are normalized between zero and one.

RBM versus Boltzmann Machines

Boltzmann Machines (**BMs**) can be thought of as a particular form of log-linear Markov random field, for which the energy function is linear in its free parameters. To increase their representation capacity for complicated distributions, one can consider and increase the number of variables that are never observed, that is, hidden variables, or in this case, the hidden neurons. RBMs are built on top of BMs, in which the restrictions are applied to force no visible-visible and hidden-hidden connections.

Recurrent neural networks (RNN/LSTM)

In a convolutional neural network or typical feedforward network, the information flows through a series of mathematical operations performed on the nodes without a feedback loop or any consideration of the order of the signal. Therefore, they are not capable of handling inputs which come in a sequence.

However, in practice, we have a lot of sequential data such as sentences and time series data, which include text, genomes, handwriting, the spoken word, or numerical times-series data emanating from sensors, stock markets, and government agencies. It is not only the order that matters here. The next value in line often greatly depends on the past context (long or short). For example, to predict the next word in a sentence a lot of information is required, not just from words nearby, but sometimes the first few words in the sentence. This helps to set up the subject and content.

The **recurrent neural network** (**RNN**) are a new form of artificial neural network and are designed specifically for these types of data. It takes into account the sequence order (this sequence can be of arbitrary length) and internal loops within their architectures, meaning any configuration/states of the network are impacted, not only by the current input but also by their recent past.

Cells in RNN and unrolling

All recurrent neural networks can be thought of as a chain of repeating models/cells in the dimension of time. This repeating module/cell can simply be a single tanh layer. One way to understand this is to unroll, or unravel, the architecture into each time step, and treat each time step as a layer. We can see that the depth of the RNN is essentially decided by the length of the time steps or length of the sequences. The first element of the sequence, such as the word of a sentence, is equivalent to the first layer.

The following figure shows the unrolling of the single recurrent cell in the timeline:

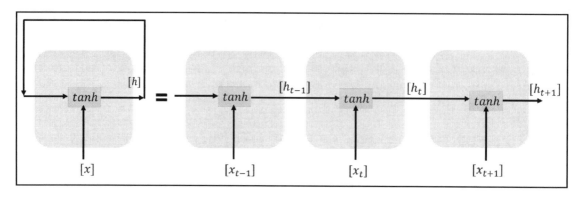

The unrolling of RNN. The repeating module in a standard RNN actually contains a single layer

Backpropagation through time

In feedforward networks, **backpropagation** (**BP**) starts with calculating the final error at the output layer and then moving backward towards the inputs, layer by layer. At each step, it calculates the partial derivatives of the error versus the weights $\partial E/\partial w$. Then through the optimization approach (for example, gradient descent), those derivatives are used to adjust the weights up or down in the direction that reduces the error.

Similarly in recurrent networks, after the unroll of the networks through time, BP can be thought of as an extension over the time dimension, this is called **backpropagation through time** or **BPTT**. The calculation is very similar, only that the series of layers has been replaced by a series of similar cells in the timeline.

Vanishing gradient and LTSM

Similar to all deep architectures, the deeper the networks get, the more severe the vanishing gradient problem gets. What's happening is that the weights at the beginning of the network change less and less. Given that the network's weights are generated randomly, with non-moving weights, we are learning very little from the data. This so-called *vanishing gradient* problem also affects RNN.

Each of the time steps in RNN can be thought of as a layer. Then, during backpropagation, errors are going from one time step to the previous one. So the network can be thought of as being as deep as the number of time steps. In many practical problems, such as word sentences, paragraphs, or other time-series data, the sequences fed into RNN can be very long. The reason that RNN is good at sequence-related problems is that they are good at retaining important information from the previous inputs and using this *past* context information to modify the current output. If the sequences are very long, and the gradients computed during training/BPTT either vanish (as a result of multiple multiplications of $0 <$ values < 1, given that unrolled RNN is deep) or explode, the networks would learn very slowly.

For example, if we are learning from sentences to predict the following word, the first word in the sentence might be very important to the subject, for setting up the context for the whole sentence, or even important for predicting the last word in the sentence. With weights that are not learned correctly backward through timelines, we might have lost such information.

In the mid-90s, a variation of the recurrent net with so-called Long Short-Term Memory units, or LSTMs, was proposed by the German researchers Sepp Hochreiter and Juergen Schmidhuber as a solution to the vanishing gradient problem.

LSTM addresses the problem of training over long sequences and retaining memory by introducing a few more gates that control access to the cell state. The new cell structure helps to maintain a more constant error so that it allows recurrent nets to continue to learn over many time steps (which sometimes can be over 1000).

In addition to incorporating the previous output (in the timeline) and the current input to generate the output, LTSM differs from a typical RNN by keeping the hidden state information, incorporating it to generate the output, and updating the new cell states. This means, the current output of RNN is decided by two terms: the current input and the previous output. The current output of LTSM is decided by three terms: the current input, the previous output, and the previous state. The RNN cell will only output the hidden value, while the LTSM cell will output the hidden value with new cell states.

Cells and gates in LTSM

LSTM networks consist of many connected LSTM cells, and each of them can be thought of as being composed of three important gates. Those gates decide whether the information from the past/present flow through.

The following figure shows a standard LSTM memory cell. In this cell, vector multiplication and vector addition are denoted by a round blue circle with a sign inside. Multiplying a vector with another vector that is in the range of [0,1] is called **gating**. Generating the vector in [0,1] can be thought of as a *filtering* process. $C_{t-1}$is the previous (in time) cell state. C_t is the updated cell state by the current input. h_t is the current prediction/output and h_{t-1} is the previous prediction/output (if only one LSTM cell is utilized in the network, h_t is essentially the prediction output, if more than one LSTM cell is stacked in the architecture, h_t is considered the hidden output of the current LSTM cell:

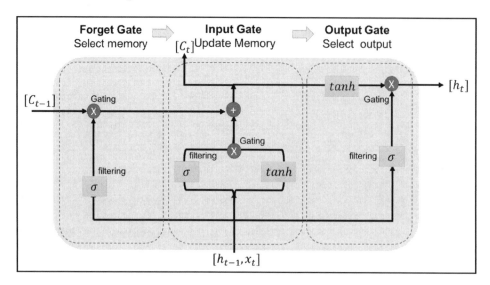

The repeating module/cell in an LSTM architecture that contains three gates

Within each cell, three steps are performed on the incoming information: the current input x_t, the previous output h_{t-1} of the cell, and the cell state C_{t-1} from last time. In the figure, and h_{t-1} are combined together with concatenation.

Step 1 – The forget gate

The **forget gate** decides which memory we'd like to keep or throw away from the past cell state C_{t-1}. This is achieved by piping the $[h_{t-1}, x_t]$ through an activation/squashing function (sigmoid) to obtain an indicator vector, and then multiplying this vector (gating) by the previous cell state vector C_{t-1}.

The result f_t represents the kept information memorized from the previous states that we think is going to be useful for the current value.

Step 2 – Updating memory/cell state

The next step is to update the cell state from C_{t-1} to C_t. The selected hidden memory from step 1 is combined additively with a filtered version of the current input. The filtering is conducted again by the so-called **input gate**, which is a sigmoid layer that decides which values we'd like to update. This filtering decision is multiplied by the activation results by tanh and then added to the selected memory vector from the forget gate. The result is used to update the cell state C_t.

Step 3 – The output gate

The **output gate** decides what we're going to output, that is, selectively decide what part of the current cell state we want to output as the new hidden state/output/prediction. Again, the sigmoid node is used to generate the filtering vector from $[h_{t-1}, x_t]$ (decides what parts of the current cell state would be selected). Then, the current cell state C_t is put through a tanh (for the purpose of squashing the value to between -1 and 1), and multiplied by the output of the sigmoid gate. Then we get our final output h_t.

Practical examples

In this section, we provide a practical problem that can be solved using a neural network. We will introduce the problems and build our neural network model using TensorFlow to solve the problems.

TensorFlow setup and key concepts

We recommend readers follow the instructions at `https://www.tensorflow.org/install/` to install TensorFlow. We will use Python as our programming language. There are mainly three key concepts that are used in the code sample:

- **Tensor**: Tensor is the central data unit in TensorFlow. We may think of it as a matrix of any number of dimensions. The entries within the tensor are primitive values. For example, see the following:

```
5 is a scalar and a rank 0 tensor
  [[0, 1, 2], [3, 4, 5]] is a matrix with shape [2, 3] and a rank 2
tensor
```

- **TensorFlow session**: A TensorFlow session encapsulates the control and state of the TensorFlow runtime.
- **Computation graph**: A set of TensorFlow operations that are arranged into a computation graph of nodes. The edges of the graph are tensors. The nodes can be tensors or operations. In TensorFlow, we need to build the computation graph and run the computation graph. For example, the following code builds a graph consisting of three nodes, where node1 and node2 output constants and node 3 is an addition operation that adds the two constants from node 1 and node 2:

```
node1 = tf.constant(1.0, dtype=tf.float32)
node2 = tf.constant(2.0, dtype=tf.float32)
node3 = tf.add(node1, node2)]
```

Then we can use the following code to run the graph:

```
sess = tf.Session()
print("sess.run(node3):", sess.run(node3))
```

The output of the preceding code is as follows:

```
sess.run(node3):3.0
```

Handwritten digits recognition

The challenge of handwritten digit recognition is to recognize digits from images of handwritten digits. It is useful in many scenarios, for example recognizing zip codes on envelopes. In this example, we will use the MNIST dataset to develop and evaluate our neural network model for handwritten digit recognition.

MNIST is a computer vision dataset hosted at: http://yann.lecun.com/exdb/mnist/. It consists of grayscale images of handwritten digits along with the correct digit labels. Each image is 28 pixels by 28 pixels. Sample images are shown as follows:

Sample images from MNIST dataset

The MNIST data is split into three parts: 55,000 images of training data, 10,000 images of test data, and 5,000 images of validation data. Each image is accompanied by its label, which represents a digit. The goal is to classify the images into digits, in other words, associate each image with one of the ten classes.

We can represent the image using a 1 x 784 vector of floating point numbers between 0 and 1. The number 784 is the number of pixels in the 28 x 28 image. We obtain the 1 x 784 vector by flattening the 2D image into 1D vector. We can represent the label as a 1 x 10 vector of binary values, with one and only one element being 1, the rest being 0. We are going to build a deep learning model using TensorFlow to predict the 1 x 10 label vector given the 1 x 784 data vector.

We first import the dataset:

```
from tensorflow.examples.tutorials.mnist import input_data
mnist = input_data.read_data_sets('MNIST_data', one_hot=True)
```

We then define some basic building blocks of our CNN:

- Weights:

```
def weight_variable(shape):
    # initialize weights with a small noise for symmetry breaking
    initial = tf.truncated_normal(shape, stddev=0.1)
    return tf.Variable(initial)
```

- Bias:

```
def bias_variable(shape):
    # Initialize the bias to be slightly positive to avoid dead
    # neurons
    initial = tf.constant(0.1, shape=shape)
     return tf.Variable(initial)
```

- Convolution:

```
def conv2d(x, W):
    # First dimension in x is batch size
    return tf.nn.conv2d(x, W, strides=[1, 1, 1, 1],
                        padding='SAME')
```

- Max pooling:

```
def max_pool_2x2(x):
    return tf.nn.max_pool(x, ksize=[1, 2, 2, 1],
                          strides=[1, 2, 2, 1], padding='SAME')
```

Now we build the neural network model through a computation graph using the basic building blocks. Our model consists of two convolution layers with pooling after each layer and a fully connected layer at the end. The graph can be illustrated in the following figure:

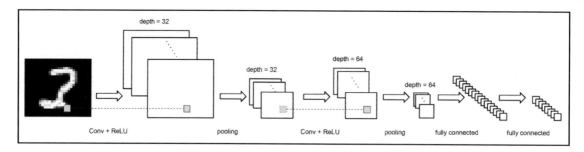

Convolutional neural network architecture for digit recognition

The following code implements this convolutional neural network architecture:

```
x = tf.placeholder(tf.float32, shape=[None, 784])
y_ = tf.placeholder(tf.float32, shape=[None, 10]) # ground-truth label
# First convolution layer
W_conv1 = weight_variable([5, 5, 1, 32])
b_conv1 = bias_variable([32])
# first dimension of x_image is batch size
x_image = tf.reshape(x, [-1, 28, 28, 1])
h_conv1 = tf.nn.relu(conv2d(x_image, W_conv1) + b_conv1)
h_pool1 = max_pool_2x2(h_conv1)
# Second convolution layer
W_conv2 = weight_variable([5, 5, 32, 64])
b_conv2 = bias_variable([64])
h_conv2 = tf.nn.relu(conv2d(h_pool1, W_conv2) + b_conv2)
h_pool2 = max_pool_2x2(h_conv2)
# Fully connected layer
```

```
W_fc1 = weight_variable([7 * 7 * 64, 1024])
b_fc1 = bias_variable([1024])
h_pool2_flat = tf.reshape(h_pool2, [-1, 7*7*64])
h_fc1 = tf.nn.relu(tf.matmul(h_pool2_flat, W_fc1) + b_fc1)
```

We can also reduce overfitting using dropout:

```
keep_prob = tf.placeholder(tf.float32)
h_fc1_drop = tf.nn.dropout(h_fc1, keep_prob)
```

We now build the last layer, the readout layer:

```
W_fc2 = weight_variable([1024, 10])
b_fc2 = bias_variable([10])
# Readout layer
y_conv = tf.matmul(h_fc1_drop, W_fc2) + b_fc2
h_fc1_drop = tf.nn.dropout(h_fc1, keep_prob)
```

Now we define the cost function and training parameter:

```
cross_entropy = tf.reduce_mean(
tf.nn.softmax_cross_entropy_with_logits(labels=y_, logits=y_conv))
train_step = tf.train.AdamOptimizer(1e-4).minimize(cross_entropy)
```

Next, we define evaluation:

```
correct_prediction = tf.equal(tf.argmax(y_conv, 1), tf.argmax(y_, 1))
accuracy = tf.reduce_mean(tf.cast(correct_prediction, tf.float32))
```

Lastly, we can finally run the graph in a session:

```
with tf.Session() as sess:
    sess.run(tf.global_variables_initializer())
    for i in range(2000):
      batch = mnist.train.next_batch(50)
      if i % 20 == 0:
        train_accuracy = accuracy.eval(feed_dict={
            x: batch[0], y_: batch[1], keep_prob: 1.0})
        print('step %d, training accuracy %g' % (i, train_accuracy))
      train_step.run(feed_dict={x: batch[0], y_: batch[1],
                            keep_prob: 0.5})
print('test accuracy %g' % accuracy.eval(
      feed_dict={
          x: mnist.test.images,
          y_: mnist.test.labels,
          keep_prob: 1.0}))
```

At the end, we achieve 99.2% accuracy on the test data for this MNIST dataset using a simple CNN.

Summary

In this chapter, we started with the basic multilayer perceptron network. From there, we have talked about the basic structures, such as the input/output layers as well as various types of *activation functions*. We have also given detailed steps on how the network learns with the focus on backpropagation and a few other important components. With these fundamentals in mind, we introduced three types of popular network: CNN, Restricted Boltzmann machines, and recurrent neural networks (with its variation, LSTM). For each particular network type, we gave detailed explanations for the key building blocks in each architecture. At the end, we gave a hands-on example as an illustration of using TensorFlow for an end-to-end application. In the next chapter, we will talk about applications of neural networks in computer vision, including popular network architectures, best practices, and real work examples.

4

Deep Learning in Computer Vision

In the previous chapter, we covered the basics of a neural network and how it is trained and applied for solving a specific **artificial intelligence (AI)** task. As outlined in the chapter, one of the most popular deep learning models that are broadly used in the field of computer vision is a convolutional neural network, also known as a CNN. This chapter aims to cover CNNs in more detail. We will go over core concepts that are essential to the working of a CNN, and how they can be used to solve real-world computer vision problems. We will specifically answer the following questions:

- How did CNNs originate and what is their historical significance?
- What core concepts form the basis for understanding CNNs?
- What are some of the popular CNN architectures in use today?
- How do you implement basic functionality of a CNN using TensorFlow?
- How do you fine-tune a pre-trained CNN and use it in your application?

Origins of CNNs

Walter Pitts and Warren McCulloch are often credited with the first computer model in 1943, which was inspired by the neural network-based structure of the human brain. They proposed a technique that inspired the notion of logic-based design and provided a formalism under which future refinements led to the invention of Finite Automata. The **McCulloch-Pitts** network was a directed graph where each node was a neuron and edges were marked as either excitatory (1) or inhibitory (0), and used a *threshold logic* to replicate the human thought process.

One of the challenges in this design was the learning of thresholds or weights, as would be defined later. Henry J. Kelley provided the first version of this learning algorithm in the form of a continuous **backpropagation model** in 1960 followed by an improvement by Arthur Bryson. The **chain rule** was developed by Stuart Dreyfus as a simplification of the original backpropagation model. Though the model and learning algorithm were designed early on, their inefficiency led to a delayed adoption by the research community.

The earliest working implementation of deep learning algorithms came from Ivakhnenko and Lapa in 1965. They used models with polynomial activation functions, which were further statistically analyzed. From each layer, they selected the statistically best feature and forwarded it to the next layer, which was often a slow and manual process. In their 1971 paper, they also described a deep neural network system called **alpha**, which had eight layers trained by the **group method of data handling** algorithm. However, none of these systems was particularly used for machine perception or vision tasks. The earliest inspiration for this line of work came from Hubel and Wiesel [5,6] in the 1950s and 1960s. They showed the visual cortex in both a cat and a monkey contains neurons that respond individually to a small region in the visual field, also known as the **receptive field**.

One of the key observations made by them was that neighboring cells have similar and overlapping receptive fields, and such receptive fields are tiled across the full visual cortex. They also discovered that cells in the visual cortex are composed of *simple cells* and *complex cells*. Simple cells respond to straight edges and have specific orientations with respect to their receptive fields. Complex cells, on the other hand, are formed due to the projection of various simple cells. Though they respond to the same orientation of edges as their corresponding simple cells, they integrate responses of all inherent simple cells over a wider receptive field. This causes complex cells to be translation-invariant or insensitive to the exact location of the edges in receptive fields. This is one of the architecture principles behind the design and implementation of CNNs in practice today.

The first real-world system inspired by the work of Hubel and Wiesel was **neocognitron,** developed by Kunihiko Fukushima. Neocognitron is often referred to as the first CNN implementation in the real world. Neocognitron's primary focus is to learn handwritten digits from zero to nine. In this particular design, neocognitron consisted of nine layers where each layer consisted of two groups of cells: s layer of simple cells, **S-cells**, and a layer of complex cells, **C-cells**. Each layer is further divided into a varying number of planes, however each plane within the layer has the same number of neurons, also referred to as **processing elements.** Each layer has a different number of planes of simple and complex cells. For example, U_{S1} has 12 planes of **19 x 19** simple cells.

The correct classification of input digits is made by the class with the strongest response in the rightmost C-cell layer. These early models provided an elegant formalism for mathematical modeling of the visual cortex. However, learning the parameters of such models was still considered a difficult task. It was not until 1985 when Rumelhart, Williams, and Hinton applied back propagation-based techniques to learn neural networks. They showed that using back propagation, neural networks can learn interesting distributional representations. The success of backpropagation continued when Yann LeCun demonstrated the practical application of backpropagation for handwritten digit recognition from bank checks. These advanced models needed more computation power than what was available during this time. However, not long after, the development of modern-day **graphics processing units** (**GPU**) in the early 2000s increased computation speeds by 1000 times. This paved the way for the real-world application of deep CNN models on large sets of imagery data as we know today.

Convolutional Neural Networks

We learned from the previous chapter that neural networks are made up of neurons, which have weights and biases learned over a training dataset. This network is organized into layers where each layer is composed of a number of different neurons. Neurons in each layer are connected to neurons in the next layer through a set of edges that carry a weight that is learned from a training dataset. Each neuron also has a pre-selected activation function. For every input it receives, a neuron computes its dot product with its learned weight and passes it through its activation function to generate a response.

Though this architecture works well for small-scale datasets, it has a scale challenge:

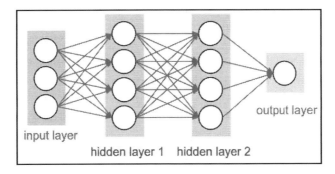

Architecture of a multi-layer neural network (Source: https://raw.githubusercontent.com/cs231n/cs231n.github.io/master/assets/nn1/neural_net2.jpeg)

Imagine you are trying to train an image recognition system through a neural network. The input images are 32 x 32 x 3, meaning they have three color channels, red, green, and blue (RGB), and each channel image is 32 pixels wide and 32 pixels high. If you were to input this image and fully connect the neurons in the first layer to the next layer, each neuron will have 32 x 32 x 3 = 3072 edges or weights, as shown in the *Architecture of a multi-layer neural network* figure. To learn a good weight representation over this large space, you would need lots of data and compute power. This scale challenge will grow polynomially if you increase the size of an image from 32 x 32 to, for example, 200 x 200. Not only will this pose compute challenges, this parameter explosion will invariably lead to **overfitting**, which is a very common machine learning pitfall.

CNNs are specifically designed to overcome this problem. CNNs work well if the inputs to them have a typical grid-like structure, as found in images. Unlike regular neural networks, CNNs organize the input data in a three-dimensional tensor-like structure representing **width**, **height**, and **depth**. To prevent a parameter explosion, each volume in one layer is connected only to a spatially relevant region in the volume of the next layer. This ensures that as the number of layers increases, each neuron has a local influence on its location (figure *Architecture of a convolutional layer in CNN*). Finally, the output layer is able to reduce the high dimensional input image into a single vector of output classes:

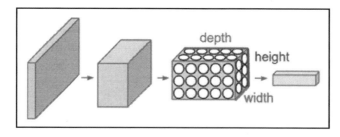

Architecture of a convolutional layer in CNN (Source: https://github.com/cs231n/cs231n.github.io/blob/master/assets/cnn/cnn.jpeg)

One of the most important ideas, after which CNN is named, is the convolution operation. A convolution operation can be understood as the interpolation of two real-valued signals. To describe it as an example, let's say you have a lake with a clear stream of water. You decide to pick up a rock from the shore and throw it in the pond. When this rock hits the surface of the water, it creates a ripple across the lake originating from the point of impact of the rock with the water's surface. In terms of convolution, you can explain this ripple effect as the result of a convolution operation of the rock on the water. The process of convolution measures the impact of one signal when it is integrated with another signal. One of its primary applications is in finding patterns in signals.

One such example is an averaging filter commonly used in image processing. Sometimes, when the images captured have very sharp edges, you might want to add a blurring effect, also known as the **averaging filter**. Convolution is often the most commonly-used tool to achieve this effect. As shown in the *Example of convolution operation* figure, the matrix on the left (**input data**), when convolved with a matrix (**kernel**) on the right, generates an output also known as a **feature map**:

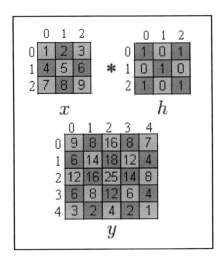

Example of convolution operation.(Source: https://upload.wikimedia.org/wikipedia/commons/f/f4/Wik_Kaminari3400_splot_2D_my.PNG)

Mathematically, convolution can be defined as follows:

$$s(t) = (x \circledast w)(t) = \int_{-\infty}^{\infty} x(k)w(t-k)\partial k$$

Here, x is the input data, w is the kernel, and s is the feature map.

Data transformations

Often, in any real-world implementation of a CNN, data processing and transform is a key step to achieving good accuracy. In this section, we will cover some basic but important data transformation steps that are more commonly used in practice today.

Input preprocessing

Let's assume that our dataset, X, has N images and each image has D flattened out pixels. The following three processing steps are usually performed on X:

- **Mean subtraction**: In this step, we compute a mean image across the whole dataset and subtract this mean image from each image. This step has the effect of centering the data across the origin along each of the feature dimensions. To implement this step in Python:

  ```
  import numpy as np

  mean_X = np.mean(X, axis=0)
  centered_X = X - mean_X
  ```

- **Normalization**: The mean subtraction step is often followed by a normalization step, which has the effect of scaling each feature dimension along the same scale. This is done by dividing each feature column by its standard deviation. The *Example of data normalization* figure illustrates the effect of normalization on the input data. It can be implemented in Python as follows:

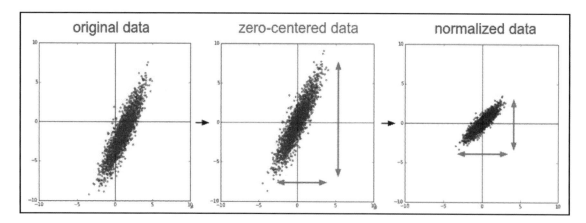

Example of data normalization (Source: https://raw.githubusercontent.com/cs231n/cs231n.github.io/master/assets/nn2/prepro1.jpeg)

The code for obtaining a normalized data is as follows:

```
std_X = np.std(centered_X, axis=0)
normalized_X = centered_X / std_X
```

- **PCA whitening**: One other important transformation step used for neural networks, in general, is whitening using **Principal Component Analysis (PCA)**. Although this method is not widely used with CNNs, it is an important step worth describing here. Whitening can be understood as the process where data is de-correlated by computing the covariance matrix and using it to reduce the dimensionality of the data to the highest principal components, as desired. The *Example of data whitening* figure shows the geometric interpretation of this step. It can also be implemented in Python as follows:

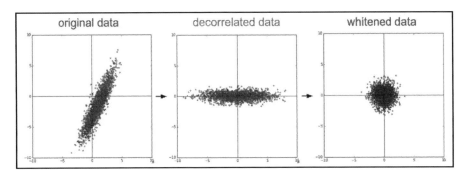

Example of data whitening (Source: https://raw.githubusercontent.com/cs231n/cs231n.github.io/master/assets/nn2/prepro2.jpeg)

```
# Compute the covariance matrix from the centered data
cov_matrix = np.dot(centered_X.T, centered_X) / centered_X.shape[0]
# Perform Singular Valued Decomposition
U,S,V = np.linalg.svd(cov_matrix)
# Compute the whitened data without dimensionality reduction
decorr_X = np.dot(centered_X, U) # decorrelate the data
# Compute the whitened data
whitened_X = decorr_X / np.sqrt(S + 1e-5)
```

Data augmentation

One of the most common tricks for improving the recognition performance is to augment the training data in an intelligent way. There are multiple strategies to achieve this effect:

- **Translation and rotation invariance**: For the network to learn translation as well as rotation invariances, it is often suggested to augment a training dataset of images with the different perspective transformation of images. For instance, you can take an input image and flip it horizontally and add it to the training dataset. Along with horizontal flips, you can translate them by a few pixels among other possible transformations.

- **Scale invariance**: One of the limitations of a CNN is its ineffectiveness to recognize objects at different scales. To address this shortcoming, it is often a good idea to augment the training set with random crops of the input images. These random crops act as a sub-sampled version of training images. You can also take these random crops and up-sample them to the original height and width of the input image.
- **Color perturbation**: One of the more interesting data transformations is perturbing the color values of the input image directly.

Network layers

As introduced in previous chapters, a typical CNN architecture consists of a series of layers, each of which transforms an input image tensor to an output tensor. Each of these layers may belong to more than one class. Each class of layers has a specific purpose in the network. The *Sample ConvNet architecture* figure shows an example of such a network, which is composed of **input layer, convolutional layer, pooling layer**, and **fully connected layer** (**FC**). A typical ConvNet can have an architecture such as [INPUT -> CONV -> POOL -> FC]. In this section, we will describe each of these layers in more detail and go over their role and significance for image processing:

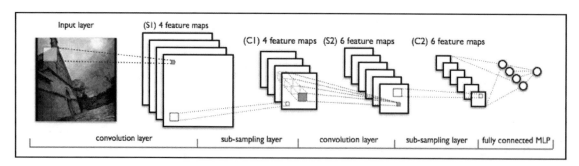

Sample ConvNet architecture (Source: http://deeplearning.net/tutorial/_images/mylenet.png)

Convolution layer

One of the core building blocks of CNNs, the convolutional layer is responsible for applying a specific convolution filter to an input image. This filter is applied on each sub-region of the image, which is further defined by the local connectivity parameter of the layer. Each filter application produces a scalar value for a specific pixel location, which when combined across all pixel locations is often referred to as a **feature map.** For example, if you use eight filters to convolve a 32 x 32 image at every single pixel location, you will produce 12 output feature maps each of the size 32 x 32. In this case, each of the feature maps will be computed corresponding to a particular convolution filter. The *Example of a convolution layer* figure illustrates this concept in more detail.

One of the important questions that arise from this discussion is, how does one choose a particular filter to convolve the image with? To answer this question, this filter is, in fact, an actual learnable parameter of the model that must be learned over a given training dataset. As such, the design of this filter becomes an extremely important step in ensuring the high performance of the network. A typical filter may be five pixels high and five pixels wide. However, a combination of such filters applied across the whole input volume acts as a potent feature detector. The training process of such filters is also relatively simple. First, you decide the number and size of filters be applied at each convolution layer in the network. During the start of the training process, starting values for these filters are chosen randomly. During the forward pass of the backpropagation algorithm, each filter is convolved at every possible pixel value in the input image to generate a feature map. These feature maps now act as the input image tensor for subsequent layers leading to the extraction of higher level image features from the raw image.

One important point to note is that computing a feature map value for every input pixel location is computationally inefficient and redundant. For example, if the input volume has a size of [32 x 32 x 3], and the filter size is 5 x 5, then each neuron in the convolution layer will be connected to a [5 x 5 x 3] region in the input volume, generating a total of 5 * 5 * 3 = 75 weights (and +1 bias parameter). To reduce this parameter explosion, we sometimes use a parameter referred to as **stride length**. Stride length denotes the gap between two subsequent filter application locations, thereby reducing the size of the output tensor significantly.

One of the post-processing layers often applied right after convolution is the **Rectified Linear Unit (ReLU)**. ReLU computes the function $f(x) = max(0, x)$. One of the advantages of ReLU is that it greatly accelerates the convergence of learning algorithms such as **stochastic gradient descent (SGD)**:

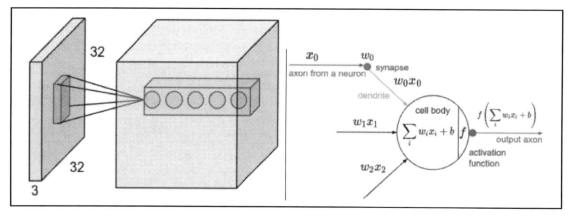

Example of a convolution layer (Source: https://raw.githubusercontent.com/cs231n/cs231n.github.io/master/assets/cnn/depthcol.jpeg, https://raw.githubusercontent.com/cs231n/cs231n.github.io/master/assets/nn1/neuron_model.jpeg)

Pooling or subsampling layer

A pooling or subsampling layer often immediately follows a convolution layer in CNN. Its role is to downsample the output of a convolution layer along both the spatial dimensions of height and width. For example, a 2 x 2 pooling operation on top of 12 feature maps will produce an output tensor of size [16 x 16 x 12] (see the *Example of Pooling/Subsampling layer* figure).

The primary function of a pooling later is to reduce the number of parameters to be learned by the network. This also has the additional effect of reducing overfitting and thereby increasing the overall performance and accuracy of the network.

There are multiple techniques around pooling. Some of the most common pooling techniques are:

- **Max pooling**: In this case, a feature map for each pooled area (2 x 2 in the previous example) is replaced by a single value, which is the **maximum** of the four values inside the pooled area

- **Average pooling**: In this case, a feature map for each pooled area (2 x 2 in the preceding example) is replaced by a single value, which is the **average** of the four values inside the pooled area

In general, a pooling layer accepts the following:

- Input volume of size: $[W_1 * H_1 * D_1, W_1 * H_1 * D_1]$
- Requires two parameters:
  - Their spatial extent $[F_x, F_y]$
  - The stride $[S_x, S_y]$
- Produces a volume of size $[W_2 * H_2 * D_2, W_2 * H_2 * D_2]$ where:
  - $W_2 = (W_1 - F_x)/S_x + 1$
  - $H_2 = (H_1 - F_y)/S_y + 1$
  - $D_2 = D_1$

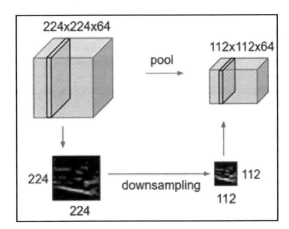

Example of Pooling/Subsampling layer (Source: https://raw.githubusercontent.com/cs231n/cs231n.github.io/master/assets/cnn/pool.jpeg)

Fully connected or dense layer

One of the final layers in a CNN is often the fully connected layer, which is also known as a **dense layer**. Neurons in this layer are fully connected to all the activations in a previous layer. The output of this layer is usually the class score, where the number of neurons in this layer equals the number of classes typically.

Using the combination of the layers previously described, a CNN converts an input image to the final class scores. Each layer works in a different way and has different parameter requirements. The parameters in these layers are learned through a gradient descent-based algorithm in a back propagation way.

Network initialization

One of the most seemingly trivial, yet crucial, aspects of CNN training is network initialization. Every CNN layer has certain parameters or weights that get trained over the training set. The most popular algorithm to learn this optimal weight is SGD. Inputs to SGD include an initial set of weights, a loss function, and labeled training data. SGD will use the initial weights to compute a loss value given the labels in the training data and adjust its weight to reduce the loss. This adjusted weight will now be fed to the next iteration where the previous process continues until convergence is achieved. As can be seen from this process, the choice of initial weight for network initialization plays a crucial role on the quality and speed of convergence of network training. Hence, a number of strategies have been applied to address this issue. Some of them are as follows:

- **Random initialization**: In this scheme, all weights are randomly assigned some value initially. One good practice with random assignment is to ensure random samples come from a zero mean and unit standard deviation Gaussian distribution. The idea behind randomization is simple—imagine if the network had very similar or identical weights assigned to each neuron, every neuron will compute exactly the same loss value and make the same gradient update at every iteration. This means every neuron will learn similar features and the network won't be diverse enough to learn interesting patterns from the data. To ensure diversity in a network, random weights are used. This would ensure weights are assigned asymmetrically, leading to diverse learning by the network. One trick with random initialization though is the network variance. If you define weights randomly, the distribution of output from neurons will have a much higher variance. One recommendation is to normalize the weights with the number of inputs to the layer.

- **Sparse initialization**: Used by Sutskever et al., in this scheme, we choose a neuron randomly and randomly connect it to K neurons in the previous layer. Weights for each neuron are assigned randomly as described earlier. A typical number of K is 10-15. The core intuition behind this idea is to decouple the number of connections to each unit from the number of units in previous layers. It is often a good idea to initialize the biases to 0 in this particular case. In case of ReLU, you might want to choose a small constant such as 0.01 to ensure some gradients are propagated forward.

- **Batch normalization**: Invented by Ioffe and Szegedy, batch normalization aims to be robust to problems of poor network initialization. The central idea in this scheme is to force the whole network to normalize itself on a unit Gaussian distribution at the start of the training phase. It takes two parameters, γ and β, and generates a batch normalized version: $BN(X_i)$ of input X_i as:

$$\mu_B = \frac{1}{m} \sum_{i=1}^{M} X_i; \sigma_B^2 = \frac{1}{m} \sum_{i=1}^{M} (X_i - \mu_b)^2$$

$$\hat{X}_i = \frac{X_i - \mu_B}{\sqrt{\sigma_B^2 + \epsilon}}$$

$$BN(X_i) = \gamma * \hat{X}_i + \beta$$

Regularization

One of the challenges in training CNNs is overfitting. Overfitting can be defined as a phenomenon where CNN, or in general any learning algorithm, performs very well in optimizing training error, but is not able to generalize well on test data. The most common trick used in the community to address this issue is **regularization**, which is simply adding a penalty to the loss function being optimized. There are various ways of regularizing the network. Some of the common techniques are explained as follows:

- **L2 regularization**: One the most popular forms of regularization, an L2 regularizer implements a squared penalty on the weights, meaning, the higher the weights, the higher the penalty. This ensures once the network is trained, the value of optimal weights is smaller. Intuitively, this means that the network having smaller weights will use all of its inputs appropriately and will be more diversified. Having higher weights in a network will make the network depend more on neurons with higher weights, eventually making it biased. The *Effect of regularization* figure illustrates this effect visually where, after L2 regularization, you see more weights concentrated around **-0.2** to **+0.2** as opposed to **-0.5** to **+0.5** before regularization.

- **L1 regularization**: One of the issues with L2 regularization is that even though the resulting weights are smaller, they are mostly positive. This means the network is taking multiple inputs even if it weighs them lower. This becomes a problem when you are dealing with noisy inputs. You want to completely eliminate taking noisy inputs and ideally, you would like to place a 0 weight on such inputs. This paves the path for L1 regularization. In this case, you add a first-order penalty on weights instead of a second-order penalty such as L2. The resulting effect of this regularization can be seen in the *Effect of regularization* figure. You can see fewer weight bins are now non-empty, suggesting that the network has learned sparse weights, which are more robust to noisy inputs. You can also combine both L1 and L2 regularization in a single regularization scheme, which is also referred to as **elastic net regularization**.

- **Max-norm constrained regularization**: In this scheme, you constrain the maximum possible norm of weight vectors to lie following a pre-specified value such as $\|\hat{W}\|_2 \leq k$. This ensures that network weights and updates are always bounded and do not depend on factors such as the speed of the learning rate of the network.

- **Dropout regularization**: One of the recent advances in regularization is dropout. The idea here is to use a parameter, p, which defines a probability with which you only use activations of certain neurons in the next layer. The *Example of Dropout-based regularization* figure shows an example. With a dropout parameter of 0.5 and four neurons, you randomly select two neurons (0.5 * 4) whose activation will be forwarded to the next layer. Since you are dropping out activations during training, you need to scale the activations properly as well so that the testing phase remains unchanged. To do this, you also do an **inverted dropout**, which scales the activation by a factor of $\frac{1}{p}$:

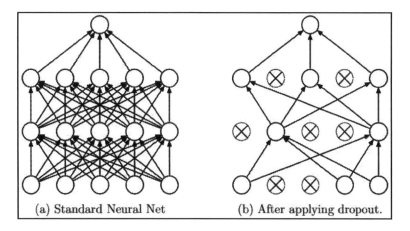

Example of Dropout-based regularization (Source: https://raw.githubusercontent.com/cs231n/cs231n.github.io/master/assets/nn2/dropout.jpeg)

You can add a dropout layer in TensorFlow using the following single line of code:

```
dropout_rate = 0.5
fc = tf.layers.dropout(fc, rate=dropout_rate, training=is_training)
```

Loss functions

So far, we have seen a CNN is trained using a gradient descent-based algorithm that tries to minimize a loss function given the training data. There are multiple ways to define how to choose this loss function. In this section, we will look at some of the most commonly used loss functions used for CNN training:

- **Cross-entropy loss:** This is one of the most popularly used loss functions for CNNs. It is based on the notion of cross-entropy, which is a measure of distance between a true distribution p and an estimated distribution q, and can be defined as $H(p,q) = -\sum_x p(x) \log(q(x))$. Using this measure, the cross-entropy loss can be defined as follows:

$$L_i = -f_{a_i} + \log(\sum_j e^{f_j})$$

- **Hinge loss:** Hinge loss can be simply defined as follows:

$$L_i = \sum_{j \neq y_i} \max(0, w_j^T x_i - W_{y_i}^T x_i + \delta)$$

Let us understand this loss function with an example. Let's assume we have three classes, and for a given data point a CNN outputs three scores for each of the classes in the following order: [10, -5, 5]. Let us also assume that the correct class for this data point is the first class and the value of δ is 10. In this case, the hinge loss would be computed as follows:

$$L_i = \max(0, -5 - 10 + 10) + \max(0, 5 - 10 + 10)$$

As shown precedingly, the total loss function would compute to 5. This seems intuitive since the loss value is smaller because the correct class one has the highest score, 10 in this case.

Model visualization

One of the important aspects of a CNN is that once it's trained, it learns a set of feature maps or filters, which act as feature extractors on natural scene images. As such, it would be great to visualize these filters and get an understanding of what the network has learned through its training. Fortunately, this is a growing area of interest with lots of tools and techniques that make it easier to visualize the trained filters by the CNN. There are two primary parts of the network that are interesting to visualize:

- **Layer activation:** This is the most common form of network visualization where one visualizes the activation of neurons during the forward pass of the network. This visualization is important for multiple reasons:
  - It allows you to see how each learned filter responds to each input image. You can use this information to get a qualitative understanding of what the filter has learned to respond to.

- You can easily debug the network by seeing if most of the filters are learning any useful feature, or are simply blank images suggesting issues during network training. The following *Visualizing activations of layers* figure shows this step in more detail:

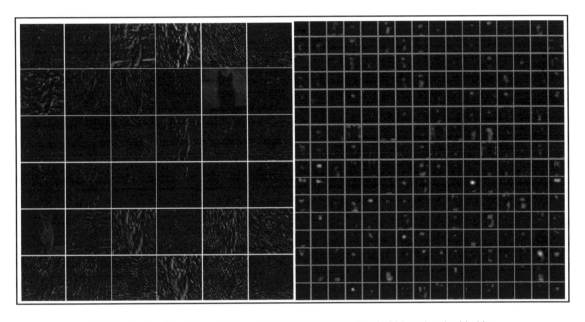

Visualizing activations of layers (Source: https://raw.githubusercontent.com/cs231n/cs231n.github.io/master/assets/cnnvis/act1.jpeg, https://raw.githubusercontent.com/cs231n/cs231n.github.io/master/assets/cnnvis/act2.jpeg)

- **Filter visualization**: Another common use case for visualization is to visualize the actual filter values themselves. Remember that CNN filters can also be understood as **feature detectors**, which when visualized can demonstrate what kind of image feature each filter can extract. For example, the preceding *Visualizing activations of layers* figure illustrates that CNN filters can be trained to detect and extract edges in different orientations as well as different color combinations. Noisy filter values can also be easily detected during this technique to provide a feedback on poor training quality for the network:

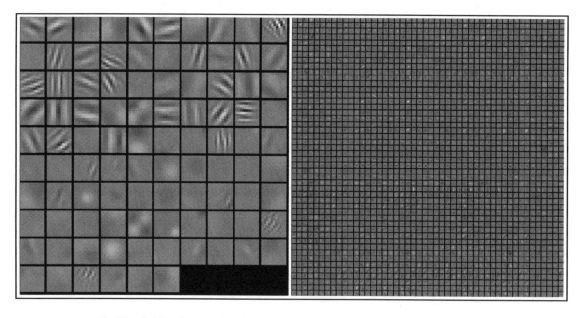

Visualizing trained filters (Source: https://raw.githubusercontent.com/cs231n/cs231n.github.io/master/assets/cnnvis/filt1.jpeg, https://raw.githubusercontent.com/cs231n/cs231n.github.io/master/assets/cnnvis/filt2.jpeg)

Handwritten digit classification example

In this section, we will show how to implement a CNN to recognize 10 class handwritten digits using TensorFlow. We will use the MNIST dataset for this challenge, which consists of 60,000 training examples and 10,000 test examples of the handwritten digits zero to nine, where each image is a 28 x 28-pixel monochrome image.

Let us assume all features are present in the `features` variable and labels in the `labels` variable. We begin with importing the necessary packages and adding the input layer from the pre-loaded `features` variable:

```
import numpy as np
import tensorflow as tf

# import mnist
mnist = tf.contrib.learn.datasets.load_dataset("mnist")
features = mnist.train.images # Returns np.array

# Input Layer
INPUT = tf.reshape(features, [-1, 28, 28, 1])
```

We will use a network architecture that consists of two convolution layers, two pooling layers, and two fully-connected layers in the following order: [INPUT -> CONV1 -> POOL1 -> CONV2 -> POOL2 -> FC1 -> FC2]. We use 32 filters each of size 5 x 5 for CONV1 and 2 x 2 filters for POOL1 with two strides. It is implemented in TensorFlow as follows:

```
CONV1 = tf.layers.conv2d(
    inputs=INPUT,
    filters=32,
    kernel_size=[5, 5],
    padding="same",
    activation=tf.nn.relu)

POOL1 = tf.layers.max_pooling2d(inputs=CONV1, pool_size=[2, 2], strides=2)
```

We use 64 filters of size 5 x 5 for CONV2 and 2 x 2 POOL2 filters again with two strides. We also connect these layers to the previous layers, as follows:

```
CONV2 = tf.layers.conv2d(
    inputs=POOL1,
    filters=64,
    kernel_size=[5, 5],
    padding="same",
    activation=tf.nn.relu)

POOL2 = tf.layers.max_pooling2d(inputs=CONV2, pool_size=[2, 2], strides=2)
```

The output of POOL2 is a two-dimensional matrix, which needs to be flattened out since we need to connect a dense or fully-connected layer. Once flattened, we connect it to a fully-connected layer with 1024 neurons:

```
POOL2_FLATTENED = tf.reshape(POOL2, [-1, 7 * 7 * 64])
FC1 = tf.layers.dense(inputs=POOL2_FLATTENED, units=1024,
activation=tf.nn.relu)
```

To improve the network training, we need to add a regularization scheme. We use a dropout layer with a dropout rate of 0.5 and connect it to a fully connected layer. Finally, this layer is connected to a final layer with 10 neurons - one neuron for each digit class:

```
DROPOUT = tf.layers.dropout(
     inputs=FC1, rate=0.5, training=mode == tf.estimator.ModeKeys.TRAIN)
FC2 = tf.layers.dense(inputs=DROPOUT, units=10)
```

Now that the network is fully configured, we need to define a loss function and start training. As described precedingly, we choose cross-entropy loss, as follows:

```
# Calculate Loss (for both TRAIN and EVAL modes)
  onehot_labels = tf.one_hot(indices=tf.cast(labels, tf.int32), depth=10)
  loss = tf.losses.softmax_cross_entropy(onehot_labels=onehot_labels,
logits=FC2)
```

We now set up learning parameters for gradient descent and commence training:

```
# Configure the Training Op (for TRAIN mode)
optimizer = tf.train.GradientDescentOptimizer(learning_rate=0.001)
train_op = optimizer.minimize(loss=loss,
global_step=tf.train.get_global_step())
train_input_fn = tf.estimator.inputs.numpy_input_fn(
       x={"x": features},
       y=labels,
       batch_size=100,
       num_epochs=None,
       shuffle=True)
mnist_classifier = tf.estimator.EstimatorSpec(mode=mode, loss=loss,
train_op=train_op)
mnist_classifier.train(input_fn=train_input_fn,steps=20000)
```

Fine-tuning CNNs

Though CNNs can be easily trained given enough computing power and labeled data, training a high-quality CNN takes lots of iterations and patience. It is not always easy to optimize a huge number of parameters, often in the range of millions, while training a CNN from scratch. Moreover, a CNN is especially suited to problems with large datasets. Often, you are faced with a problem that has a smaller dataset and training a CNN on such datasets may lead to overfitting on training data. Fine-tuning a CNN is one such technique that aims to address this pitfall of CNNs. The fine-tuning of a CNN implies that you never train the CNN from scratch. Instead, you start from a previously trained CNN model and finely adapt and change the model weights to better suit your application context. This strategy has multiple advantages:

- It exploits the large number of pre-trained models readily available for adaptation
- It reduces the compute time since the network has already learned stable filters, and it converges quickly to refine the weights on a new dataset
- It can also work on a smaller dataset and avoid overfitting completely

There are multiple ways to perform fine-tuning with CNNs. They are listed as follows:

- **CNN feature extractor**: Often, you are faced with an image classification task that has a specific number of class labels, say 20. Given this task, one obvious question is, how do you take advantage of existing pre-trained CNN models that have as high as 1000 class labels and use them for fine-tuning? The CNN feature extractor is a technique that answers this question. In this technique, we take a pre-trained CNN model such as AlexNet, which has 1000 classes, and remove the last fully connected layer and retain the rest of the network as is. We then perform a forward pass for each input image and capture the activations of all convolutional layers, such as **Conv5** or even the penultimate fully connected layer, such as **fc6**. For example, if you choose fc6, your total number of activations is 4096, which now acts as a 4096-dimensional feature vector. This feature vector can now be used with any existing machine learning classifier, such as SVM, to train a simple 20-class classification model.

- **CNN adaptation**: Sometimes, you would like to take advantage of fully connected layers in the networks themselves for your classification task. In such scenarios, you can replace the last fully connected layer of the pre-trained network with your own version of a fully connected layer that has the right number of output classes for your application—for example, 20 classes in the preceding example. Once this new network is configured, you copy over the weights from the pre-trained network and use it to initialize the new network. Finally, the new network is run through back propagation to adapt the new network weights to your particular application and data. This method has the obvious advantage of not needing any additional classifiers for your task, and with little modification, you are able to use a pre-trained model as well as a pre-trained network architecture to achieve your task. This strategy also works well with a small amount of training data since the pre-trained network has already been trained with large volumes of data.

- **CNN retraining**: This strategy is useful when you need to train a CNN from scratch. Usually, full training of a CNN may span days, which is not very useful. To avoid this multi-day training, it is often recommended to initialize the weights of your network with a pre-trained model and start the training of your network from the point where the pre-trained network stopped its training. This ensures every step of training is adding more learnable filters to your model instead of wasting precious compute hours in re-learning old filters that have already been learned by lots of pre-trained models. Usually, it is advisable to use smaller learning rates when using retraining.

Popular CNN architectures

Designing a perfect CNN architecture involves a large amount of experimentation and compute power. Hence, it is often non-trivial to achieve optimal CNN architecture design. Fortunately, a number of CNN architectures exist today that act as a good starting point for many developers and researchers as they wet their feet in designing a CNN network from scratch. In this section, we will go over some popular CNN architectures known today.

AlexNet

One of the earliest works in popularizing the use of CNNs in large-scale image classification, AlexNet was proposed by Alex Krizhevsky and their co-authors in 2012. It was submitted as an entry to the ImageNet challenge in 2012 and significantly outperformed its runner-up with a 16% top-5 error rate. AlexNet consists of eight layers in the following order:

[INPUT -> CONV1 -> POOL1 -> CONV2 -> POOL2 -> CONV3 -> CONV5 -> CONV5 -> POOL3 -> FC6 -> FC7 -> FC8].

CONV1 is a convolutional layer with 96 filters of size 11 x 11. CONV2 has 256 filters of size 5 x 5, CONV3 and CONV4 have 384 filters of size 3 x 3, followed by CONV5 with 256 filters of size 3 x 3. All pooling layers, POOL1, POOL2, and POOL3, have 3 x 3 pooling filters. Both FC6 and FC7 have 4096 neurons with the last layer being FC8 with 1000 neurons, which is equal to the 1000 output classes in the labeled data. It is a very popular architecture and often the first CNN architecture applied to large-scale image recognition tasks today.

Visual Geometry Group

This architecture from Simonyan and their co-authors [17] was the runner-up in the ImageNet challenge in 2014. It is designed on the core idea that deeper networks are better networks. Though they provide a higher level of accuracy, they have an inherently larger number of parameters (~140M) and use a lot more memory than AlexNet. **Visual Geometry Group (VGG)** has smaller filters than AlexNet, where each filter is of size 3 x 3 but with a lower stride of one, which effectively captures the same receptive field as a 7 x 7 filter with four strides. It has typically 16-19 layers depending on the particular VGG configuration. The *VGG CNN architecture* figure illustrates this architecture:

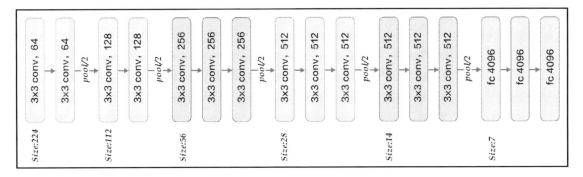

VGG CNN architecture (Source: https://raw.githubusercontent.com/PaddlePaddle/book/develop/03.image_classification/image/vgg16.png)

GoogLeNet

While VGG was the runner-up in the ImageNet 2014 challenge, GoogLeNet, also known as **inception,** was the winning submission. It has 22 layers in total with no fully-connected layer at all. One of the primary contributions of inception was its hugely reduced parameter set of 5M from 60M in AlexNet. Though the number of parameters is reduced, it is computationally more expensive than any of its predecessor networks. The *GoogLeNet Inception architecture* figure illustrates this architecture:

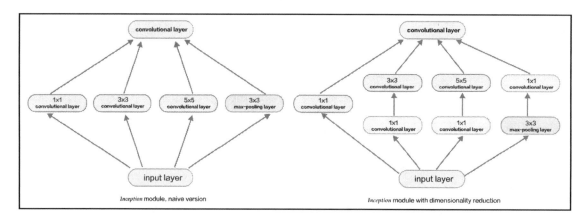

GoogLeNet Inception architecture (Source: http://book.paddlepaddle.org/03.image_classification/image/inception_en.png)

ResNet

ResNet is currently the state-of-the-art architecture for large-scale image recognition. One of the themes in common with previous architectures is that the deeper the network is, the better the performance. However, with increasing depth of the network, the problem of **vanishing gradients** is also amplified since each layer successively computes its gradient with respect to the gradient from the previous layer. The larger the number of layers, the smaller the gradients become, eventually vanishing to 0. To avoid this problem, ResNet introduces a shortening edge, where instead of computing the gradient over $F(x)$, you now compute the gradient over $F(x) + x$, where x is the original input to the network. This alleviates the effect of $F(x)$ getting successively smaller. The advantage of this strategy is that now you can create deeper networks with as many as 150 layers, which was not possible before.

The following *ResNet ReLU illustration* figure illustrates this network architecture in more detail:

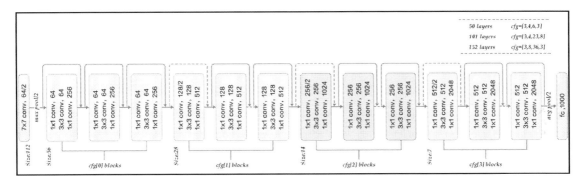

ResNet ReLU illustration (Source: https://raw.githubusercontent.com/PaddlePaddle/book/develop/03.image_classification/image/resnet.png)

Summary

In this chapter, we described the core concepts of a convolutional neural network in more detail. We provided a summarized history of the CNN and how it originated. We covered the basics of CNNs, ranging from network architecture, layers, loss function, and regularization techniques. We also outlined practical recommendations for each of these concepts and also illustrated how to implement a simple digit classification system using TensorFlow. We also outlined how to use a pre-trained model for a custom application development. Finally, we illustrated popular CNN architectures that often serve as the initial choice of developers for any computer vision task. In next chapter, we will look at how deep learning techniques are applied to the field of natural language processing.

5
NLP - Vector Representation

Natural language processing (**NLP**) is one of the most important technologies in machine learning. Understanding complex language is a crucial part of **artificial intelligence** (**AI**). The applications of NLP are almost everywhere, as we communicate mostly through language and store human knowledge mostly in language as well. This includes web searches, advertisements, emails, customer service, machine translation, and so on. Some of the hot research areas include language modeling (speech recognition, machine translation), word-sense learning and disambiguation, reasoning over knowledge bases, acoustic modeling, part-of-speech tagging, name-entity recognition, sentiment analysis, chatbot, question/answering, and others. Each of these tasks requires a deep understanding of the task or the application, as well as effective and fast machine learning models.

Similar to computer vision, extracting features out of text is of fundamental importance. Recently, deep learning approaches have obtained significant progress regarding representation learning for text data. This chapter will describe the word embedding in NLP. We will talk about three state-of-the-art embedding models: Word2Vec, Glove, and FastText. We will show an example of how to train Word2Vec in TensorFlow, and how to do visualization. We will also talk about the differences between Word2Vec, Glove, and FastText, and how to use them in applications such as text classification.

Traditional NLP

Extracting useful information for text-based information is no easy task. For a basic application, such as document classification, the common way of feature extraction is called **bag of words** (**BoW**), in which the frequency of the occurrence of each word is used as a feature for training the classifier. We will briefly talk about BoW in the following section, as well as the tf-idf approach, which is intended to reflect how important a word is to a document in a collection or corpus.

Bag of words

BoW is mainly for categorizing documents. It is also used in computer vision. The idea is to represent the document as a bag or a set of words, disregarding the grammar and the order of the word sequences.

After the preprocessing of the text, often called the **corpus**, a set of vocabulary is generated and BoW representation for each document is built on top of it.

Take the following two text samples as an example:

```
"The quick brown fox jumps over the lazy dog"
"never jump over the lazy dog quickly"
```

The corpus (text samples) then form a dictionary with the key as the word and the second column as the word ID:

```
{
    'brown': 0,
    'dog': 1,
    'fox': 2,
    'jump': 3,
    'jumps': 4,
    'lazy': 5,
    'never': 6,
    'over': 7,
    'quick': 8,
    'quickly': 9,
    'the': 10,
}
```

The size of the vocabulary (V=10) is the number of unique words from the corpus. Sentences will be then represented as a length 10 vector, where each entry corresponds to one word in the vocabulary. The value of this entry is determined by the number of times the corresponding word occurs in the document or sentence.

In this case, these two sentences will be encoded as 10-element vectors, like so:

```
Sentence 1:  [1,1,1,0,1,1,0,1,1,0,2]
Sentence 2:  [0,1,0,1,0,1,1,1,0,1,1]
```

Each element of the vector represents the number of occurrences for each word in the corpus (text sentence). Therefore, in the first sentence, there is 1 count for `brown` (at position 0 in the vector), 1 for the `dog`, 1 for `fox`, and so on. Similarly, for the second sentence, there is no occurrence of `brown`, so we get 0 for position 0, 1 count for the `dog` (at position 1 of the array vector), 0 counts for `fox`, and so on and so forth.

Weighting the terms tf-idf

In most languages, some words tend to appear more often than others but may not contain much differentiative information regarding judging the similarity of two documents. Examples are words such as *is*, *the*, and *a*, which are all very common in English. If we only consider their raw frequency as we did in the previous session, we might not be able to effectively differentiate between different classes of documents or retrieve the similar documents that match the core content.

One approach to tackle this problem is called **term frequency and inverse document frequency (tf-idf)**. Like its name, it takes into account two terms: **term frequency (tf)** and **inverse document frequency (idf)**.

With tf, *tf(t,d)*, the simplest choice is to use the raw count of a term in a document; that is, the number of times that term t occurs in document d. However, to prevent a bias towards longer documents, a common way is to take the raw frequency divided by the maximum frequency of any terms in the document:

$$\text{tf}(t, d) = 0.5 + 0.5 \cdot \frac{f_{t,d}}{\max\{f_{t',d} : t' \in d\}}$$

In this eqution, $f_{t,d}$ is the number of occurrences of the term (raw count) in the document.

The *idf* measures how much information the word provides; that is, whether the term is common or rare in all documents. One common way to determine this term is to take the log of the inverse of the proportion of documents containing the term:

$$log(\frac{total\ document\ count}{documents\ containing\ term})$$

By multiplying both values, tf-idf is calculated as:

$$\text{TFIDF}(t, d, D) = \text{tf}(t, d) \cdot \text{idf}(t, D)$$

A tf-idf is often used in information retrieval and text mining.

Deep learning NLP

Deep learning brings multiple benefits in learning multiple levels of representation of natural language. In this section, we will cover the motivation of using deep learning and distributed representation for NLP, word embeddings and several methods to perform word embeddings, and applications.

Motivation and distributed representation

Like in many other cases, the representation of the data, which is how the information is encoded and shown to machine learning algorithms, is often the most important and fundamental part in all pipelines of learning or AI. The effectiveness and scalability of the representation largely determine for the performance of the downstream machine learning model and application.

As mentioned in the previous section, traditional NLP often uses one-hot encoding to represent the word in a fixed vocabulary and uses a BoW to represent documents. Such an approach treats each word as, for example, house, road, tree, as an atomic symbol. The one-hot encoding will generate representations like [0 0 0 0 0 0 0 0 0 1 0 0 0 0]. The length of the representation is the size of the vocabulary. With such representation, one often ends up with huge sparse vectors. For example, in a typical speech application, vocabulary size can be from 20,000 to 500,000. However, it has an obvious problem, which is that the relationship between any pair of words is ignored, for example, motel [0 0 0 0 0 0 0 0 0 0 1 0 0 0 0] and hotel [0 0 0 0 0 0 1 0 0 0 0 0 0 0] = 0. Also, encodings are actually arbitrary, for example in one setting, *cat* may be represented as *Id321* and *dog* as *Id453*, meaning the 453rd entry of the long sparse vector is 1. Such representation provides no useful information to the system regarding the interactions or similarities that may exist between individual symbols.

This makes the learning of the model difficult because the model won't be able to leverage much of what it has learned about *cat* when it is processing the data regarding *dog*. Therefore, discrete IDs separate the actual semantic meaning of the word from its representation. Although some statistical information can be calculated at the document level, information at the atomic level is extremely limited. This is where distributed vector representation, and deep learning in particular, comes to help.

Deep learning algorithms attempt to learn multiple levels of representation of increasing complexity/abstraction.

There are multiple benefits we get from using deep learning for NLP problems:

- As often directly derived from the data or the problem, improve the incompleteness and over-specification of a hand-crafted feature. Handcrafting features is often very time consuming and may need to be performed again and again for each task or domain-specific problem. Features learned from one field often show little generalization ability toward other domains or areas. On the contrary, deep learning learns information from the data and the representation across multiple levels, in which the lower level corresponds to more general information that can be leveraged by other areas directly or after fine-tuning.

- Learning features that are not mutually exclusive can be exponentially more efficient than nearest-neighbour-like or clustering-like models. Atomic symbol representations do not capture any semantic interrelationship between words. With words being treated independently, NLP systems can be incredibly fragile. The distributional representation that captures these similarities in a finite vector space provides the opportunity to the following NLP system to do more complex reasoning and knowledge derivation.

- Learning can be done unsupervised. Given the current scale of data, there is a great need for unsupervised learning. It is often not realistic to acquire labels in many practical cases.

- Deep learning learns multiple levels of representation. This is one of the most important advantages of deep learning, for which the learned information is constructed level-by-level through composition. The lower level of representation often can be shared across tasks.

- Naturally handles the recursivity of human language. Human sentences are composed of words and phrases with a certain structure. Deep learning, especially recurrent neural models, is able to capture the sequence information in a much better sense.

Word embeddings

The very fundamental idea of distributional similarity-based representations is that a word can be represented by the means of its neighbors. As said by J. R. Firth 1957: 11:

You shall know a word by the company it keeps

This is perhaps one of the most successful ideas of modern statistical NLP. The definition of neighbors can vary to take account of either local or larger contexts to get a more syntactic or semantic representation.

Idea of word embeddings

First of all, a word is represented as a dense vector. A word embedding can be thought as a mapping function from the word to an n-dimensional space; that is, $W : words \rightarrow R_n$, in which W is a parameterized function mapping words in some language to high-dimensional vectors (for example, vectors with 200 to 500 dimensions). You may also consider W as a lookup table with the size of $V \ X \ N$, where V is the size of the vocabulary and N is the size of the dimension, and each row corresponds to one word. For example, we might find:

```
W("dog")=(0.1, -0.5, 0.8, ...)
W("mat")=(0.0, 0.6, -0.1, ...)
```

Here, W is often initialized to have random vectors for each word, then we let the network learn and update W in order to perform some tasks.

For example, we can train the network to let it predict whether an n-gram (sequence of n words) is valid. Let's say we got one sequence of words as *a dog barks at strangers*, and take this as an input with a positive label (meaning valid). We then replace some of the words in this sentence with the random word and transfer it to *a cat barks at strangers*, and the label is as negative since that will almost certainly mean that this 5-gram is nonsensical:

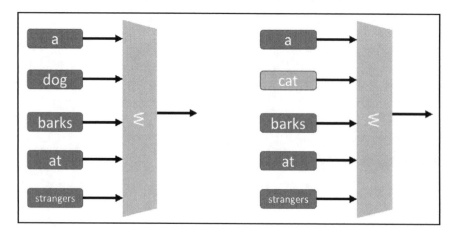

As shown in the preceding figure, we train the model by feeding the *n*-gram through the lookup matrix **W** and get a vector that represents each word. The vectors are then combined through the output neuron, and we compare its results with the target value. A perfect prediction would result in the following:

```
R(W("a"), W("dog"), W('barks"), W("at"), W("strangers"))=1
R(W("a"), W("cat"),  W('barks"), W("at"), W("strangers"))=0
```

The differences/errors between the target value and the prediction will be used for updating W and R (the aggregation function, for example, sum).

The learned word embeddings have some interesting properties.

First, the location of the word representations in the high-dimensional space is determined by their meanings, such that words with close meanings are clustered together:

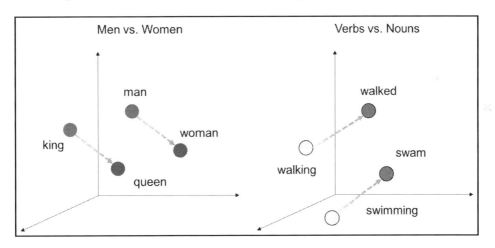

Linear relationship between embeddings learned from the model

Second, which is even more interesting, is that word vectors have linear relationships. The relationship between words can be thought as the direction and the distance formed by a pair of words. For example, starting from the location of the word **king**, move the same distance and direction between **man** and **woman**, and one will get the word **queen**, that is:

$$[king] - [man] + [woman] \sim = [queen]$$

Researchers found that if training using a large amount of data, the resulting vectors can reflect very subtle semantic relationships, such as a city and the country it belongs to. For example, France is to Paris as Germany is to Berlin.

Another example is to find a word that is similar to small in the same sense as biggest is similar to big. One can simply compute *vector X = vector(biggest) − vector(big) + vector(small)*. Many other kinds of semantic relationships can also be captured, such as opposite and, comparative. Some nice examples can be found in Mikolov's publication, *Efficient Estimation of Word Representations in Vector Space* (`https://arxiv.org/pdf/1301.3781.pdf`), as shown in the following figure:

Type of relationship	Word Pair 1		Word Pair 2	
Common capital city	Athens	Greece	Oslo	Norway
All capital cities	Astana	Kazakhstan	Harare	Zimbabwe
Currency	Angola	kwanza	Iran	rial
City-in-state	Chicago	Illinois	Stockton	California
Man-Woman	brother	sister	grandson	granddaughter
Adjective to adverb	apparent	apparently	rapid	rapidly
Opposite	possibly	impossibly	ethical	unethical
Comparative	great	greater	tough	tougher
Superlative	easy	easiest	lucky	luckiest
Present Participle	think	thinking	read	reading
Nationality adjective	Switzerland	Swiss	Cambodia	Cambodian
Past tense	walking	walked	swimming	swam
Plural nouns	mouse	mice	dollar	dollars
Plural verbs	work	works	speak	speaks

An example of five types of semantic and nine types of syntactic questions in the Semantic Syntactic Word Relationship test set from the paper by Mikolov and their co-authors in *Efficient Estimation of Word Representations in Vector Space*

Advantages of distributed representation

There are many advantages of using distributed word vectors for NLP problems. With the subtle semantic relationships being captured, there is great potential in improving many existing NLP applications, such as machine translation, information retrieval, and question answering system. Some obvious advantages are:

- Capturing local co-occurrence statistics
- Produces state-of-the-art linear semantic relationships
- Efficient use of statistics
- Can train on (comparably) little data and gigantic data
- Fast, only non-zero counts matter
- Good performance with small (100-300) dimension vectors that are important for downstream tasks

Problems of distributed representation

Keep in mind that no approach can solve everything, and similarly, a distributed representation is not a silver bullet. To use it properly, we need to understand some of its known issues:

- **Similarity and relatedness are not the same**: With great evaluation results presented in some publications, there is no guarantee for the success of its practical application. One reason is that the current standard evaluation is often on the degree of correlation versus a set of words created by humans. It's possible that representations from the model correlate with human evaluation well, but do not boost performance given a specific task. This is perhaps caused by the fact that most evaluation datasets don't distinguish between word similarity and relatedness. For example, *male* and *man* are similar, whereas *computer* and *keyboard* are related but dissimilar.

- **Word ambiguity**: This problem occurs when words have multiple meanings. For example, the word *bank* has the meaning of *sloping land* in addition to the meaning of *a financial institution*. In this way, there is a limit to representing a word as one vector without considering word ambiguity. Some approaches have been proposed to learn multiple representations for each word. For example, Trask and their co-authors proposed a method that models multiple embeddings for each word based on supervised disambiguation (`https://arxiv.org/abs/1511.06388`). One can refer to those approaches when it's necessary for a task.

Commonly used pre-trained word embeddings

The following table lists a few commonly used pre-trained word embeddings:

Name	Year	URL	Comments
Word2Vec	2013	`https://code.google.com/archive/p/word2vec/`	A multilingual pre-trained vector is available at `https://github.com/Kyubyong/wordvectors`.

GloVe	2014	`http://nlp.stanford.edu/projects/glove/`	Developed by Stanford, it is claimed to be better than Word2Vec. GloVe is essentially a count-based model that combines global matrix decomposition and local context window.
FastText	2016	`https://github.com/icoxfog417/fastTextJapaneseTutorial`	In FastText, the atomic unit is n-gram characters, and a word vector is represented by the aggregation of the n-gram characters. Learning is quite fast.
LexVec	2016	`https://github.com/alexandres/lexvec`	LexVec performs factorization of the **positive pointwise mutual information (PPMI)** matrix using **window sampling and negative sampling (WSNS)**. Salle and others, in their work of *Enhancing the LexVec Distributed Word Representation Model Using Positional Contexts and External Memory*, suggest that LexVec matches and often outperforms competing models in word similarity and semantic analogy tasks.
Meta-Embeddings	2016	`http://cistern.cis.lmu.de/meta-emb/`	By Yin and others, *Learning Word Meta-Embeddings*, 2016. It combines different public embedding sets to generate better vectors (meta-embeddings).

In the following sections, we will mainly talk about three popular ones: Word2Vec, GloVe, and FastText. In particular, we will dive deeper into Word2Vec for its core ideas, its two distinct models, the process of training, and how to leverage the open source pre-trained Word2Vec representations.

Word2Vec

Word2Vec is a group of efficient predictive models for learning word embeddings from raw text. It maps words to vectors. In the mapped vector space, the words that share common context are located close to one another. In this section, we will discuss in detail Word2Vec and its two specific models. We will also describe how to train a Word2Vec using TensorFlow.

Basic idea of Word2Vec

Word2Vec models only have three layers; the input layer, the projection layer, and the output layer. There are two models that come with it, namely the **Continuous Bag of Words (CBOW)** model and the Skip-Gram model. They are very similar but differ in how the input layer and output layer are constructed. The Skip-Gram model has each target word (for example, *mat*) as the input and predicts the context/surrounding words as the output (*the cat sits on the*). On the other hand, CBOW starts from source context words (*the cat sits on the*), does aggregation and transformation using the middle layer, and predicts the target word (*mat*). The following figure illustrates the differences:

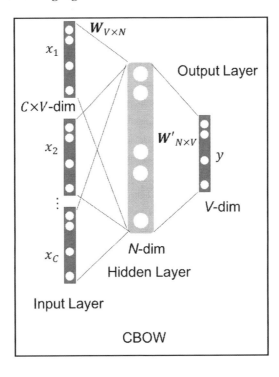

Take the CBOW model as an example. Each word in the training set is represented as a one-hot encoded vector. $x_1, x_2,..., x_c$ is the one-hot encoding for the context word. The target word is also represented by one-hot encoding y. The hidden layer has N nodes. Matrix $W_{V \times N}$ represents the weight matrix (connections) between the input layer and hidden layer whose row represents the weights corresponding to the word in the vocabulary. This weight matrix is what we are interested in learning because it contains the vector encodings of all of the words in our vocabulary (as its rows). $W'_{N \times V}$ is the output matrix (connections) connecting the hidden layer, with the output layer, which is also called the context word matrix. This is the matrix that each output word vector is associated with. In the Skip-Gram model, the input is the target word representation vector x, the output is a vector of length V, and each entry corresponds to one word in the vocabulary. For the same target word x, multiple pairs (x, y_1), (x, y_2), and (x, y_c) are generated for training. The goal is that, through the transform of the network, given an input one-hot encoded word x, the prediction (a *1 X V* length vector) should have a higher number at the entry which corresponds to the one-hot encoded vector of the context word.

The word windows

Remember that from the section on the idea of word embedding, we know that a word can be represented by its context, or more specifically, its so words. Therefore, we can use a window to determine how many surrounding words (before and after) we'd like to learn together with the target word in the center, as shown in the following figure:

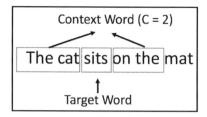

In this case, the window size is **2**. In order to learn the target word **sits**, nearby words up to two words away from the target word will be included to generate the training pairs. Then we slide the window along structured texts.

Generating training data

In the Skip-Gram model, we generate pairs of words for training as follows:

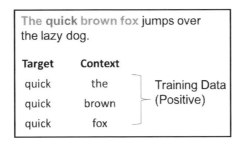

An example of generating positive training pairs, in which the window covers the beginning of the document

A positive training pair can be generated as follows:

The quick brown fox jumps over the lazy dog.

Target	Context	
fox	quick	Training Data
fox	brown	(Positive)
fox	jumps	
fox	over	

An example of generating positive training pairs

From these illustration, one can easily see that the network is going to learn the statistics from the number of times each pairing (target, context) shows up. For example, the model may see more samples of *York, New* or *New, York* rather than *Old, York*. Therefore, at the testing stage, if you give the word *York* as input, it will output a much higher probability for *New*.

From the way that the training data is generated, one can notice that the trained neural network will not know anything regarding the offset of the output context word relative to the target word. Take the example shown in the preceding figure, the model will not take into account that in the sentence, **quick** is further away than **brown**, and **quick** is before the target word **fox**, while **jump** is after. The information that has been learned is that all these context words are in the vicinity of the target word regardless of their order or position. Therefore, the predicted probability of a context word given an input target word only represents the probability that it occurs in the vicinity.

Negative sampling

From the loss function, we can see that computing the softmax layer can be very expensive. The cross-entropy cost function requires the network to produce probabilities, which means the output score from each neuron needs to be normalized to generate the actual probabilities of each class (for example, a word in the vocabulary in the Skip-Gram model). The normalization requires computation of the hidden-layer output with every word in the context-word matrix. In order to deal with this issue, Word2Vec uses a technique called **negative sampling (NEG)**, which is similar to **noise-contrastive estimation (NCE)**.

The core idea of NCE is to convert a multinomial classification problem, such as the case of predicting a word based on the context, where each word can be considered as a class, into a binary classification problem of *good pair* versus *bad pair*.

During training, the network is fed with the *good pair*, which is the target word paired with the other word in the context window, and a few randomly generated *bad pairs*, which consist of the target word and a *randomly* selected word from the vocabulary.

The network is therefore forced to distinguish the good ones from the bad ones, which ultimately leads to the learning of the representation based on context.

Essentially, NEG keeps the softmax layer but with a modified loss function. The goal is to force the embedding of a word to be similar to the embeddings of words in the context, and different from the embeddings of the words that are far away from the context.

The sampling process selects a couple of out-of-window context pairs according to some specifically designed distribution, such as unigram distribution, which can be formalized as:

$$P(w_i) = \frac{f(w_i)}{\sum_{j=0}^{n} f(w_j)}$$

In some implementations of Word2Vec, the frequency is raised to the power of ¾, which is an empirical value:

$$P(w_i) = \frac{f(w_i)^{3/4}}{\sum_{j=0}^{n} f(w_j)^{3/4}}$$

In this equation, $f(w_i)$ is the word frequency. Selecting by this distribution essentially favors frequent words to be drawn more often. Changing the sampling strategy can have a significant impact on the learning results.

The following figure illustrates the way of pairing the target word with a word outside the context, randomly selected from the vocabulary:

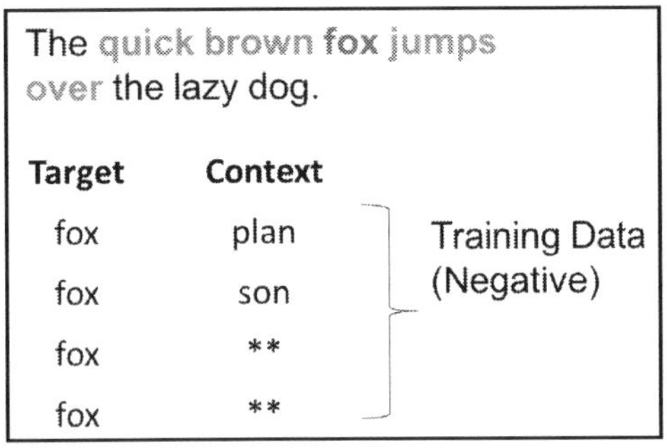

Hierarchical softmax

Computing the softmax is expensive because for each target word, we have to compute the denominator to obtain the normalized probability. However, the denominator is the sum of the inner product between the hidden layer output vector, h, and the output embedding, W, of every word in the vocabulary, V.

To solve this problem, many different approaches have been proposed. Some are softmax-based approaches such as hierarchical softmax, differentiated softmax, and CNN softmax so on, while others are sampling-based approaches. Readers can refer to `http://ruder.io/word-embeddings-softmax/index.html#cnnsoftmax` for a deeper understanding of approximating softmax functions.

Softmax-based approaches are methods that keep the softmax layer intact but modify its architecture to improve its efficiency (for example, hierarchical softmax).

Sampling-based approaches, however, will completely remove the softmax layer and instead optimize a newly designed loss function to approximate the softmax. For example, approximating the denominator that is cheap to compute, like NEG. A good explanation can be found at Yoav Goldberg and Omer Levy's paper, *word2vec Explained: deriving Mikolov and et al.'s negative-sampling word-embedding method*, 2014 (`https://arxiv.org/abs/1402.3722`).

For hierarchical softmax, the main idea is to build a Huffman tree based on word frequencies, where each word is a leaf of this tree. The computation of the softmax value for a particular word is then translated into computing the multiplication of probabilities of the nodes in the tree, from the root to the leaf, that represents the word. At each subtree split point, we calculate the probability to go either to the right branch or the left branch. The sum of the probability of the right and left branch equals to one; this guarantees that the sum of all the probabilities of leaf nodes equals to one. With a balanced tree, this can reduce the computational complexity from $O(V)$ to $O(logV)$, where V is the vocabulary size.

Other hyperparameters

On top of the novelty of the new algorithms, such as Skip-Gram models (with negative sampling), CBOW (with hierarchical softmax), NCE, and GloVe, compared to traditional count-based approaches, there are also many new hyperparameters or preprocessing steps that can be tuned to improve performance. For example, subsampling, removing rare words, using dynamic context windows, using context distribution smoothing, adding context vectors, and more. Each one of them, if used properly, would greatly help boost performance, especially in practical settings.

Skip-Gram model

We now focus on an important model architecture in Word2Vec, the Skip-Gram model. As described in the beginning of this section, the Skip-Gram model predicts the context word given the input target word. The word embedding we want is in fact the weight matrix between the input layer and the hidden layer. Next, we explain the Skip-Gram model in details.

The input layer

Well, we can't feed a word directly as a text string to the neural network. Instead, we need something mathematically. Suppose we have a vocabulary of 10,000 unique words; by using one-hot encoding, we can represent each word as a vector of length 10,000, with one entry as one in the position corresponding to the word itself, and zero in all of the other positions.

The input of the Skip-Gram model is a single word represented (one-hot encoded) with length equal to the size of the vocabulary, V, and output is determined by the generated pairs.

The hidden layer

The hidden layer, in this case, does not have any activation functions. The connection between the input layer and the hidden layer can be thought of as a weight matrix, W_{VXN}, where N is the number of the neurons in the hidden layer. W_{VXN} is with V rows, that is one for every word in the vocabulary, and N columns, that is one for every hidden neuron. The number N will be the embedding vector length. There is another auxiliary matrix, W'_{NXV}, which connects the hidden layer and the output layer, and the similarity of the word, W, with the *hallucinated* context word (out-of-window word) is minimized.

The output layer

The output layer is a softmax regression classifier. It takes a vector of arbitrary real-valued scores (z) and squashes it to a vector of values between zero and one that sums to one:

$$p(c_i|w) = \frac{e^{f_i}}{\sum_{j=1}^{V} e^{f_j}}$$

The output from the hidden layer (the word vector for the input target word, w) is multiplied with the auxiliary matrix W'_{NXV} where each column of it represents a word (let's assume a word, c). The dot product produces a value which, after normalization, represents the probability of having context word, c, given the input target word, w.

Here's an illustration of calculating the output of the output neuron for the word *car* and applying the softmax function:

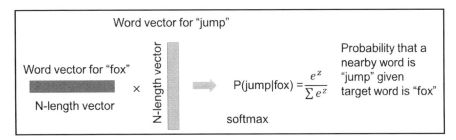

The loss function

The loss function is the negative logarithm of the output of the softmax:

$$L_i = -log(\frac{e^{f_i}}{\sum_{j=1}^{V} e^{f_j}})$$

Remember that the total loss for the dataset is the mean of L_i overall training examples together with a regularization term, $R(W)$.

From an **information theory** point of view, this is essentially a cross-entropy loss function.

We can understand it in the following way.

The cross-entropy is defined as:

$$H(p,q) = H(p) + D_{KL}(q||p)$$

With the actual distribution p as a delta function, its entropy term is $H(p) = 0$.

Therefore:

$$H(p,q) = D_{KL}(q||p) = -\sum p(x)log(q(x))$$

In this equation, $p(x)$ is the actual distribution and $q(x)$ is the estimation of the distribution.

In our case, $q(x)$ is essentially the softmax output, which is $e^{f_i}/\sum e^{f_j}$, and with $p = [0,0,\ldots 1,0,0]$ where only the jth entry is 1. The preceding equation can be simplified as:

$$H(p,q) = -log(q_i) = -log(\frac{e^{f_i}}{\sum e^{f_j}})$$

So, minimizing the loss function here is equivalent to minimizing the cross-entropy value.

From a **probabilistic interpretation** point of view, $e^{f_i}/\sum e^{f_j}$ can be interpreted as the (normalized) probability assigned to the correct label. We are actually minimizing the negative log likelihood of the correct class, that is, performing **maximum likelihood estimation (MLE)**.

Continuous Bag-of-Words model

For the **Continuous Bag-of-Words (CBOW)** model, the idea is even more straightforward, because the model uses the surrounding context to predict the target word. The inputs are still basically the surrounding context with a fixed window size, C; the difference is that we aggregate them (adding their one-hot encoding) first, then input to the neural network. These words will then be processed through the middle layer, and the output is the target word in the center.

Training a Word2Vec using TensorFlow

In this section, we will explain step-by-step how to build and train a Skip-Gram model using TensorFlow. For a detailed tutorial and source code, please refer to `https://www.tensorflow.org/tutorials/word2vec`:

1. We can download the dataset from `http://mattmahoney.net/dc/text8.zip`.
2. We read in the content of the file as a list of words.
3. We set up the TensorFlow graph. We create placeholders for the input words and the context words, which are represented as integer indices to the vocabulary:

```
train_inputs = tf.placeholder(tf.int32, shape=[batch_size])
train_labels = tf.placeholder(tf.int32, shape=[batch_size, 1])
```

Note that we train in batches, so `batch_size` refers to the size of the batch. We also create a constant to hold the validation set indices, where `valid_examples` is an array of integer indices to the vocabulary for validation:

```
valid_dataset = tf.constant(valid_examples, dtype=tf.int32)
```

We perform validation by computing the similarity between word embeddings in the validation set and the vocabulary, and find the words in the vocabulary that are most similar to the words in the validation set.

4. We set up the embedding matrix variable:

```
embeddings = tf.Variable(
    tf.random_uniform([vocabulary_size, embedding_size],
                        -1.0, 1.0))
embed = tf.nn.embedding_lookup(embeddings, train_inputs)
```

5. We create the weights and biases that connect the hidden layer with the output softmax layer. The weights variable is a matrix of size `vocabulary_size` × `embedding_size`, where `vocabulary_size` is the size of the output layer and `embedding_size` is the size of the hidden layer. The size of the `biases` variable is the size of the output layer:

```
weights = tf.Variable(
    tf.truncated_normal([vocabulary_size, embedding_size],
                        stddev=1.0 / math.sqrt(embedding_size)))
biases = tf.Variable(tf.zeros([vocabulary_size]))
hidden_out = tf.matmul(embed, tf.transpose(weights)) + biases
```

Now, we apply softmax to the `hidden_out` and use cross-entropy loss to optimize the weights, biases, and embedding. In the following code, we also specify a gradient descent optimizer with the learning rate of `1.0`:

```
train_one_hot = tf.one_hot(train_context, vocabulary_size)
cross_entropy = tf.reduce_mean(
    tf.nn.softmax_cross_entropy_with_logits(logits=hidden_out,
                                            labels=train_one_hot))
optimizer =
    tf.train.GradientDescentOptimizer(1.0).minimize(cross_entropy)
```

For efficiency, we can change the loss function from `cross_entropy` loss to NCE loss. NCE loss was originally proposed in Michael Gutmann and their co-authors paper, *Noise-contrastive estimation: A new estimation principle for unnormalized statistical models*:

```
nce_loss = tf.reduce_mean(
    tf.nn.nce_loss(weights=weights,
                   biases=biases,
                   labels=train_context,
                   inputs=embed,
                   num_sampled=num_sampled,
                   num_classes=vocabulary_size))
optimizer =
    tf.train.GradientDescentOptimizer(1.0).minimize(nce_loss)
```

For validation, we compute cosine similarity between word embeddings in the validation set and the word embeddings in the vocabulary. Later, we will print the top K words in the vocabulary that have the closest embeddings to validation words. The cosine similarity between embedding A and B is defined as:

$$similarity = \frac{A \cdot B}{\|A\|_2 \|B\|_2}$$

This translates to the following code:

```
norm = tf.sqrt(tf.reduce_sum(tf.square(embeddings), 1,
keep_dims=True))
normalized_embeddings = embeddings / norm
valid_embeddings = tf.nn.embedding_lookup(
    normalized_embeddings, valid_dataset)
similarity = tf.matmul(
    valid_embeddings, normalized_embeddings, transpose_b=True)
```

6. Now we are ready to run the TensorFlow graph:

```
with tf.Session(graph=graph) as session:
  # We must initialize all variables before we use them.
  init.run()
  print('Initialized')
  average_loss = 0
  for step in range(num_steps):
    # This is your generate_batch function that generates input
    # words and context words (labels) in a batch from data.
    batch_inputs, batch_context = generate_batch(data,
        batch_size, num_skips, skip_window)
    feed_dict = {train_inputs: batch_inputs,
                 train_context: batch_context}
    # We perform one update step by evaluating the optimizer op
    # and include it in the list of returned values for
    # session.run()
    _, loss_val = session.run(
        [optimizer, cross_entropy], feed_dict=feed_dict)
    average_loss += loss_val
    if step % 2000 == 0:
      if step > 0:
        average_loss /= 2000
      # The average loss is an estimate of the loss over
      # the last 2000 batches.
      print('Average loss at step ', step, ': ', average_loss)
      average_loss = 0
  final_embeddings = normalized_embeddings.eval()
```

7. In addition, we want to print out the words that are most similar to our validation words—we do this by calling the similarity operation we defined earlier, and sorting the results. Note that this is an expensive operation, so we do it only once every 10,000 steps:

```
if step % 10000 == 0:
    sim = similarity.eval()
    for i in range(valid_size):
        # reverse_dictionary - maps codes(integers) to words(strings)
        valid_word = reverse_dictionary[valid_examples[i]]
        top_k = 8  # number of nearest neighbors
        nearest = (-sim[i, :]).argsort()[1:top_k + 1]
        log_str = 'Nearest to %s:' % valid_word
        for k in range(top_k):
            close_word = reverse_dictionary[nearest[k]]
            log_str = '%s %s,' % (log_str, close_word)
        print(log_str)
```

It is interesting to notice that for the first iteration, the top eight nearest words to *four* are lanthanides, dunant, jag, wheelbase, torso, bayesian, hoping, and serena, but after 30,000 steps, the top eight nearest words to *four* are six, nine, zero, two, seven, eight, three, and five. We can use t-SNE by Maaten and Hinton, from *Visualizing Data using t-SNE* (2008) http://www.jmlr.org/papers/volume9/vandermaaten08a/vandermaaten08a.pdf, to visualize the embeddings using the following code:

```
from sklearn.manifold import TSNE
import matplotlib.pyplot as plt
tsne = TSNE(perplexity=30, n_components=2,
            init='pca', n_iter=5000, method='exact')
plot_only = 500
low_dim_embs = tsne.fit_transform(final_embeddings[:plot_only, :])
# reverse_dictionary - maps codes(integers) to words(strings)
labels = [reverse_dictionary[i] for i in xrange(plot_only)]
plt.figure(figsize=(18, 18))  # in inches
for i, label in enumerate(labels):
    x, y = low_dim_embs[i, :]
    plt.scatter(x, y)
    plt.annotate(label,
                 xy=(x, y),
                 xytext=(5, 2),
                 textcoords='offset points',
                 ha='right',
                 va='bottom')
```

In the following figure, we visualize the Word2Vec embedding, and find that words with similar meaning are close to each other:

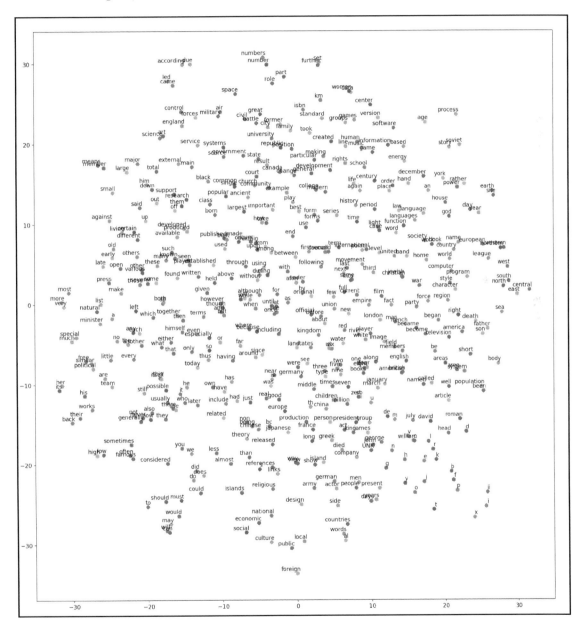

Visualization of Word2Vec embeddings using t-SNE

Using existing pre-trained Word2Vec embeddings

In this section, we will be going through the following topics:

- Word2Vec from Google News
- Using the pre-trained Word2Vec embeddings

Word2Vec from Google News

The Word2Vec model trained by Google on the Google News dataset has a feature dimension of 300. The number of features is considered as a hyperparameter which you can, and perhaps should, experiment with in your own applications to see which setting yields the best results.

In this pretrained model, some stop words such as *a*, *and*, and *of* are being excluded, but others such as *the*, *also*, and *should* are included. Some misspelled words are also included, for example, both *mispelled* and *misspelled*—the latter is the correct one.

You can find open source tools such as `https://github.com/chrisjmccormick/inspect_word2vec` to inspect the word embeddings in the pre-trained model.

Using the pre-trained Word2Vec embeddings

In this section, we will briefly explain how to use pre-trained vectors. Before reading this section, download Word2Vec pre-trained vectors from `https://drive.google.com/file/d/0B7XkCwpI5KDYNlNUTTlSS21pQmM/edit`, and load the model:

```
from gensim.models import KeyedVectors
# Load pre-trained model
model = KeyedVectors.load_word2vec_format(
    './GoogleNews-vectors-negative300.bin', binary=True)
```

Then, we find the top 5 words that are similar to woman and king, but dissimilar to man:

```
model.wv.most_similar(positive=['woman', 'king'],
                      negative=['man'], topn=5)
```

We see the following:

```
[(u'queen', 0.7118192911148071),
 (u'monarch', 0.6189674139022827),
 (u'princess', 0.5902431607246399),
 (u'crown_prince', 0.5499460697174072),
 (u'prince', 0.5377321243286133)]
```

This makes sense, since `queen` shares similar attributes to a `woman` and a `king`, but does not share attributes with a `man`.

Understanding GloVe

GloVe is an unsupervised learning algorithm for obtaining vector representations (embeddings) for words. It has been seen that with similar training hyperparameters, the embeddings generated using the two methods tend to perform very similarly in downstream NLP tasks.

The differences are that Word2Vec is a predictive model, which learns the embeddings to improve their predictive ability by minimizing the prediction loss, that is, the loss (target word | context words; *W*). In Word2Vec, it's been formalized as a feed-forward neural network and uses an optimization approach such as SGD to update the network.

On the other hand, GloVe is essentially a count-based model, where a co-occurrence matrix is first built. Each entry in this co-occurrence corresponds to the frequency we see the target word (rows), at the same time, that we see the context word (the columns). Then, this matrix is factorized to yield a lower-dimensional (word x features) matrix, where each row now yields a vector representation for each word. This is where the dimension reduction flavor comes in, as the goal is to minimize the reconstruction loss and find the lower-dimensional representations to explain most of the variance in the high-dimensional data.

There are some benefits though for GloVe over Word2Vec, as it is easier to parallelize the implementation such that the model can be trained on more data.

There are many resources online. For implementation using TensorFlow, one can look at `https://github.com/GradySimon/tensorflow-glove/blob/master/Getting%20Started.ipynb`.

FastText

FastText (https://fasttext.cc/) is a library for efficient learning of word representations and sentence classification. The main advantage of FastText embeddings over Word2Vec is to take into account the internal structure of words while learning word representations, which could be very useful for morphologically rich languages, and also for words that occur rarely.

The main difference between Word2Vec and FastText is that for Word2Vec, the atomic entity is each word, which is the smallest unit to train on. On the contrary, in FastText, the smallest unit is character-level n-grams, and each word is treated as being composed of character n-grams. For example, the word vector of *happy* with an n-gram of minimum size three and maximum size six, can be decomposed to:

<ha, <hap, <happ, <happy, hap, happ, happy, happy>,app,appy, appy>, ppy, ppy>, py>

Because of this, FastText typically generates better word embeddings for rare words as even at the word level they are rare, and the composed n-gram characters can still be seen and shared with other words. While in Word2Vec, a rare word often has fewer neighbors, so fewer resulting training instances to learn from. Also, Word2Vec has a fixed vocabulary size, and vocabulary is configured through preprocessing based on the given training data. When facing a new word that is not in the vocabulary, both Word2Vec and GloVe will have no solution for it. However, since FastText is on the character n-gram level, as long as the n-grams from the rare word have appeared in the training corpus, FastText will be able to construct the word-level vector by summing up the character n-gram vectors.

Because of the finer granularity, FastText also takes a longer time and more memory to learn. Therefore, one needs to carefully choose the hyperparameters that control the size of the n-gram, such as the n-gram max and n-gram min. With a pre-set n-gram min/max, one can tune the min word count, which determines the minimum frequency a word needs to be seen in the corpus to be included in the vocabulary. The parameter-bucket number is to control the number of buckets that word and character n-gram features are hashed into (picking of a vector for n-grams is a hashing function). This helps to limit the memory usage of the model. For setting up the bucket size, if the number of n-grams is not huge, it is recommended to use a smaller bucket size.

Readers can find the pre-trained word vectors for 294 languages at https://github.com/facebookresearch/fastText/blob/master/pretrained-vectors.md.

Applications

In this section, we talk about some example use cases and fine-tuning of NLP models.

Example use cases

With the pre-trained Word2Vec embedding, the downstream applications can be many for NLP, for example, document classification or sentiment classification. One example is called **Doc2Vec**, which, in the simplest form, takes the Word2Vec vectors of every word in the document and aggregates them by either taking a normalized sum or arithmetic mean of the terms. The resulting vector for each document is used for text classification. This type of application can be thought of as the direct application of the learned word embeddings.

On the other hand, we can apply the idea of Word2Vec modeling to other applications, for example, finding similar items in an e-commerce environment. During each session window, an online user may be browsing multiple items. From such behavior, we can look for similar or related items using behavior information. In such cases, each item with a unique ID can be thought of as a word, and items within the same session can be thought of as the context words. We can do similar training data generation and pipe the generated pairs into the network. The embedding results can then be used for calculating the similarity between items.

Fine-tuning

Fine-tuning refers to the technique of initializing a network with parameters from another task (such as an unsupervised training task) and then updating these parameters based on the task at hand. For example, NLP architecture often uses pre-trained word embeddings such as Word2Vec, and these word embeddings are then updated during training or through continued training for a specific task such as sentiment analysis.

Summary

In this chapter, we introduced the basic ideas and models for using a neural network to learn distributed word representation. We particularly dove into the Word2Vec model and have shown how to train a model, as well as how to load the pre-trained vectors for downstream NLP applications. In the next chapter, we will talk about more advanced deep learning models in NLP, such as recurrent neural network, long-term short memory model, and several real-world applications.

6

Advanced Natural Language Processing

In the previous chapter, we covered the basics of **natural language processing** (NLP). We covered simple representations of text in the form of the bag-of-words model, and more advanced word embedding representations that capture the semantic properties of the text. This chapter aims to build upon word representation techniques by taking a more model-centric approach to text processing. We will go over some of the core models, such as **recurrent neural networks** (RNNs) and **Long Short-Term Memory** (LSTM) networks. We will specifically answer the following questions:

- What are some core deep learning models for understanding text?
- What core concepts form the basis for understanding RNNs?
- What core concepts form the basis for understanding LSTMs?
- How do you implement basic functionality of an LSTM using TensorFlow?
- What are some of the most popular text processing applications of an RNN/LSTM?

Deep learning for text

We have seen various different techniques so far, which employ variants of neural networks for text processing. Word-based embedding is one such common application of neural networks. As seen in the previous chapter, word-based embedding techniques are feature-level, or representation learning, problems. In other words, they solve a very specific problem: Given a text block, represent it in some feature form that is used for a downstream text mining application, such as classification, machine translation, attribute labeling, and so on. A number of machine learning techniques exist today that can apply text mining at varying accuracy levels. In this chapter, we focus on an entirely different model of text processing. We look into the core deep learning models that are suited to text processing applications and can perform both:

- Representation learning or feature extraction
- Downstream text mining application in a unified model

Before we begin our understanding of deep learning models for text, let's revisit neural networks for a moment and try to understand why they are not suited for some of the important text mining applications.

Limitations of neural networks

Neural networks are a very potent tool for approximating any non-linear function—a problem that arises very frequently in any pattern recognition or machine learning task. Though they are very powerful in their modeling approach, they have certain limitations, which makes them limited in their abilities for various pattern recognition tasks. A few of those limitations are:

- **Fixed sized inputs**: A neural network architecture has a fixed number of input layers. As such, it can only take a fixed sized input and output for any task. This is a limiting factor for many pattern recognition tasks. For example, imagine an image captioning task, where the goal of the network is taking an image and generating words as captions. A typical neural network cannot model this task as for every image, a number of words in the captions are going to be different. Given a fixed output size, it is not possible for a neural network to efficiently model this task. Another example is the task of sentiment classification. In this task, a network should take a sentence as its input and output a single label (for example, positive or negative). Given a sentence has a varying number of words, the input for this task has a variable number of inputs. Hence, a typical neural network cannot model this task. This type of task is often referred to as a *sequence classification* task.

- **Lack of memory:** Another limitation of neural networks is their lack of memory. For example, for the task of sentiment classification, it is important to remember the sequence of words to classify the sentiment of the whole sentence. For a neural network, each input unit is processed independently of each other. As such, the next word token in the sentence has no correlation to any previous word token in the sentence, which makes the task of classifying the sentence extremely difficult. A good model that can perform well at such tasks needs to maintain context or memory:

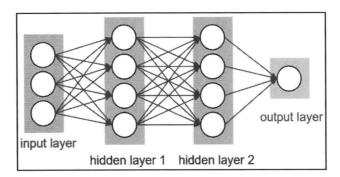

Fixed sized inputs of neural networks (Source: https://raw.githubusercontent.com/cs231n/cs231n.github.io/master/assets/nn1/neural_net2.jpeg)

To address these limitations, an RNN is used. This class of deep learning model is our primary focus in this chapter.

Recurrent neural networks

The basic idea behind recurrent neural networks is the vectorization of data. If you look at figure *Fixed sized inputs of neural networks,* which represents a traditional neural network, each node in the network accepts a scalar value and generates another scalar value. Another way to view this architecture is that each layer in the network accepts a vector as its input and generates another vector as its output. Figure *Neural network horizontally rolled up* and figure *Neural network vertically rolled up* illustrate this representation:

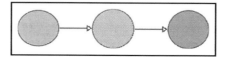

Neural network horizontally rolled up

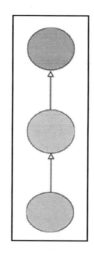

Neural network vertically rolled up

The figure *Neural network vertically rolled up* is a simple RNN representation, which is a one-to-one RNN; one input is mapped to one output using one hidden layer.

RNN architectures

Typically, RNNs have many different architectures. In this section, we will go over some basic architectures of RNNs and discuss how they fit various, different text mining applications:

- **One-to-many RNN**: Figure *RNN: One-to-many architecture* illustrates the basic idea of a one-to-many RNN architecture. As shown in the following figure, in this architecture a single input unit of RNN is mapped to multiple hidden units as well as multiple output units. One application example of this architecture is image captioning. As described previously, in this application the input layer accepts a single image and maps it to multiple words in the caption:

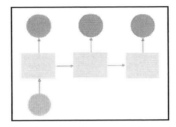

RNN: One-to-many architecture

- **Many-to-one RNN**: Figure *RNN: Many-to-one architecture,* illustrates the basic idea of a many-to-one RNN architecture. As shown in the following figure, in this architecture multiple input units of RNN are mapped to multiple hidden units but only a single output unit. One application example of this architecture is sentiment classification. As described previously, in this application the input layer accepts multiple word tokens from a sentence and maps them to a single sentiment of the sentence as positive or negative:

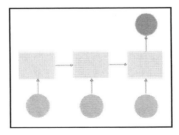

RNN: Many-to-one architecture

- **Many-to-many RNN**: Figure *RNN: Many-to-many architecture* illustrates the basic idea of a many-to-many RNN architecture. As shown in the following, in this architecture multiple input units of RNN are mapped to multiple hidden units and multiple output units. One application example of this architecture is a machine translation. As described previously, in this application the input layer accepts multiple word tokens from a source language and maps them to multiple word tokens from a target language:

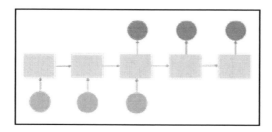

RNN: Many-to-many architecture

Basic RNN model

Figure *Basic RNN model* describes a basic RNN model in more detail. As you can see, this is a simple one-to-many RNN model. If you just focus on nodes X_1, h_1, and Y_1, they are very similar to a one-layer neural network. The only additions to this RNN model are the steps in time when hidden neurons take on different values, such as h_2 and h_3. The overall sequence of operations in this RNN model is as follows:

- Time step t1 where X_1 is input to the RNN model
- Time step t1 where h1 is computed based on input X1
- Time step t1 where Y1 is computed based on input h1
- Time step t2 where h2 is computed based on input h1
- Time step t2 where Y2 is computed based on input h2
- Time step t3 where h3 is computed based on input h2
- Time step t3 where Y_3 is computed based on input h_3

Using this model, we can generate multiple output vectors based on each time step. Hence, such models are widely applicable to a number of time-series or sequence-based data models.

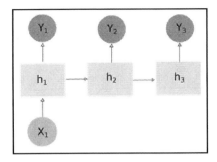

Basic RNN model

Training RNN is tough

In this section, we will look at some of the existing limitations of training RNN. We will also dive deeper and understand why it is tough to train RNN.

The traditional method of training neural networks is through the backpropagation algorithm. In the case of RNN, we need to perform a backpropagation of gradient through time, often referred to as **backpropagation through time (BPTT)**. Although it's numerically possible to compute backward propagation of gradients through time, it often results in poor results due to the classic vanishing (or exploding) gradient problem as shown in figure vanishing *gradient problem in RNN with multiplicative gradients*:

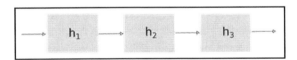

Vanishing gradient problem in RNN with multiplicative gradients

To understand this concept in more detail, let's take a look at figure *Basic RNN model*. It shows a single layer of hidden neurons through three-time steps. To compute a forward pass of the gradient across this, we need to compute a derivative of a composite function as follows:

$$H = h_3\left(h_2\left(h_1\left(x\right)\right)\right)$$

$$\frac{\partial H}{\partial x} = \frac{\partial h_3}{\partial h_2}\frac{\partial h_2}{\partial h_1}\frac{\partial h_1}{\partial x}$$

As you can imagine, each gradient computation here successively becomes smaller, and multiplying a smaller value with a bigger value leads to diminishing the overall gradient when computed through a large time step. Hence RNNs cannot be trained in an efficient manner with longer time steps using this approach. One way to solve this approach is to use a gating logic as shown in figure *Solution to vanishing gradient problem with additive gradients:*

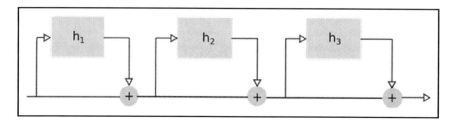

Solution to vanishing gradient problem with additive gradients

In this logic, instead of multiplying the gradients together, we add them as follows:

$$H = h_1(x) + h_2(x) + h_3(x)$$

$$\frac{\partial H}{\partial x} = \frac{\partial h_1}{\partial x} + \frac{\partial h_2}{\partial x} + \frac{\partial h_3}{\partial x}$$

As can be seen from the preceding equation, the overall gradient can be computed as a sum of smaller gradients, which do not diminish even when passed through longer time steps. This addition is achieved due to the gating logic, which adds the output of the hidden layer with the original input at every time step, thereby reducing the impact of diminishing gradients. This gating architecture forms the basis of a new type of RNN also known as Long Short-Term Memory networks or LSTMs. LSTMs are the most popular way to train RNNs on a long sequence of temporal data and have been shown to perform reasonably well on a wide variety of text mining tasks.

Long short-term memory network

So far, we have seen that RNNs perform poorly due to the vanishing and exploding gradient problem. LSTMs are designed to help us overcome this limitation. The core idea behind LSTM is a gating logic, which provides a memory-based architecture that leads to an additive gradient effect instead of a multiplicative gradient effect as shown in the following figure. To illustrate this concept in more detail, let us look into LSTM's memory architecture. Like any other memory-based system, a typical LSTM cell consists of three major functionalities:

- Write to memory
- Read from memory
- Reset memory

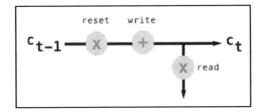

LSTM: Core idea (Source: https://ayearofai.com/rohan-lenny-3-recurrent-neural-networks-10300100899b)

Figure *LSTM: Core idea* illustrates this core idea. As shown in the figure LSTM: Core idea, first the value of a previous LSTM cell is passed through a reset gate, which multiplies the previous state value by a scalar between 0 and 1. If the scalar is close to 1, it leads to the passing of the value of the previous cell state (remembering the previous state). In case it is closer to 0, this leads to blocking of the value's previous cell state (forgetting the previous state). Next, the write gate simply writes the transformed output of the reset gate. Finally, the read gate reads a view of the output from the write gate:

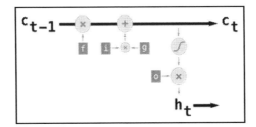

LSTM: Gating functions in the cell (Source: https://ayearofai.com/rohan-lenny-3-recurrent-neural-networks-10300100899b)

Understanding LSTM's gating logic can be quite complex. To describe this more succinctly, let us take a detailed look into the cell architecture of LSTM without any inputs as shown in figure *LSTM: Core idea*. The gating functions now have well-defined labels. We can call them as follows:

1. **f gate**: Often referred to as the forget gate, this gate applies a sigmoid function to the input cell value from a previous time step. Since a sigmoid function takes any value between 0 and 1, this gate amounts to forgetting a portion of the previous cell state value based on the activation of the sigmoid function.

2. **g gate**: The primary function of this gate is to regulate the additive factor of the previous cell state value. In other words, the output of the f gate is now added with a certain scalar controlled by the g gate. Typically, a tanh function between -1 and 1 is applied in this case. As such, this gate often acts as an incrementing or decrementing a counter.

3. **i gate**: Though g gates regulate the additive factor, the *i* gate is another tanh function between 0 and 1 that dictates what portion of the g gate can actually be added to the output of the f gate.

4. **o gate**: Also known as the *output gate*, this gate also uses a sigmoid function to generate a scaled output, which is then inputted to the hidden state in the current time step:

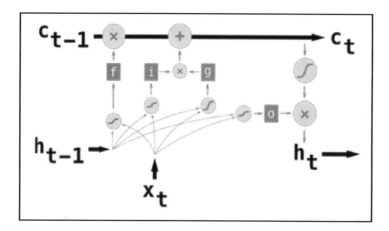

LSTM: Basic cell architecture (Source: https://ayearofai.com/rohan-lenny-3-recurrent-neural-networks-10300100899b)

Figure *LSTM: Gating functions in the cell* shows the full LSTM cell with both inputs and hidden states from previous and current time steps. As shown here, each of the preceding four gates receives inputs from both the hidden state from the previous time step as well as input from the current time step. The output of the cell is passed to the hidden state of the current time step, as well as carried forward to the next LSTM cell. Figure *End-to-end LSTM network* describes this connection visually.

As shown here, each LSTM cell acts as a separate unit between the input neuron and hidden neuron across all time steps. Each of these cells is connected across time steps using a two-channel communication mechanism sharing both the LSTM cell output as well as hidden neuron activations across different time steps:

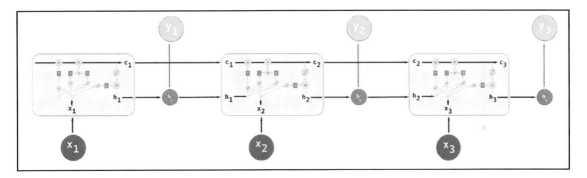

End-to-end LSTM network (Source: https://ayearofai.com/rohan-lenny-3-recurrent-neural-networks-10300100899b)

LSTM implementation with tensorflow

In this section, we will look at an example of using LSTM in TensorFlow for the task of sentiment classification. The input to LSTM will be a sentence or sequence of words. The output of LSTM will be a binary value indicating a positive sentiment with 1 and a negative sentiment with 0. We will use a many-to-one LSTM architecture for this problem since it maps multiple inputs onto a single output. Figure *LSTM: Basic cell architecture* shows this architecture in more detail. As shown here, the input takes a sequence of word tokens (in this case, a sequence of three words). Each word token is input at a new time step and is input to the hidden state for the corresponding time step.

For example, the word *Book* is input at time step *t* and is fed to the hidden state h_i:

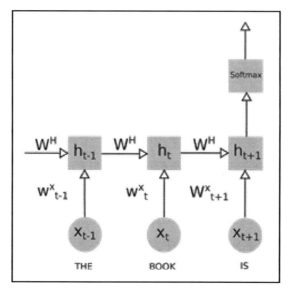

Sentiment analysis using LSTM

To implement this model in TensorFlow, we need to first define a few variables as follows:

```
batch_size = 4
lstm_units = 16
num_classes = 2
max_sequence_length = 4
embedding_dimension = 64
num_iterations = 1000
```

As shown previously, `batch_size` dictates how many sequences of tokens we can input in one batch for training. `lstm_units` represents the total number of LSTM cells in the network. `max_sequence_length` represents the maximum possible length of a given sequence. Once defined, we now proceed to initialize TensorFlow-specific data structures for input data as follows:

```
import tensorflow as tf

labels = tf.placeholder(tf.float32, [batch_size, num_classes])
raw_data = tf.placeholder(tf.int32, [batch_size, max_sequence_length])
```

Given we are working with word tokens, we would like to represent them using a good feature representation technique. We propose using word embedding techniques from the chapter 5, NLP- Vector Representation, for this task. Let us assume the word embedding representation takes a word token and projects it onto an embedding space of dimension, `embedding_dimension`. The two-dimensional input data containing raw word tokens is now transformed into a three-dimensional word tensor with the added dimension representing the word embedding. We also use pre-computed word embedding, stored in a `word_vectors` data structure. We initialize the data structures as follows:

```
data = tf.Variable(tf.zeros([batch_size, max_sequence_length,
embedding_dimension]),dtype=tf.float32)
data = tf.nn.embedding_lookup(word_vectors,raw_data)
```

Now that the input data is ready, we look at defining the LSTM model. As shown previously, we need to create `lstm_units` of a basic LSTM cell. Since we need to perform a classification at the end, we wrap the LSTM unit with a dropout wrapper. To perform a full temporal pass of the data on the defined network, we unroll the LSTM using a `dynamic_rnn` routine of TensorFlow. We also initialize a random weight matrix and a constant value of `0.1` as the bias vector, as follows:

```
weight = tf.Variable(tf.truncated_normal([lstm_units, num_classes]))
bias = tf.Variable(tf.constant(0.1, shape=[num_classes]))
lstm_cell = tf.contrib.rnn.BasicLSTMCell(lstm_units)
wrapped_lstm_cell = tf.contrib.rnn.DropoutWrapper(cell=lstm_cell,
output_keep_prob=0.8)
output, state = tf.nn.dynamic_rnn(wrapped_lstm_cell, data,
dtype=tf.float32)
```

Once the output is generated by the dynamic unrolled RNN, we transpose its shape, multiply it by the weight vector, and add a bias vector to it to compute the final prediction value:

```
output = tf.transpose(output, [1, 0, 2])
last = tf.gather(output, int(output.get_shape()[0]) - 1)
prediction = (tf.matmul(last, weight) + bias)
weight = tf.cast(weight, tf.float64)
last = tf.cast(last, tf.float64)
bias = tf.cast(bias, tf.float64)
```

Since the initial prediction needs to be refined, we define an objective function with cross-entropy to minimize the loss as follows:

```
loss =
tf.reduce_mean(tf.nn.softmax_cross_entropy_with_logits(logits=prediction,
labels=labels))
optimizer = tf.train.AdamOptimizer().minimize(loss)
```

After this sequence of steps, we have a trained, end-to-end LSTM network for sentiment classification of arbitrary length sentences.

Applications

Today, RNNs (for example, LSTM) have been used in a variety of different applications ranging from time series data modeling, image classification, and video captioning, as well as textual analysis. In this section, we will cover some important applications of RNNs for solving different natural language understanding problems.

Language modeling

Language modeling is one of the fundamental problems in **natural language understanding** (NLU). The core idea of a language model is to model important distributional properties of the words in a given language. Once such a model is learnt, it can be applied to a sequence of new words to generate the most likely next word token given the learned distributional representation. More formally, a language model computes a joint probability over a sequence of words as follows:

$$P(W_1, W_2, W_3, \ldots, W_n) = \prod_i P(W_i | W_1, W_2, \ldots, W_{i-1})$$

Estimating this probability is computationally expensive, hence a number of estimation techniques exist, which make certain assumptions about the time range dependence of the word tokens. Some of them are as follows:

- **Unigram model**: It assumes that each word token is independent of the sequence of words before and after it:

$$P(W_1, W_2, W_3, \ldots, W_n) \approx \prod_i P(W_i)$$

- **Bigram model**: It assumes that each word token is dependent on only the word token immediately before it:

$$P(W_1, W_2, W_3, \ldots, W_n) = \prod_i P(W_i | W_{i-1})$$

We can solve the language model estimation problem efficiently through the use of an LSTM-based network. The following figure illustrates a specific architecture that estimates a three-gram language model. As shown here, we take a many-to-many LSTM and chunk the whole sentence into a running window of three-word tokens each. For example, let us assume a training sentence is: [**What, is, the, problem**]. The first input sequence is: [**What, is, the**] and the output is [**is, the, problem**]:

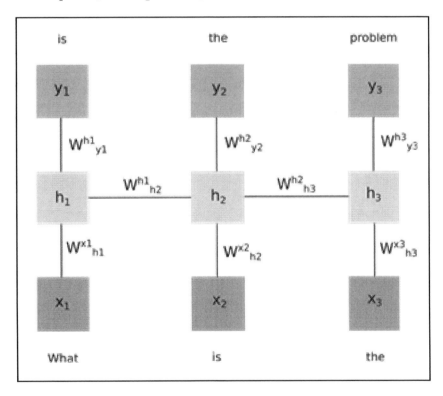

Language modeling with traditional LSTM

Sequence tagging

Sequence tagging can be understood as a problem where the model sees a sequence of words or tokens for each word in the sequence and it is expected to emit a label. In other words, the model is expected to tag the whole sequence of tokens with an appropriate label from a known label dictionary. Sequence tagging has some very interesting applications in natural language understanding such as named entity recognition, part of speech tagging, and so on:

- **Named Entity Recognition**: Also known as **NER**, Named Entity Recognition is an information extraction technique that aims to recognize named entities in the given sequence of text tokens (for example, words). Some of the common named entities include person, location, organization, currency, and so on. For example, when you input a sequence *IBM opens an office in Peru* to an NER system, it can recognize the presence of two named entities *B-ORG* and *B-LOC*, and label them appropriately to tokens *IBM* and *Peru* respectively.

- **Part of Speech tagging**: Also known as POS tagging, POS tagging is an information extraction technique that aims to recognize parts of speech in text. Some of the common parts of speech classes are NN (noun, singular), NNS (noun, plural), NNPS (proper noun, singular), VB (verb, base form), CC (coordinating conjunction), CD (cardinal number), and so on:

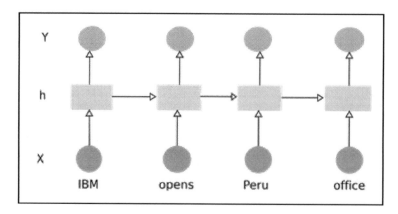

Sequence tagging with traditional LSTM

As shown in the preceding figure, *Sequence Tagging with Traditional LSTM*, one can model this problem with a simple LSTM. One important point to note from this figure is LSTM is only able to make use of the previous context of data. For example, in hidden state at time t, the LSTM cell sees input from time t and output from hidden state at time t-1. There is no way to make use of any future context from time greater than t in this architecture. This is a strong limitation of traditional LSTM models for the task of sequence tagging.

To address this issue, bi-directional LSTM or B-LSTMs are proposed. The core idea of a bi-directional LSTM is to have two LSTM layers, one in a forward direction and another in a backward direction. With this design change, you can now combine information from both directions to get previous context (forward LSTM) and future context (backward LSTM). Figure *Language modeling with traditional LSTM* shows this design in more detail. B-LSTMs are one of the most popular LSTM variants used for sequence tagging tasks today:

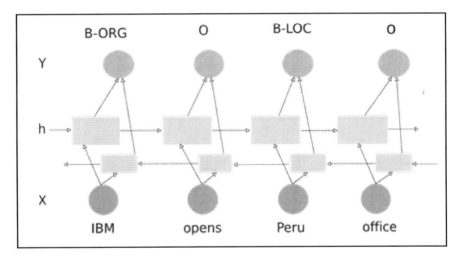

Sequence tagging with bi-directional LSTM

To implement B-LSTM in TensorFlow, we define two LSTM layers, one for forward and one for backward direction as follows:

```
lstm_cell_fw = tf.contrib.rnn.BasicLSTMCell(lstm_units)
lstm_cell_bw = tf.contrib.rnn.BasicLSTMCell(lstm_units)
```

In the previous implementation, we unrolled the LSTM using a dynamic RNN. TensorFlow provides a similar routine for bidirectional LSTM which we can use as follows:

```
(output_fw, output_bw), state =
tf.nn.bidirectional_dynamic_rnn(lstm_cell_fw,lstm_cell_bw, data,
dtype=tf.float32)
context_rep = tf.concat([output_fw, output_bw], axis=-1)
context_rep_flat = tf.reshape(context_rep, [-1, 2*lstm_units])
```

Now, we initialize weights and bias like before (note, `weight` has twice the number of `lstm_units` as before, one for each directional layer of LSTM):

```
weight = tf.Variable(tf.truncated_normal([2*lstm_units, num_classes]))
bias = tf.Variable(tf.constant(0.1, shape=[num_classes]))
```

Now, you can generate predictions based on the current value of weights and compute a loss value. In the previous example, we computed a cross entropy loss. For sequence labeling, it is often useful to have a **conditional random field** (**CRF**)-based loss function. You can define these loss functions as follows:

```
prediction = tf.matmul(context_rep_flat, weight) + bias
scores = tf.reshape(prediction, [-1, max_sequence_length, num_classes])
log_likelihood, transition_params = tf.contrib.crf.crf_log_likelihood(
scores, labels, sequence_lengths)
loss_crf = tf.reduce_mean(-log_likelihood)
```

The model can now be trained as follows:

```
optimizer = tf.train.AdamOptimizer().minimize(loss_crf)
```

Machine translation

Machine translation is one of the most recent success stories of NLU. The goal of this problem is to take a text sentence in a source language, such as English and convert it into the same sentence in a given target language, such as Spanish. Traditional methods of solving this problem relied on using phrase-based models. These models typically chunk the sentences into shorter phrases and translate each of these phrases one by one into a target language phrase.

Though translation at phrase-level works reasonably well, when you combine these translated phrases into the target language to generate a fully translated sentence, you find occasional choppiness, or *disfluency*. To avoid this limitation of phrase-based machine translation models, the **neural machine translation** (**NMT**) technique is proposed, which utilizes a variant of RNN to solve this problem:

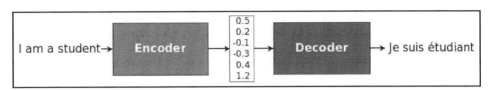

Neural machine translation core idea (Source: https://github.com/tensorflow/nmt)

The core idea of an NMT can be described in figure *Neural machine translation core idea*. It consists of two parts: (a) **Encoder** and (b) **Decoder**.

The role of the encoder is to take a sentence in the source language and convert it into a vector representation (also known as **thought vector**) that captures the overall semantics and meaning of the sentence. This vector representation is then inputted to a decoder, which then decodes this into a target language sentence. As you can see, this problem is a natural fit for a many-to-many RNN architecture. In the previous application example for sequence labeling, we introduced the concept of B-LSTM that can map an input sequence to a set of output tokens. Even B-LSTM is unable to map an input sequence to an output sequence. Hence, to solve this problem with an RNN architecture, we introduce another variant of RNN also known as the *Seq2Seq* model.

Figure *Neural machine translation architecture with Seq2Seq model* describes the core architecture of a Seq2Seq model applied for the task of NMT:

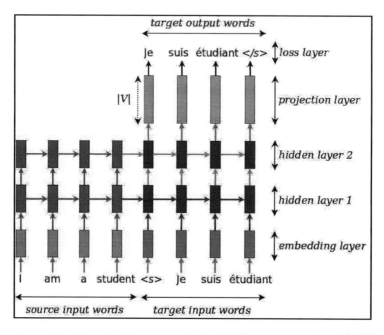

Neural machine translation architecture with Seq2Seq model (Source: https://github.com/tensorflow/nmt)

A Seq2Seq model, as shown in Figure *Neural machine translation architecture with Seq2Seq model* is essentially composed of two groups of RNNs, Encoders and Decoders. Each of these RNNs may be composed of either uni-directional LSTM or bidirectional LSTM, may be composed of multiple hidden layers, and may either use LSTM or GRU as its basic cell unit type. As shown, an encoder RNN (shown on left) takes source words as its inputs and projects it onto two hidden layers. These two hidden layers when moved across the time step, invoke the decoder RNN (shown on right) and project the output onto a projection and loss layer to generate the most likely candidate words in the target language.

To implement Seq2Seq in TensorFlow, we define a simple LSTM cell for both encoding and decoding and unroll the encoder with a dynamic RNN module as follows:

```
lstm_cell_encoder = tf.nn.rnn_cell.BasicLSTMCell(lstm_units)
lstm_cell_decoder = tf.nn.rnn_cell.BasicLSTMCell(lstm_units)
encoder_outputs, encoder_state = tf.nn.dynamic_rnn( lstm_cell_encoder,
encoder_data, sequence_length=max_sequence_length, time_major=True)
```

In case you want to use bi-directional LSTM for this step, you can do that as follows:

```
lstm_cell_fw = tf.contrib.rnn.BasicLSTMCell(lstm_units)
lstm_cell_bw = tf.contrib.rnn.BasicLSTMCell(lstm_units)
bi_outputs, encoder_state = tf.nn.bidirectional_dynamic_rnn(lstm_cell_fw,
lstm_cell_bw, encoder_data,
sequence_length=max_sequence_length, time_major=True)
encoder_outputs = tf.concat(bi_outputs, -1)
```

Now we need to perform a decoding step to generate the most likely candidate words in the target language (hypotheses). For this step, TensorFlow provides a `dynamic_decoder` function under the Seq2Seq module. We use it as follows:

```
training_helper = tf.contrib.seq2seq.TrainingHelper(decoder_data,
decoder_lengths, time_major=True)
projection_layer = tf.python.layers.core.Dense(target_vocabulary_size)
decoder = tf.contrib.seq2seq.BasicDecoder(decoder_cell, training_helper,
encoder_state, output_layer=projection_layer)
outputs, state = tf.contrib.seq2seq.dynamic_decode(decoder)
logits = outputs.rnn_output
```

Lastly, we define a loss function and train the model to minimize the loss:

```
loss =
tf.reduce_sum(tf.nn.softmax_cross_entropy_with_logits(logits=prediction,
labels=labels))
optimizer = tf.train.AdamOptimizer().minimize(loss)
```

Seq2Seq inference

During the inference phase, a trained Seq2Seq model gets a source sentence. It uses this to obtain an `encoder_state` which is used to initialize the decoder. The translation process starts as soon as the decoder receives a special symbol, **<s>**, denoting the start of the decoding process.

The decoder RNN now runs for the current time step and computes the probability distribution of all the words in the target vocabulary as defined by the `projection_layer`. It now employs a greedy strategy, where it chooses the most likely word from this distribution and feeds it as the target input word in the next time step. This process is now repeated for another time step until the decoder RNN chooses a special symbol, **</s>**, which marks the end of translation. Figure *Neural machine translation decoding with greedy search over Seq2Seq model* illustrates this greedy search technique with an example:

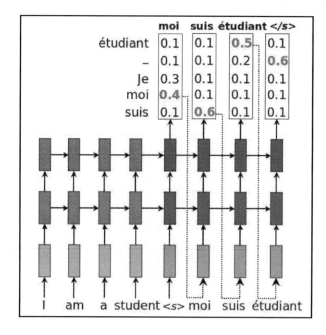

Neural machine translation decoding with greedy search over Seq2Seq model (Source: https://github.com/tensorflow/nmt)

To implement this Greedy Search strategy in TensorFlow, we use the `GreedyEmbeddingHelper` function in Seq2Seq module as follows:

```
helper = tf.contrib.seq2seq.GreedyEmbeddingHelper(decoder_data,
  tf.fill([batch_size], "<s>"), "</s>")
decoder = tf.contrib.seq2seq.BasicDecoder(
  decoder_cell, helper, encoder_state,
  output_layer=projection_layer)
# Dynamic decoding
num_iterations = tf.round(tf.reduce_max(max_sequence_length) * 2)
outputs, _ = tf.contrib.seq2seq.dynamic_decode(
  decoder, maximum_iterations=num_iterations)
translations = outputs.sample_id
```

Chatbots

Chatbots are another example of an application that lends itself very well to RNN models. Figure *Sequence tagging with traditional LSTM* shows an example of a chatbot application built with the Seq2Seq model, which was described in the preceding section. Chatbots can be understood as a special case of machine translation, where the target language is replaced with a vocabulary of responses for each possible question in the chatbot knowledge base:

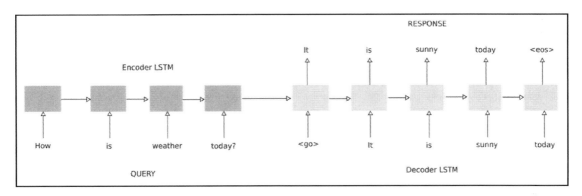

Chatbot with Seq2Seq LSTM

Summary

In this chapter, we introduced some core deep learning models for understanding text. We described the core concepts behind sequential modeling of textual data, and what network architectures are more suited to this type of data processing. We introduced basic concepts of recurrent neural networks (RNN) and showed why they are difficult to train in practice. We describe LSTM as a practical form of RNN and sketched their implementation using TensorFlow. Finally, we covered a number of natural language understanding applications that can benefit from the application of various RNN architectures.

In next chapter, chapter 7, we will look at how deep learning techniques can be applied to tasks involving both NLP and images.

7
Multimodality

With the exciting progress of deep learning in different areas such as computer vision, **natural language processing** (**NLP**), robotics, and so on, there is an emerging trend to leverage multiple data sources to develop more powerful applications. This is called **multimodality**, which is a way of unifying different information sources, including images, text, speech, and so on.

In this chapter, we will discuss some fundamental progress in multimodality of using deep learning and share with you some advanced novel applications.

What is multimodality learning?

Before we dive deeper, the first question to ask is, what is multimodality/multimodal?

Modality refers to a certain type of information and/or the representation format in which information is stored. For example, humans have various sensory modalities, such as light, sound, and pressure. In our case, we are talking more about how the data is acquired and stored. For example, commonly available modalities include natural language (both spoken or written), visual information (from images or videos), audio (including voice, sounds, and music), **Light Detection and Ranging** (**LIDAR**) data, depth images, infrared images, functional MRI and physiological signals, **electrocardiogram** (**ECG**), and so on.

The path of leveraging multiple data sources for creating real-world applications is more of a need rather than choice, as in reality, dealing with multimodal data is inevitable. For example, when we watch videos, we consume both visual and audio information. When making a decision while driving, we are leveraging visual, audio, touch sensory, and all other information to jointly make the decision. For an application that would perform perfectly for even a simplest human task, information from various data sources is necessary and needs to be jointly processed.

In the past, since feature extraction is mostly hand-crafted, the traditional way of handling multimodality data is to learn models separately on each individual modality and combine the results by voting, using a weighted average, or other probabilistic method. Some very important aspects, for example, joint learning/feature embedding or learning of the association between different modalities, have been missed. This is where deep learning provides great opportunities. As a representation learning approach, deep learning is capable of extracting task-specific features from single-modality or multiple-modality data. The shared representation captures the relationship between different sources, which can help with the following:

- Learning the transformation from one modality to another modality, and the other way around
- Handling missing modalities as long as the relationship between the absent modality has been effectively learned
- Generating joint representation for downstream prediction/decision making

Challenges of multimodality learning

To use the multimodality information, we will face a few core challenges, such as representation, translation, alignment, fusion, and co-learning (non-exclusive). In this section, we will briefly talk about each of them.

Representation

Representation refers to the *computer-interpretable description of the multimodal data* (for example, vector and tensor). It covers the following, but is not limited to:

- How to handle different symbols and signals—for example, in machine translation, Chinese characters and English characters are two distinct linguistic systems; in a self-driving system, point clouds from LIDAR sensors and image pixels from the RGB camera are two distinct sources with distinct characteristics
- How to handle different granularities
- Modality can be either static or sequential
- Different noise distribution
- Unbalanced proportions.

Translation

Translation/mapping refers to *the process of changing data from one modality to another*, for example, image captioning, speech synthesis, visual animations, and so on. Some known challenges include:

- Different representations
- Multiple source modalities
- Open-ended translations
- Subjective evaluation
- Repetitive processes

Alignment

Alignment refers to *identifying relations between elements from two or more different modalities*. The Application examples include image caption alignment, video description alignment, language-gesture co-reference, and lip reading. The following figure shows an example of image caption alignment:

Example of alignment from Andrej Karpathy's paper *Deep Fragment Embeddings for Bidirectional Image Sentence Mapping*

Some known challenges are:

- Long-range dependencies
- Ambiguous segmentation
- Limited annotated datasets with explicit alignments
- One-to-many relationships

Fusion

Fusion refers to *the process of joining information from two or more modalities to perform a prediction*. Example applications include audio-visual speech recognition, multimodal emotion recognition, multimedia event detection, and image-LIDAR joint learning for self-driving. Some known challenges are:

- Different similarity metrics
- Temporal contingency
- Varying predictive power
- Different noise topology
- Ambiguous correspondence

Co-learning

Co-learning refers to *transferring knowledge between modalities and their representations*. Some challenges are as follows:

- Partially-observable views
- Pivot identification
- Collaborative overfitting
- Imperfect predictions
- Potential divergence

In the following section, we will cover a few application cases for some recent benchmarks of multimodality learning. We will be focusing on a high-level introduction of these different fields to give you a better overview and a starting point for how each application can be implemented. With them as an anchor point, you should be able to start your own exploration of deep learning on multimodalities.

Image captioning

With the advanced progress in both computer vision and NLP areas, more and more researchers are starting to look at potential applications in their intersect areas.

One type of application is called **image captioning,** or **im2text**, which is for automatically generating descriptions for a given image. It requires the joint use of technologies in both computer vision and NLP. For a given image, the goal is to analyze its visual content and generate a realistic textual description to describe the major content or most salient aspect of the image. For example, the human in a picture.

To achieve this goal, the caption generation model has to have at least two capabilities:

- Understand the visual cues
- Be able to generate realistic natural language

Understanding the visual cues can be very task-specific; that is, the focus can be different in different scenarios. This is very much like human perception. For example, with the same image but a different focus, the interpretation of the image can be different. It's similar for the text generation step, the same meaning can have a different presentation.

In the following sessions, we will first discuss deep learning techniques, in particular the *show and tell* approach proposed by Oriol Vinyals, to give you a flavor of how deep learning is handling this problem. For this part, we will combine deep learning techniques such as **Convolutional Neural Network (CNN)** (developed in the computer vision area) and **recurrent neural network (RNN)** or **Long Short-Term Memory (LSTM)** (developed in the natural language area) to tackle the problem. It is strongly recommended for the reader to read and understand the content of Chapter 4, *Deep Learning in Computer Vision*, Chapter 5, *NLP - Vector Representation*, and Chapter 6, *Advanced Natural Language Processing*, as they are a preliminary foundation for this chapter.

Following that, we will also briefly discuss some other types of approaches, including traditional methods, such as retrieval-based or template-based approaches for image caption generation.

Certainly, there is more to just generating captions for images at the intersection of these two unrelated fields. Not only can this technique bring us some straightforward applications, such as captioning unlabeled images for better retrieval, tagging, and generating summaries for videos, but it can also potentially help to improve the quality of life for a wide range of the population, for example helping blind people to understand the content captured by a camera or video as a guiding tool. Technologies like this have the potential to make our world more accessible.

Show and tell

One of the fundamental approaches for image captioning is proposed in Oriol Vinyals' paper *Show and Tell: Lessons learned from the 2015 MSCOCO Image Captioning Challenge* (https://arxiv.org/abs/1609.06647). This session provides a deeper dive into the *show and tell* algorithm. At a high-level, the caption model contains two stages: the encoder stage and the decoder stage. The encoder generates an image embedding as the initial input of the decoder, and the decoder transforms the image representation to the natural language description space.

A similar process can be seen in the area of machine translation, where the goal is to translate the content written in one language to another.

Mathematically, this single joint model takes an image, I, as input, and is trained to maximize the conditional likelihood of $p(S|I)$, producing a target sequence of words, $S = \{S_1, S_2, \ldots\}$, that can describe the given image accurately/adequately (is the description generated correctly) and fluently (is output grammatical and fluent). Each word, S_t, in this sequence is a one-hot vector representing words from a given dictionary. A similar process can be seen in the area of machine translation, where the goal is to translate the content written in one language to another; that is, given a source sentence, maximize the likelihood of the target sentence $p(T|S)$, where T is the translated sentence, and S is the source sentence. In fact, the approach here is inspired by the machine learning system.

An illustration from Vinyals' paper can be seen as follows:

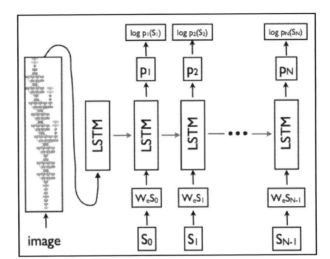

The preceding illustration shows the LSTM model combined with a CNN image embedder and word embeddings from Oriol Vinyals' paper, *Show and Tell: Lessons learned from the 2015 MSCOCO Image Captioning Challenge*. The unrolling of the LSTM is pictured in blue (dark gray in hard copies). All LSTMs share the same parameters. To understand what *unrolling* is, please refer to `Chapter 3`, *Getting Started with Neural Networks*.

The following sessions describe each important component in a detailed manner.

Encoder

First, the input image will be encoded by a deep Convolutional Neural Network and generate a vector representation to capture the image information/visual cues in the image.

The CNN can be thought of as an encoder. The last hidden state of the CNN is connected to the decoder, where the state of the neural nodes in this layer is considered as the visual features (for example, with 4096 dimensions). Note that the features are always extracted from the hidden layers of the CNN rather than the last output layer.

Decoder

The decoder, which often uses an RNN or LSTM, will perform language modeling to transform the image representation to sentences. The input to the very first stage of the decoder (at t = -1) is the output from the encoder. This is to inform the RNN/LSTM about the image content. During the training stage, we use a embeding transform W_e to embed a word at time t from the ground truth sentence, represented by $W_e S_t$, and feed this embeding to the LSTM at time t to predict the probability distribution of words at time $t+1$, represented by p_{t+1}. The embeding transform W_e can be learned from Word2Vec or other types of embeding techniques.

Training

The output from the last hidden state of the CNN (encoder) is given to the first time step of the decoder. We set x_1 = *<START>* vector and the desired label y_1 equals the first word in the sequence. Analogously, we set x_2 equals to the word vector of the first word, and expect the network to predict the distribution of second word. Finally, on the last step, x_T equals to the last word, and the target label y_T =*<EOS>* token. During training, the correct input is given to the decoder at every time step, even if the decoder made a mistake before. Finally, the loss function is defined as the sum of negative log likelihood of the ground truth words:

$$L(I, S) = - \sum_{t=1}^{N} \log p_t(S_t)$$

Testing/inference

At the inference stage, the image representation is provided to the first time step of the decoder. Set x_1 =*<START>* vector and compute the distribution over the first word, y_1. One could either sample a set of words from the distribution, or greedily choose the argmax over the computed probability of the next word, or sample the top ones from the returned candidates (Beam Search). If using LSTM, both the current state and the output will be used in the next time step as input information. The system repeats this process until it hits an *<EOS>* token.

During testing, the output of the decoder at time t is fed back and becomes the input of the decoder at time $t + 1$ (RNN/LSTM unrolling):

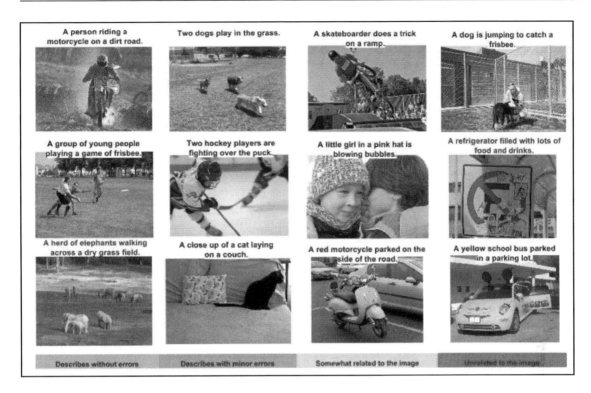

The preceding figure shows a selection of evaluation results, grouped by human rating with four levels—describes without errors, describes with minor errors, somewhat related to the image, and unrelated to the image, from *Show and Tell: Lessons learned from the 2015 MSCOCO Image Captioning Challenge.*

Beam Search

Beam Search is a heuristic search algorithm that explores a graph by expanding the most promising node in a limited set. It can be considered as an optimization of the best-first search that reduces its memory requirements. Basically, it's an iterative approach where, at each step or time t, only consider the set of k best sentences (with length = t) to generate the sentence of $t + 1$. For all resulting sentences with length equals $t + 1$, only keep the best k of them.

Other types of approaches

In general, image captioning approaches can be categorized into two categories—generating the description from scratch, searching, and retrieving from a visual space and or a multimodal space:

- Description as generation from visual input
- Description as a retrieval in visual space or multimodal space

The show and tell model can be considered as generating descriptions from scratch (using an RNN).

For the category of the retrieval types of approaches, there are also two types.

The first type is to treat the problem as a retrieval problem from a joint multimodal space. The training set contains image-description pairs or image patches—sentence segment pairs and a joint model is trained using both visual and textual information. An embedding step is included to build the multimodel space, and a deep learning type of network can be applied in this case. The learnt common representation can be used for cross-modal retrieval, from image to description or from description to image.

The second type is to cast the problem as a retrieval problem in visual space. For example, the system can first explore the similarities in the visual space to collect a set of descriptions. Then, the retrieved top descriptions are used to form the description for the query image.

One problem of the retrieval approach is that it does not aim to generate the novel text. Also, it typically requires a large amount of training data in order to provide a relevant description.

In the past, there have also been approaches that build on top of object detection and recognition, then use a template-based text generation schema or language model to output text. The following figure shows an example of generating tags for image patches through object detection and recognition, then from the generated blobs, construct sentences to generate possible candidates. Candidates are then ranked and the most probable one is chosen as the description. Obviously, one can see that this process did not optimally associate the image and the text. For example, the word **holding** from the final caption is detected and labeled from the women in purple in the image, but is used for describing the woman in brown:

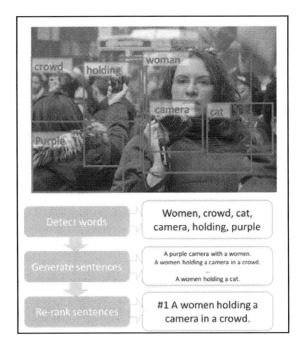

Image captions are generated by detecting and recognizing objects first, then form sentences to select the best possible candidate.

Datasets

There are a few datasets that consist of image and sentence pairs in English describing the content of the images that are available publicly for evaluation purposes:

- Basketball player has fallen on the court while another grabs at the ball from out of frame.
- Two basketball players are scrambling for the ball on the court.
- Two basketball players, one on the floor, struggle to gain possession of a basketball.
- Two high school basketball players reach to grab the ball, one falling to the floor.
- Two men in uniforms playing basketball, struggle for the ball.

The following table lists some basic information:

Dataset name	#Images	#Text	Object	Link	Description	Reference
Pascal VOC 2008	1000	5	No	`http://nlp.cs. illinois.edu/ HockenmaierGroup/ pascal-sentences/ index.html`	It consists of 1,000 images randomly selected from the training and validation set of the PASCAL 2008 object recognition challenge. Each image is associated with five different captions that describe the entities and events depicted in the image that were collected using crowdsourcing from Amazon Mechanical Turk.	A. Farhadi, M. Hejrati, M. A. Sadeghi, P. Young, C. Rashtchian, J. Hockenmaier, and D. Forsyth, *Every picture tells a story: Generating sentences from images*, in ECCV, 2010.

Flickr8K	8,092	5	No	`http://nlp.cs.illinois.edu/HockenmaierGroup/8k-pictures.html`	A collection of 8,000 described images taken from `https://www.flickr.com/`. Each image is associated with five different captions that describe the entities and events depicted in the image that were collected using crowdsourcing from Amazon Mechanical Turk. It mainly contains *action* images of scenes featuring people and animals.	C. Rashtchian, P. Young, M. Hodosh, and J. Hockenmaier, *Collecting image annotations using amazon's mechanical turk*, in NAACL HLT Workshop on Creating Speech and Language Data with Amazon's Mechanical Turk, 2010, pp. 139–147.
Flickr30K	31,783	5	No	`http://shannon.cs.illinois.edu/DenotationGraph/`	Contains 31,783 images collected from Flickr. Most of these images depict humans performing various activities. Each image is paired with five crowdsourced captions.	P. Young, A. Lai, M. Hodosh, and J. Hockenmaier, *From image descriptions to visual denotations: New similarity metrics for semantic inference over event descriptions*, in ACL, 2014.

MSCOCO	164,062	5	Partial	`http://mscoco.`
				`org/dataset/`
				`#overview`
					The largest image captioning dataset, containing 82,783 images for training, 40,504 images for validation, and 40,775 images for testing. Each image has five human-annotated captions.	T.-Y. Lin, M. Maire, S. Belongie, J. Hays, P. Perona, D. Ramanan, P. Dollar, and C. L. Zitnick, *Microsoft COCO: Common Objects in Context,* `https://`
						`arxiv.org/`
						`abs/1405.`
						`0312,` 2014.

SBU1M	1,000,000	1	No	`http://vision.cs.`
				`stonybrook.edu/`
				`~vicente/`
				`sbucaptions/`
					Also from Flikr but with a totally different distribution. The dataset also comes with pre-computed descriptors. The dataset was initially developed for retrieval-type approaches. The descriptions were originally given by the Filckr user. The author of the data generated the dataset by setting rules on filtering the retrieval results.	V. Ordonez, G. Kulkarni, and T. L. Berg, *Im2text: Describing images using 1 million captioned photographs,* in NIPS, 2011.

With the exception of SBU, each image has been annotated by labelers with five sentences that are relatively visual and unbiased. SBU consists of descriptions given by image owners when they uploaded them to Flickr. As such, they are not guaranteed to be visual or unbiased and thus this dataset has more noise.

Evaluation

Evaluation of the image caption/description results is not an easy task. Similar to machine translation, some known challenges include, but are not limited to:

- Human evaluation is subjective
- How good is good enough?
- Is system A better than system B?
- Target application and context dependency

Often, two major aspects are considered—linguistic quality and semantic correctness, and two types of approaches are commonly used—human judgments and automatic measures.

The human evaluation is often used through crowdsourcing, for example Amazon Mechanical Turk. The tasks are often designed to include questions on grammar, content, and fluency. Judgers are provided with images together with the generated descriptions. In some other cases, the judger might be provided with two images, one with a random description, the other with the model-generated caption, and is asked to select one. This type of approach is good for comparing models, but lack of standardization means that results can be leveraged across different experiments. Also, a human judger may have different agreement levels. Therefore, there is a need for developing an automatic measuring metric for fairness and comparability. Some of the desired attributes of an automated metric include:

- High levels of correlation with quantified human description
- Sensitive to small differences
- Consistent for similar input image/reference pairs
- Reliable—image caption systems that score similarly will perform similarly
- Generalizable—applicable to a wide range of domains and scenarios
- Fast and lightweight, no human involvement

Some of the commonly used automatic evaluation metrics include BLEU [Papineni and their co-authors, 2002, *BLEU: a Method for Automatic Evaluation of Machine Translation*] *(precision-based, from the machine translation community)*, ROUGE [*Chin-Yew Lin, ROUGE: A Package for Automatic Evaluation of Summaries*] (recall-based), METEOR [Denkowski and Lavie, 2014, *METEOR: An Automatic Metric for MT Evaluation with Improved Correlation with Human Judgments*], CIDEr [Vedantam and their co-authors, 2015, *CIDEr : Consensus-based Image Description Evaluation*] and SPICE [Anderson and their co-authors , 2016, *SPICE : Semantic Propositional Image Caption Evaluation*].

BLEU and METEOR were originally developed for evaluating the output of machine translation engines or text summarization systems, while CIDEr and SPICE were designed specifically for image description or captioning evaluation.

All of the approaches are trying to compute the similarity between the algorithm output and one or more human-written/crowdsourced reference texts.

BLEU

Bilingual Evaluation Understudy (BLEU) is a popular metric for machine translation evaluation. It computes an n-gram based precision for the candidate sentence with respect to the references. Intelligibility or grammatical correctness are not taken into account. BLEU computes the geometric mean of the n-gram precisions and adds a brevity penalty (penalizes system results that are shorter than the general length of a reference) to discourage overly short sentences. The range of BLEU is always between zero and one. A number closer to one indicates that the candidate text is more similar to the reference texts. For multiple references, the maximum score is returned as the judgment of quality.

The most common formulation of BLEU is BLEU4, which uses 1-grams up to 4-grams, though lower-order variations such as BLEU1 (unigram BLEU) and BLEU2 (unigram and bigram BLEU) are also used.

For machine translation, BLEU is most often computed at the corpus level, where correlation with human judgment is high (the sentences are first evaluated, but then aggregated to corpus level); for image caption, it is often computed at the sentence level as the accuracies on individual sentences are more of interest.

There are however, some downsides of BLEU. For example, BLEU performs less well when applied at the sentence level or sub-sentence level, and when using only one reference. Part of the reason is because BLEU is n-gram based, and may have many zero or low counts for higher (tri-gram or higher) n-grams. In addition, clipping of n-gram counts, such that they do not exceed the count of each n-gram in the references, also complicates sub-sentential applications.

ROUGE

Recall-Oriented Understudy of Gisting Evaluation (ROUGE). It computes n-gram based recall for the candidate sentence with respect to the references. It is a popular metric for summarization evaluation, trying to answer how often the words (and/or n-grams) in the reference summaries appeared in the machine-generated summaries (compared to BLEU asking how often the words (and/or n-grams) in the machine-generated summaries appeared in the human-reference summaries).

Similar to BLEU, versions of ROUGE can be computed by varying the n-gram count. Two other versions of ROUGE are $ROUGE_s$ and $ROUGE_L$. $ROUGE_s$ computes an F-measure with a recall bias using skip-bigrams, while $ROUGE_L$ uses the longest common subsequence between the candidate and each reference sentence. Skip-bigrams are a generalization of bigrams in which the words need not be consecutive, but may leave gaps that are skipped over. For multiple references, the maximum score is returned as the judgment of quality.

Note that for computing BLEU and ROUGE, both the generated description and the reference description have to be preprocessed, including tokenization and stripping out non-alphanumeric and hyphen characters. Also, one can apply a stemmer to remove stop words before compute ROUGE scores.

METEOR

Metric for Evaluation of Translation with Explicit ORdering (METEOR) was originally used for measuring machine translation. It combines recall and precision as weighted score components by looking only at the unigram precision, and recalling and aligning output with each reference individually and taking the score of best pairing (instead of BLEU's brevity penalty). It takes into account translation variability via word inflection variations, synonymy and paraphrasing matches, which enables the match between semantic equivalents. Also, it addresses fluency via a direct penalty for word order: how fragmented is the matching of the MT output with the reference? METEOR has significantly better correlation with human judgments compared to BLEU, especially at the segment-level.

CIDEr

Consensus-based Image Description Evaluation (CIDEr) measures the similarity of a generated sentence against a set of ground-truth sentences written by humans, which is trying to solve the problem of weak correlation between the previous metrics and human judgment. CIDEr however shows higher agreement with consensus as assessed by humans. Using sentence similarity, the notions of grammaticality, saliency, importance, and accuracy (precision and recall) are inherently captured by this metric.

SPICE

Semantic Propositional Image Caption Evaluation (SPICE) is based on semantic scene graphs and has shown that it correlates much better with human judgments in comparison to the aforementioned standard measures. The author of this metric illustrated that the previous metrics are sensitive to n-gram overlap, which is neither necessary nor sufficient for two sentences to convey the same meaning. However, SPICE focuses on recovering objects, attributes, and the relations between them; it does not count in the aspects of grammar and syntax. Similar to n-gram based metrics, SPICE implicitly assumes that the caption has been well-formed. It would be recommended to include a fluency metric.

Rank position

For ranking/retrieval-based image generation systems, the ranking position of their original text description can be used for evaluating the system, such as Recall at position k (*R@k*) and median rank scores, where k = 1,3,5. Recall at position k (*R@k*) means the percentage of test queries for which a model returns the original item among the top *k* results. Differently, the median rank represents the *k* at which a system has a recall of 50% (that is the number of results one would have to consider in order to find the original item for half the queries), therefore, the smaller the *k* is, the better the performance.

Attention models

Attention mechanisms in neural networks are (very) loosely based on the visual attention mechanism found in humans. The idea is to focus on different parts of the inputs as the algorithm tries to make and refine prediction each time.

In computer vision, attention means the ability to attend/focus on a certain region of an image with high resolution while perceiving the surrounding image in low resolution to get better understanding of the salient content, and then adjusting the focal point over time. There are a few benefits of introducing the attention model into image understanding.

First, it helps the model to focus on only the salient or important objects or areas that matter to the viewer of the image (human or computer) and pay less attention or less computation to the background.

Second, it provides the ability to *attend* certain aspects of the image and perform the information extraction/understanding results in a high resolution zoomed-in for that particular region at each time. This ability gives a better chance to understand the local content more precisely. Take an image as an example, such attention helps generate embedding feature vectors that represent local information at a finer-grained level as compared to a global embedding feature vector from the entire image.

The attention model is not a new concept, and has been used in many other applications such as image tracking (Denil and their co-authors, 2011, *Learning where to Attend with Deep Architectures for Image Tracking*).

Attention has also been used in natural language processing. We will have a brief introduction to its usage in NLP first in the following session, as this will help us to understand its use in computer vision better.

Attention in NLP

In this session, we will talk about the use of the attention model in RNNs for machine translation.

The problem of machine translation can be formularized as an optimization problem over P $(T|S)$, where S is the source sentence and T is the translated sentence. The machine translation system has two major components: encoder and decoder.

Given an input, *S*, and each word in this sentence, we can unroll the RNN, so for each time step, the RNN takes an input word together with the previous state to update its internal state. For example, in the following figure, the input words are fed into the RNN's encoder; after the last word, the generated state is essentially the vector representation of the entire sentence. Then, the decoder takes it as an input to generate the probabilities of each translated word in a sequence until it hits an **<EOS>** mark; that is, basically it is reversing a sentence:

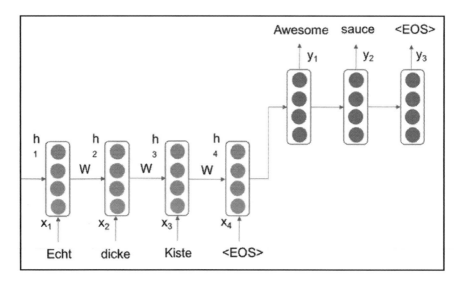

You might wonder how effectively an entire sentence can be represented by a single vector. Indeed, researchers have found that if you plot the sentence embedding to a low dimensional space, sentences with similar meanings would be closer to each other. However, problems do occur when you have longer sentences (we briefly mentioned this in Chapter 5, *NLP - Vector Representation*, when comparing RNNs and LSTM, as LSTM was able to partially solve this problem). The figure below shows that similar sentences are close together in summary-vector space (shown on the left). It also shows the problem with longer sentences:

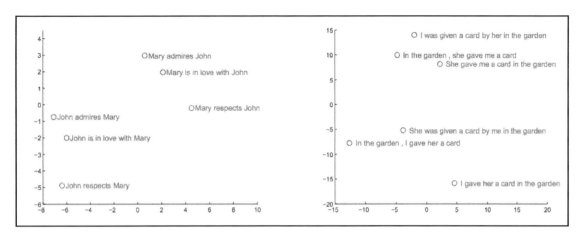

Two-dimensional visualization of sentence representations from Sutskever and their co-authors' publication *Sequence to Sequence Learning with Neural Networks*

In addition, the problem can get worse if the ways of constructing the sentence in two languages have significant differences in order. For example, in some languages, such as Japanese, the last word might be very important to predict the first word, while translating English to French might be easier as the order of the sentences (how the sentence is organized) is more similar to each other.

One solution is to focus on a part of the sentence, and for each part we generate the prediction of the next word. This sounds like a divide and conquer technique in which we divide the sentences into smaller parts, and assume that in both the source sentence and the target sentence there are local connections between different parts of the sentence.

This saves us the effort of encoding the full-source sentence into a fixed-length vector. So, now the prediction of the word does not singularly depend on the final sentence embedding, or the previous state of the decoder, but on a weighted combination of all states of the encoder, with larger weights on the most correlated parts. The weight of each state reflects how much the prediction of the decoder depends on each input word.

The question now is, how do we generalize or utilize such an idea in computer vision applications?

Attention in computer vision

Similar to the attention mechanism used in machine translation, which helps the neural network to focus on specific parts of the input, such as one to two words at each time step, the attention model also helps the image neural network to focus on different spatial regions or some salient regions for better understanding the image content.

Recall that in the previous session, we discussed how to encode the input image first and use the image embedding as the first time input of the following RNN/LTSM network. Now, the system needs to differentiate different patches/spatial areas of the image as they are not equally important from the perspective of how humans understand the image. Therefore, Xu and their co-authors, in their ground work *Show, attend and tell: Neural Image Caption Generation with Visual Attention*, proposed a way of incorporating an attention mechanism into the system.

Unlike previous work, where feature embeddings are extracted from the fully-connected layers (consider such embeddings are representing the full image, similarly to what we mentioned about the embedding that represents the entire sentence), they first extract the feature from the lower convolutional layer. This allows the decoder to selectively focus on certain parts of an image by selecting a subset of all the feature vectors. The following figure illustrates the architect in the paper of *Show, attend and tell*:

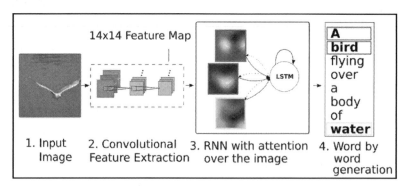

Algorithm architect from Show, Attend and Tell: Neural Image Caption Generation with Visual Attention

As a result, different from the previous model where a single vector/embedding is formed to represent the image information, this time a matrix is formed to represent multiple patches (step two in the preceding figure):

$$a = \{a_1, a_2, \ldots, a_L\}\, a_i \in R^D$$

Where each column is a D-dimensional representation corresponding to a part of the image, and the whole image is represented by a set of L vectors.

Recall that in `Chapter 3`, *Getting Started with Neural Networks,* where we introduced LSTM, we talked about that at each time step, an LSTM cell has three inputs from the actual input data, the forget gate, and the memory gate.

Suppose the hidden state at *t-1* can be denoted by h_{t-1}. An attention model, which is also a multilayer perceptron model, outputs the positive weight for each image patch:

$$e_{ti} = f_{att}(a_i, h_{t-1})$$

$$\alpha_{ti} = \frac{e^{e_{ti}}}{\sum_{k=1}^{L} e^{e_{tk}}}$$

Where α_{ti} is the weight for patch i at time t. Note that they are typically normalized to sum to one, to form a distribution over the input states. So α_{ti} represents the probability that location/patch i is the right place to focus to produce the next word, or the importance of patch i in all the L patches. With this weight, all the image patch information is dynamically combined together with focus/importance varying each time to generate a context vector, which is used in updating the LSTM cell state and generating the prediction output.

At the training stage, not only have the parameters of the LSTM cell been updated, so has the multilayer perceptron model that determines the weight or importance of each patch.

The following figures are from *Show, Attend and Tell: Neural Image Caption Generation with Visual Attention,* where the first figure illustrates the change of attention over time, and the second figure illustrates attending a particular object in the image and generating the correct word:

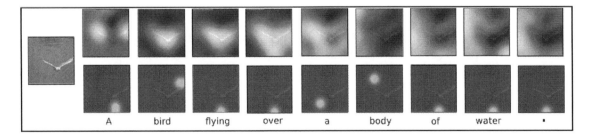

The illustration from *Show, Attend and Tell: Neural Image Caption Generation with Visual Attention* shows the attention changes over time as the model generates each word, where the highlighted parts reflects the relevant parts of images regarding the word. The top row is the result of soft attention, and the bottom row is from the hard attention:

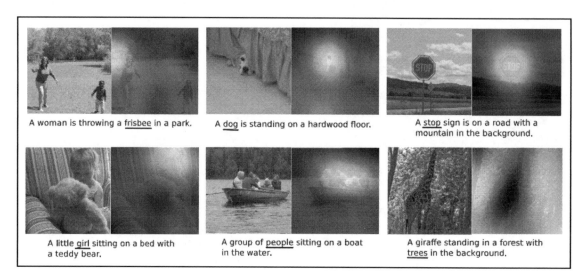

The illustration from *Show, Attend and Tell: Neural Image Caption Generation with Visual Attention* shows the correspondence of the attended parts of image (white highlighted part) versus the words that describe that part (with underline).

The difference between hard attention and soft attention

There are two types of attention models: hard attention and soft attention.

In hard attention, each part in a sentence or patch in an image is either used to obtain the context vector or is discarded. In this case, α_{ti} represents the probability of the part/patch being used; that is, the probability of indicator $St, i = 1$. For example, in Xu's *Show, Attend and Tell*, the context vector in the hard attention senario is computed as:

$$z_i = \sum_i s_{t,i} \alpha_i$$

Given the sum-to-one criterion, it can be seen clearly that hard attention selects the element with the highest probability. This is definitely more philosophically appealing, and is also more scalable and efficient regarding computation. However, such a definition is not differentiable. In Xu's paper, they use Monte Carlo methods to approximate derivatives. Readers can look into the Reinforcement Learning literature for more details.

On the other hand, the soft attention does not have such restriction. Therefore, soft attention is differentiable and one can simply back-propagate the errors to learn the model by gradient descent.

Visual question answering

The task of **visual question answering** (**VQA**) is the task of answering an open-ended text question about a given image. VQA was proposed by Antol and its co-authors in 2015 (`https://www.cv-foundation.org/openaccess/content_iccv_2015/papers/Antol_VQA_ Visual_Question_ICCV_2015_paper.pdf`). This task lies at the intersection of computer vision and natural language processing. It requires the understanding of the image and the parsing and understanding of the text question. Due to its multimodality nature and its well-defined quantitative evaluation metric, VQA is considered an important artificial intelligence task. It also has potential practical applications, including helping the visually impaired.

A few examples of the VQA task are illustrated in the following table:

Q: How many giraffes can be seen? A: 2	Q: Is the bus door open? A: Yes	Q: If you were to encounter this sign, what would you do? A: Stop

Several datasets have been proposed for visual question answering, including, but not limited to, the VQA v1 (`http://visualqa.org/vqa_v1_download.html`), VQA v2 (`http://visualqa.org/download.html`), visual genome dataset (`http://visualgenome.org/`), and freestyle multilingual *Image Question and Answering* (FM-IQA) dataset (`http://idl.baidu.com/FM-IQA.html`).

In this chapter, we mainly focus on the VQA v1 and v2 datasets. The questions in the VQA dataset are mostly about specifics of the images, so one to three words are often enough for an answer. Let's use the preceding figure as an example. The question is, if you were to encounter this sign, what would you do? We can answer with one word, **Stop**. There are mainly three types of answers: yes/no, number, and other open-ended answers. Experimental results show that machine learning systems get the highest accuracy on yes/no answers, followed by number answers, and other answers. There are also answers that can be obtained from common sense without looking at the image, for example, what is the color of the fire hydrant?

In addition, good performance can be obtained by relying on language-based priors. In other words, just by looking at the questions and training question/answer pairs, one can infer the answer without looking at the image. So VQA v2 uses balanced pairs to emphasize the role of computer vision. It provides two images for one question, and each image leads to a different answer. This discourages blind guesses from questions alone or heavy language-based priors. The VQA v2 dataset consists of 204,721 COCO images, 1,105,904 questions, and 11,059,040 answers provided by human annotators.

The evaluation metric for the VQA dataset (with 10 human annotators) is that, for a particular answer produced by AI, the accuracy of it is:

$$Accuracy(AI_{answer}) = \min\left(\frac{\text{number of humans said } AI_{answer}}{3}, 1\right)$$

Then, it is averaged over $\binom{10}{9}$ sets of human annotators. If the answers were freestyle phrases or sentences, not just one to three words, then BLEU, METEOR, or CIDEr, introduced earlier in this chapter, can be used. Gao and others in their paper *Are You Talking to a Machine? Dataset and Methods for Multilingual Image Question Answering* proposed the *Visual Turing Test* for freestyle answers. Essentially, a human judge is presented with answers from the human annotators or a machine learning model, then he or she needs to decide whether the answer comes from a human or a machine.

A popular paradigm for solving the visual question answering problem is to pose the problem as a classification problem, then use a **Convolutional Neural Network** (**CNN**) for encoding the image, a **recurrent neural network** (**RNN**) for encoding the questions, combining them, and feeding to a multilayer perceptron classifier. The following figure illustrates this concept:

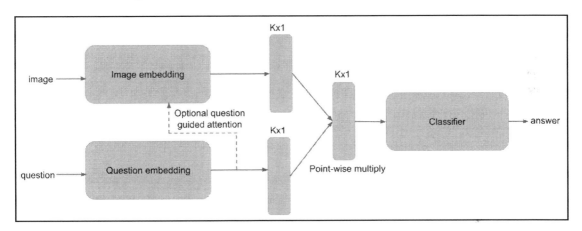

The image embedding can often be done using a CNN model that is pre-trained. For example, we can use the last hidden layer of the VGG network (`http://www.robots.ox.ac.uk/~vgg/research/very_deep/`) as the image embedding. The pre-trained weights can be found at `http://www.cs.toronto.edu/~frossard/post/vgg16/`. Another approach is to bring question-guided attention to the image embedding.

For example, we can pre-train a CNN model to produce M x K features, where M is the number of locations in the image, and K is the feature vector dimension. Then, we concatenate the question, embedding with each of the feature vectors at different locations in the image, and compute a weight. The reader can refer to `https://arxiv.org/abs/1708.02711` for details on weight computation. The final image embedding is the weighted average of the M feature vectors.

To embed the question, we cap the question to a certain length, then encode each word with a 300-dimensional vector, using a fully-connected layer and tanh non-linearity, then feed each of the word embeddings in the question to the RNN, for example, long short term memory networks. We use the final state of this RNN as the question embedding.

Finally, we point-wise multiply the image and word embeddings and feed it to the multi-layer perceptron classifier to produce the result. As of December 2017, the best performing model on the VQA dataset has 69% accuracy over all types of questions, and human accuracy is about 83%. This big gap indicates that visual question answering is a challenging AI task and there is still significant room to improve.

Multi-source based self-driving

Is autonomous driving far from us? Perhaps not. If you look at the following road map published by Morgan Stanley Research, it is expected that in around 10-15 years we can safely let cars drive for us without much interference:

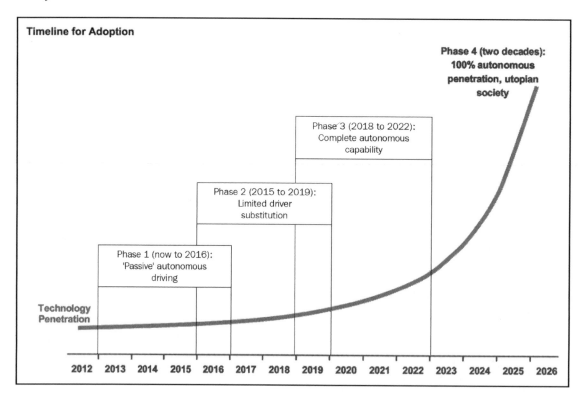

Great applications need powerful tools to realize them, and deep learning has been recognized as one such tool. Deep learning can potentially help in solving many problems that exist in the self-driving car system, for example:

- Lane detection
- Pedestrian detection
- Road sign recognition
- Traffic light detection
- Face detection/recognition
- Car detection
- Obstacle detection
- Environment recognition
- Human action recognition
- Blind-spot monitoring

And for all of these problems, it's possible that we can leverage multiple data sources to gain better accuracy and speed. Basically, a self-driving car can be equipped with various sensors, such as visible-light or infrared cameras, LIDARs, radars, ultrasonics, GPS/IMU, audio, and so on, to be able to see their environment. Data from these different modalities can be jointly utilized to make decisions and generate commands for driving. Different sources of data capture parts of the information from the environment in a certain format, which then can be combined to deal with:

- Localization and mapping: where is the car?
- Orientation—which direction is the car moving towards?
- Detection—what is surrounding the car, static and dynamic?
- Perception/scene understanding—what are detected objects, traffic lights, lanes, or moving pedestrian/cars?
- Prediction—how do detected objects change in the future?
- Motion planning—best car moving path and speed? How to move from A to B?
- Vehicle command—speed up, braking/slowing down, steering (left or right), changing lanes
- Driver state—what's the driver up to?

In a recently published work by Chen and others from Baidu, *Multi-View 3D Object Detection Network for Autonomous Driving*, the authors employ both LIDAR and cameras to acquire data, then proposed **Multi-View three-dimensional (MV3D)** networks to combine LIDAR and camera images in a complex neural network pipeline, as shown in the following figure:

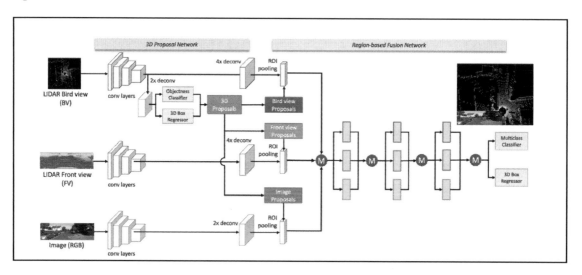

The process of execution is as follows:

1. This **Multi-View 3D** networks (**MV3D**) first utilize the bird's-eye view from the LIDAR data to generate three-dimensional bounding box proposals
2. The generated bounding box is then projected to a different direction to get the two-dimensional region of interest proposals, which are then used in RGB images and LIDAR bird's-eye view projection data and front-view projection data
3. The resulting regions of interest are fed into a multilayer network to obtain the region-based fusion results

Interested readers can refer to the above mentioned paper from Chen and others for more detailed reading.

There are not many multimodality publicly-available datasets for self-driving. A well-known one is the KITTI dataset (`http://www.cvlibs.net/datasets/kitti/`). The KITTI dataset was collected by an autonomous driving platform called **Annieway**, a project of the Karlsruhe Institute of Technology and the Toyota Technological Institute at Chicago. The dataset was captured by driving around the mid-size city of Karlsruhe, in rural areas and on highways. Overall, it contains six hours of traffic scenarios at 10–100 Hz using a variety of sensor modalities, such as high-resolution color and grayscale stereo cameras, a Velodyne 3D laser scanner, and a high-precision GPS/IMU inertial navigation system.

Data has been calibrated, synchronized, and timestamped, and provides the rectified and raw image sequences. It is suitable for tasks such as stereo, optical flow, visual odometry, 3D object detection, and 3D tracking. Accurate ground truth is provided by a Velodyne laser scanner and a GPS localization system. There are up to 15 cars and 30 pedestrians visible per image. Some object labels are available in the form of 3D tracklets. The KITTI Vision Benchmark Suite also comes with a few benchmarks for each task, as well as an evaluation metric.

 Note that this dataset is of non-commercial license.

For readers who are interested in applying deep learning to self-driving, there are many good resources out there on the internet, such as:

- End-to-end visual based self-driving: `https://devblogs.nvidia.com/parallelforall/deep-learning-self-driving-cars/`

- A self-driving course from MIT: `https://selfdrivingcars.mit.edu/`

Summary

In this chapter, we learned what is multimodality learning and its challenges, and some specific areas and applications in multimodality learning, including image captioning, visual question answering, and self-driving car. In the next chapter, we will deep dive into another multimodality learning area, audio-visual speech recognition. We will be covering the audio and visual feature extraction methods and models, and how to integrate them to perform reliable speech recognition.

8

Deep Reinforcement Learning

In previous chapters, we covered the basics of deep learning as applied to the fields of computer vision and **natural language processing** (**NLP**). Most of these techniques can be broadly classified as supervised learning techniques, where the goal is to learn patterns from training data and apply them to unseen test instances. This pattern learning is often represented as a model learnt over large volumes of training data. Obtaining such large volumes of labeled data is often a challenge. This necessitates a new approach to learning patterns from data with or without labels. To ensure correct training, minimal supervision may be provided in the form of a reward if the model correctly learns a pattern, or a penalty otherwise. Reinforcement learning provides a statistical framework to achieve this task in a principled manner. In this chapter, we will cover the basics of reinforcement learning and see how deep learning can be applied to improve its performance. We will specifically answer the following questions:

- What is **reinforcement learning** (**RL**)?
- What core concepts form the basis for understanding RL?
- What is **deep reinforcement learning** (**DRL**)?
- How do you implement basic functionality of DRL using TensorFlow?
- What are some of the most popular applications of DRL?

What is reinforcement learning (RL)?

So far in this book, we have looked at AI as a framework, to learn from vast amounts of data. For instance, if you are training an image classifier such as MNIST, you need labels for each image as to what digit they represent. Alternatively, if you are training a machine translation system, you need to provide a parallel aligned corpus of pairwise sentences, where each pair constitutes a sentence in a source language and an equivalent translation in a target language. Given such settings, it is possible to build an efficient deep learning-based AI system today.

However, one of the core challenges that still remains for mass-scale deployment and industrialization of such systems is the requirement of high-quality labeled data. Obtaining data is cheap, but curating and annotating is expensive as it requires manual intervention. One of the grand visions for the field of AI is to overcome this data limitation barrier and to build a fully autonomous system that does not need labels, but merely a weak form of supervision to learn correct patterns from data. Such a system would interact directly with the environment and learn optimal behavior over a period of time. This model is akin to learning by trial and error, where actions taken are refined over a period of time based on the outcome of each action. In the following subsections, we outline the problem setup for RL as well as traditional approaches to solving RL.

Problem setup

The core setup of RL involves two components: (a) an Agent and (b) Environment. Both of these components interact dynamically with each other. For example, an agent takes a particular action that changes the existing state of the environment. The environment, based on this change, transitions to a new state and provides feedback to the agent as to how positive or negative the action taken by the agent was. This feedback is what we refer to as the weak supervision for the agent. After receiving this feedback, the agent tries to learn and optimize its future actions so that it can maximize its positive feedback. This feedback is often referred to as the reward function. After a few iterations, when the agent has learnt well, the actions taken by it are considered the optimal actions taken. Figure *Reinforcement Learning: Basic Interaction Model*, illustrates this concept in more detail:

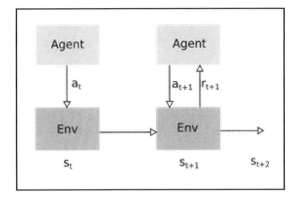

Reinforcement Learning: Basic Interaction Model

More formally, an agent, A, observes a state, S_t, from the environment at time t. The agent interacts with the environment, E, by taking an action, a_t. This action causes the environment, E, to transition to a new state, S_{t+1}, at time $t+1$. While being in this state, S_{t+1}, environment E sends a scalar reward value, r_{t+1}, to agent A. The agent now receives this reward and recomputes its strategy to take a new action a_{t+1}. Typically, this is done through a policy π which maps a given state, S, to a particular action a as : $a = \pi(s)$. An optimal policy π^* is defined as the policy that maximizes the expected reward received from the environment over a long period of time. This expected value of reward in state S and action a is often measured as a value function:

$$Q^{\pi}(s,a) = \mathbb{E}[r_{t+1} + \gamma r_{t+2} + \gamma^2 r_{t+2} + \gamma^3 r_{t+3} + \dots | s, a]$$

Here, γ is a discounting factor with a value between zero and one. There are three primary learning strategies to solve this problem:

- **Value-based RL**: The goal of this strategy is to estimate an optimal value function, $Q^*(s,a)$, and then simply pick a policy that maximizes the value function for a given state-action combination
- **Policy-based RL**: The goal of this strategy is to search for an optimal policy π^* that is able to achieve maximum future reward
- **Actor-Critic-based RL**: This is a hybrid strategy that uses both value function as well as policy-based search to solve the RL learning problem

In the following subsections, we will cover these strategies in more detail.

Value learning-based algorithms

Value learning-based RL algorithms focus on a key aspect of defining a value for every state-action pair. More formally, it is defined as the value of expected reward obtained while being in a state S and under a policy π as follows:

$$V^{\pi}(s) = \mathbb{E}(R|s, \pi)$$

Once this value function is defined, the task of choosing an optimal action (or an optimal policy) simply reduces to learning the optimal value function as follows:

$$V^{*}(s) = \max_{\pi} V^{\pi}(s), \forall s \in S$$

One of the challenges in estimating the optimal value of this function is lack of a complete state-action transition matrix that captures reward values for all possible state transitions for every possible action. One simple trick to overcome this issue is to replace this value function with a quality function, also referred to as a Q-function, as follows:

$$Q^{\pi}(s, a) = \mathbb{E}(R|s, a, \pi)$$

An important distinction to note here is that a Q-function assumes a given state and action.

Hence, the best policy can be chosen in a greedy fashion by simply taking an action that maximizes the Q function value for the current state as follows:

$$Q^{*}(s) = \arg\max_{a} Q^{\pi}(s, a)$$

The core problem that now remains is computing a good estimate of Q-function: Q^{π}. As shown previously, this can be represented as follows:

$$Q^{\pi}(s, a) = \mathbb{E}[r_{t+1} + \gamma r_{t+2} + \gamma^2 r_{t+2} + \gamma^3 r_{t+3} + \dots | s, a]$$

Using the Markov property assumption, we assume given the present state, that all future states are conditionally independent of all past states. This allows us to solve this equation in a dynamic programming framework using a backward induction technique. One of the most commonly used algorithms for this family of techniques is the Bellman equation. Using Bellman's equation, a Q-function can be unrolled recursively as follows:

$$Q^\pi(s_t, a_t) = \mathbb{E}_{s^{t+1}}\left[r_{t+1} + \gamma Q^\pi(s_{t+1}, a_{t+1}) | s_t, a_t\right]$$

This equation suggests that the value of Q^π (s,a) can be improved iteratively. This allows for a simple incremental update-based approach to learning an optimal Q function, which is also referred to as Q-learning:

$$Q^\pi(s_t, a_t) \leftarrow Q^\pi(s_t, a_t) + \alpha * \delta$$

$$\delta = Y - Q^\pi(s, a)$$

$$Y = r_t + \gamma \max_a Q^\pi(s_{t+1}, a)$$

The full Q-learning algorithm can be summarized as follows:

```
Initialize Q(s,a) arbitrarily for all state and action combinations
For each episode
    Sample a state s
    For each step t of episode
        Choose action aₜ with a greedy policy using Q(s,a)
        Take action aₜ and observe reward rₜ₊₁ and next state sₜ₊₁
        Update Q(s,a) based on the equation above
        Update state s as sₜ₊₁
    Repeat until s is a terminal state
```

Policy search-based algorithms

In contrast to value learning-based algorithms, policy search-based methods directly search for an optimal policy π^* under the policy space. This is typically done by parameterization of policy $\pi\theta$ where parameter θ is updated to maximize the expected value of the reward E $(r|\theta)$. The introduction of parameter θ serves as adding prior information to the policy search so as to restrict the search space by using this information.

Such techniques can often be used when the task is well known and integration of prior knowledge can serve well for the learning problem. Policy-based algorithms can be further sub-divided into two parts:

- **Model-free-based policy search**: These methods use the interaction values to directly update the policy. Hence they require a lot of values or samples to search an optimal policy. However, given that they do not impose a particular model structure, they are widely applicable to a number of different tasks.
- **Model-based policy search**: These methods approximate a model based on the provided interaction values and use the model to optimize the policy. Given a strict model assumption, they are only applicable in scenarios where a good model can be learnt. On the other hand, it also allows them to use fewer values to approximate a good model wherever possible.

Actor-critic-based algorithms

Both value-based and policy-based algorithms act independently without learning from each other. Actor-critic-based algorithms aim to improve upon this drawback. This algorithm combines value functions with policy iteration algorithms, so that the policy is updated at every iteration based on the updated value function. Figure, *Actor-critic-based reinforcement learning*, illustrates this workflow in more detail:

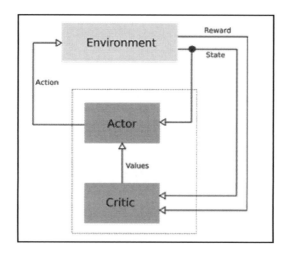

Actor-critic-based reinforcement learning

In the preceding figure, you start with an initial policy by an **Actor** (policy-based algorithm). The **Critic** or the value function receives the new state as well as reward from the **Environment** and sends updated values back to the **Actor**. The **Actor**, having received this feedback, updates its policy and generates a new action based on this policy. The process of receiving an updated value function from the **Critic** can be thought of as a way of introducing bias in the system.

Deep reinforcement learning

As explained in previous sections, there are few core components of any RL-based system. A value function $v(s,\theta)$ or a Q-function $Q(s, a, \theta)$, and a policy function $\pi(a|s, \theta)$, which could be model-free or model based. The wide scale applicability of any RL-based system depends on how good these estimations are. In practice, existing Q-learning systems suffer from multiple drawbacks:

- **Curse of dimensionality**: If you were to apply a Q-learning-based technique to a high-dimensional RL setting, such as predicting the next joystick movement based on current pixel values of screen images of a game. A 32 x 32 sized image with boolean pixel values will lead to a total number of 2^{1024} states. Q-learning will need a large number of samples to effectively deal with this state explosion.
- **Sample correlation**: Given that a Q-learning update happens in an online fashion, successive samples are often highly correlated. This leads to unstable learning by the system.

A fundamental challenge, common to these shortcomings, is the ability to succinctly represent a high-dimensional environment in the form of a compact model. This is where recent advances in deep learning come to play a major role. As seen in previous chapters, deep learning can perform reasonably well for image modeling tasks, where it can convert a high dimensional image pixel vector into a compact feature set that preserves essential semantic information about the image. This is the basis of deep reinforcement learning.

In the next few sub-sections, we will go over some of the deep learning-based techniques introduced to achieve high-performing reinforcement learning systems today.

Deep Q-network (DQN)

Q-learning has been a major backbone to a large number of RL algorithms. However, this does not scale well to a high dimensional environment, such as building a RL system to play a game by Atari. DQN uses a **Convolutional Neural Network** (**CNN**) to map this high dimensional state-action space into stable Q-value function outputs. Figure *Deep Q-network (DQN): high-level architecture*, illustrates this interaction at a high level. The core idea is that CNNs are very useful in learning correlations in structured data. Hence, they take the raw image pixel values from the game screen and learn its correlation with an optimal action value (that is, joystick position) and output a corresponding Q-value. This allows us to approximate a stable Q-function:

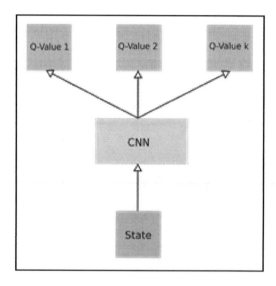

Deep Q-network (DQN): high level architecture

DQN uses a pretty standard CNN architecture with three convolutional layers and two fully-connected layers, as shown in the following table, *DQN CNN architecture details* following:

Layer	Input Size	Filter Size	Number of Filters	Stride Length	Activation Unit	Output Size
Conv-1	84 x 84 x 4	8 x 8	32	4	Rectified Linear	20 x 20 x 32
Conv-2	20 x 20 x 32	4 x 4	64	2	Rectified Linear	9 x 9 x 64
Conv-3	9 x 9 x 64	3 x 3	64	1	Rectified Linear	7 x 7 x 64

| fc4 | 7 x 7 x 64 | N/A | 512 | N/A | Rectified Linear | 512 |
| fc5 | 512 | N/A | 18 | N/A | Linear | 18 |

DQN CNN architecture details

By approximating, the CNN DQN solves the curse of the dimensionality problem. However, it still needs to deal with unstable learning due to a high correlation in the input sequence data. DQN uses a number of different tricks to handle this issue such as:

- Experience replay
- Target network
- Reward clipping

Experience replay

The core idea behind experience replay is to store past experiences in memory and sample from it during the learning phase. More specifically, at every time step t, DQN stores an experience e_t of the form $(s_t, a_t, s_{t+1}, r_{t+1})$. To reduce the correlation of sequence data, it samples an event from the event buffer using a uniform distribution as follows:

$$e \leftarrow \mathbb{U}(e_1, e_2, \ldots, e_t)$$

This allows the network to avoid overfitting due to data correlations. From an implementation perspective, this mini-batch based update can be massively parallel, leading to faster training time. This batch update also reduces the number of interactions with the environment and reduces the variance of each training update. Furthermore, a uniform sampling from historical events allows it to avoid forgetting important transitions, which will otherwise be lost in online training.

Target network

One of the other reasons for instability in Q-learning is the frequent changes to the target function. This is shown in the following equations:

$$\theta_{t+1} = \theta_t + \alpha(Y_t^Q - Q(s_t, a_t; \theta_t))\nabla\theta_t Q(s_t, a_t; \theta_t)$$

$$Y_t^Q = r_{t+1} + \gamma \max_a Q(s_{t+1}, a; \theta_t)$$

The target network trick fixes the parameter of the target function $Q(s, a; \theta_t)$ for every specified number of steps (for example, 1000 steps). At the end of each episode, the parameter is updated with the latest value from the network:

$$Y_t^{DQN} = r_{t+1} + \gamma \max_a Q(s_{t+1}, a; \theta_t^-)$$

Reward clipping

While applying DQN to different environment settings, where reward points are not on the same scale, the training becomes inefficient. For instance, in one game a positive reward leads to an addition of 100 points, versus another game, where it is only 10 points. To normalize the reward and penalty uniformly across all settings of environment, reward clipping is used. In this technique, each positive reward is clipped to +1 and each negative reward is fixed to -1. Hence this avoids large weight updates and allows the network to update its parameters smoothly.

Double-DQN

If you notice the DQN equation in the previous section, the max operator in Y_t^{DQN} uses the same values to both select as well as evaluate a specific action. This can be seen more clearly by re-writing the DQN function as follows:

$$Y_t^Q = r_{t+1} + \gamma Q(s_{t+1}, \max_a Q(s_t, a_t; \theta_t); \theta_t)$$

This often results in overestimating the values, leading to more than optimal Q value estimates. To illustrate this with an example, let us consider a scenario where for a set of actions we have identical optimal Q values. But, since estimation using Q-learning is sub-optimal, we will have Q-values higher or lower than the optimal value. Due to the max operator in the equation, we select the action with the largest positive error from the optimal value, and this error is further propagated to other states. Hence, instead of having an optimal value, states receive this additional positive bias causing the value overestimation problem.

To overcome this issue, double DQN was designed. The core idea in this network is to decouple the selection process from the evaluation step. This is achieved by learning two different value functions, one for selection and one for evaluation, θ and θ'. During each training update, one of these values is used to select the action using a greedy policy, whereas the other one is used to evaluate its updated value. This can be shown as follows:

$$Y_t^Q = r_{t+1} + \gamma Q(s_{t+1}, \max_a Q(s_t, a_t; \theta_t); \theta_t')$$

One other way to interpret this decoupling mechanism is to think of double DQN as learning two different Q functions: Q_1 and Q_2, as follows:

$$Q_1(s_t, a_t) \leftarrow r_{t+1} + \gamma Q_2(s_{t+1}, \max_a Q_1(s_{t+1}, a))$$

$$Q_2(s_t, a_t) \leftarrow r_{t+1} + \gamma Q_1(s_{t+1}, \max_a Q_2(s_{t+1}, a))$$

Prioritized experience delay

In the previous section, we learnt the importance of experience delay in stabilizing Q-learning by de-correlating the input sequential data. In experience delay, we sample an event from an experience buffer using a uniform distribution. This has the effect of treating each historical event as the same in terms of its priority. However, in practice this is not true. There are certain events that are more likely to augment the learning process than others.

One way to find such events is to look for events that do not fit with the current estimates of the Q-value. By selecting and feeding such events into the learning process, you can augment the learning capacity of the network. This can be understood intuitively; when we encounter an event in real life that is far from our expectation, we try to find more of those events and replay them so as to align our understanding and expectations closer to these events. In prioritized experience delay, we compute an error value for every event S in the experience buffer as follows:

$$error = |Q_1(s_t, a_t) - T(S)|$$

$$T(S) = r_{t+1} + \gamma Q_2(s_{t+1}, \max_a Q_1(s_{t+1}, a))$$

We then sample an event with a distribution over this error function.

Dueling DQN

So far we have seen that most Q-learning focuses on learning a state-action table $Q(s,a)$, which measures how good a particular action a is in any given state s. This is achieved by learning this function jointly to optimize both being present in a given state and taking a particular action from that state. From a learning perspective, it might be easier to simply learn the usefulness of being in a given state without caring much about the action values. Decoupling state utility from action value might help model these functions robustly. This forms the core idea behind a dueling DQN architecture.

Dueling DQN decomposes the Q-learning function into two separate functions: (a) Value function: *V(s)* and (b) Advantage function: *A (a)*, as follows:

$$Q(s,a) = V(s) + A(a)$$

Figure *Dueling deep Q-network (dueling DQN): high level architecture*, illustrates the dueling DQN architecture in more detail. As shown, the output of the CNN model is fed into two different streams, one for learning a value function and another for the advantage function. The output from both these functions is then combined in the final layer to learn the Q-value of the network:

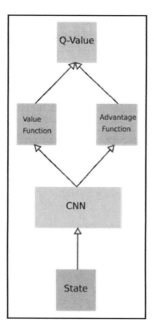

Dueling deep Q-network (dueling DQN): High level architecture

Implementing reinforcement learning

In this section, we will look at how to implement a simple reinforcement learning method. We will use OpenAI's open source toolkits, `gym` and `universe`, for this purpose. `gym` is a software framework for developing and comparing different reinforcement learning algorithms. It supports environments for different games by Atari, board games, as well as classic control tasks. `universe` on the other hand provides a wrapper on top of `gym` with modules for client and server, where you can visualize the progress of a reinforcement learning system. To install these toolkits on a macbook, we do the following:

```
pip install gym
brew install golang libjpeg-turbo
pip install universe
```

Simple reinforcement learning example

In this section, we will implement a simple reinforcement learning example for a game of `DuskDrive`:

1. We will use `gym` game environment for this purpose and `universe` Docker environment for running it:

```
import gym
import universe

env = gym.make('flashgames.DuskDrive-v0')
env.configure(remotes=1)
```

2. Once the environment is configured to run it, we reset it to a random start state as follows:

```
observations = env.reset()
```

Once the game is initialized to a random start state, we need to continuously provide an action. Since `DuskDrive` is a racing game, one simple strategy is to simply move forward using the **up arrow** key.

3. We run this strategy in an infinite loop, as follows:

```
while True:
    action = [[('KeyEvent', 'ArrowUp', True)] for obs in
observations]
    observation, reward, done, info = env.step(action)
    env.render()
```

4. Once the game is started, you can see this strategy in action live on your screen, as shown in the Figure *Playing DuskDrive with simple RL algorithm*.

This illustrates an example of how one can use **gym** and **universe** modules to perform a simple reinforcement task for common games:

Playing DuskDrive with simple RL algorithm

Reinforcement learning with Q-learning example

In this section, we will implement reinforcement learning with a TensorFlow-based Q-learning algorithm. We will look at a popular game, `FrozenLake`, which has an inbuilt environment in the OpenAI `gym` package. The idea behind the `FrozenLake` game is quite simple. It consists of 4 x 4 grid blocks, where each block can have one of the following four states:

- **S**: Starting point/Safe state
- **F**: Frozen surface/Safe state
- **H**: Hole/Unsafe state
- **G**: Goal/Safe or Terminal state

In each of the 16 cells, you can use one of the four actions, namely up/down/left/right, to move to a neighboring state. The goal of the game is to start from state **S** and end at state **G**. We will show how we can use a neural network-based Q-learning system to learn a safe path from state **S** to state **G**. First, we import the necessary packages and define the game environment:

```
import gym
import numpy as np
import random
import tensorflow as tf

env = gym.make('FrozenLake-v0')
```

Once the environment is defined, we can define the network structure that learns the Q-values. We will use a one-layer neural network with 16 hidden neurons and 4 output neurons as follows:

```
input_matrix = tf.placeholder(shape=[1,16],dtype=tf.float32)
weight_matrix = tf.Variable(tf.random_uniform([16,4],0,0.01))
Q_matrix = tf.matmul(input_matrix,weight_matrix)
prediction_matrix = tf.argmax(Q_matrix,1)
nextQ = tf.placeholder(shape=[1,4],dtype=tf.float32)
loss = tf.reduce_sum(tf.square(nextQ - Q_matrix))
train = tf.train.GradientDescentOptimizer(learning_rate=0.05)
model = train.minimize(loss)
init_op = tf.global_variables_initializer()
```

Now we can choose the action greedily:

```
ip_q = np.zeros(num_states)
ip_q[current_state] = 1
a,allQ =
sess.run([prediction_matrix,Q_matrix],feed_dict={input_matrix:[ip_q]})
if np.random.rand(1) < sample_epsilon:
    a[0] = env.action_space.sample()
next_state, reward, done, info = env.step(a[0])
ip_q1 = np.zeros(num_states)
ip_q1[next_state] = 1
Q1 = sess.run(Q_matrix,feed_dict={input_matrix:[ip_q1]})
maxQ1 = np.max(Q1)
targetQ = allQ
targetQ[0,a[0]] = reward + y*maxQ1
_,W1 =
sess.run([model,weight_matrix],feed_dict={input_matrix:[ip_q],nextQ:targetQ
})
```

Figure *RL with Q-learning example* shows the sample output of the program when executed. You can see different values of Q matrix as the agent moves from one state to the other. You also notice a value of reward **1** when the agent is in state **15**:

```
Next State = 4, Reward = 0.0, Q-Value = 0.549656867981
Next State = 4, Reward = 0.0, Q-Value = 0.558322191238
Next State = 4, Reward = 0.0, Q-Value = 0.561794042587
Next State = 4, Reward = 0.0, Q-Value = 0.605571866035
Next State = 10, Reward = 0.0, Q-Value = 0.527264535427
Next State = 0, Reward = 0.0, Q-Value = 0.58230805397
Next State = 9, Reward = 0.0, Q-Value = 0.662398397923
Next State = 6, Reward = 0.0, Q-Value = 0.342416584492
Next State = 12, Reward = 0.0, Q-Value = 0.00967993494123
Next State = 0, Reward = 0.0, Q-Value = 0.549962639809
Next State = 0, Reward = 0.0, Q-Value = 0.548377752304
Next State = 4, Reward = 0.0, Q-Value = 0.557400584221
Next State = 4, Reward = 0.0, Q-Value = 0.573505043983
Next State = 8, Reward = 0.0, Q-Value = 0.609502971172
Next State = 10, Reward = 0.0, Q-Value = 0.647010564804
Next State = 7, Reward = 0.0, Q-Value = 0.00918172858655
Next State = 0, Reward = 0.0, Q-Value = 0.567937016487
Next State = 4, Reward = 0.0, Q-Value = 0.596188902855
Next State = 8, Reward = 0.0, Q-Value = 0.615541934967
Next State = 0, Reward = 0.0, Q-Value = 0.555838167667
Next State = 4, Reward = 0.0, Q-Value = 0.554713010788
Next State = 6, Reward = 0.0, Q-Value = 0.30840498209
Next State = 6, Reward = 0.0, Q-Value = 0.373454988003
Next State = 0, Reward = 0.0, Q-Value = 0.520658791065
Next State = 13, Reward = 0.0, Q-Value = 0.777940273285
Next State = 15, Reward = 1.0, Q-Value = 0.00980058684945
Next State = 10, Reward = 0.0, Q-Value = 0.605933964252
Next State = 0, Reward = 0.0, Q-Value = 0.542133152485
Next State = 14, Reward = 0.0, Q-Value = 0.843689084053
Next State = 6, Reward = 0.0, Q-Value = 0.365039229393
```

RL with Q-learning example

Summary

In this chapter, we introduced concepts of reinforcement learning and how they are different from traditional supervised learning techniques. We described the core ideas behind RL, as well as basic modules such as Q-learning and policy learning that characterize any reinforcement learning technique today. We also presented deep learning-based advances to traditional RL techniques in form of DRL. We illustrated various different network architectures for DRL and discussed their relative merits. Finally, we sketched the core implementation of a few reinforcement learning tasks as applied to some popular computer-based games.

In next chapter, we will look at some of the practical tips and tricks used while implementing deep learning models in real world applications.

9

Deep Learning Hacks

In this chapter, we will cover many practical tips for applying deep learning, such as the best practices for network weight initialization, learning parameter tuning, how to prevent overfitting, and how to prepare your data for better learning when facing data challenges.

Readers will go through various crucial topics during their own development of deep learning models.

Massaging your data

Given different problems, the minimum requirements to successfully apply deep learning vary. Unlike benchmark datasets, such as MNIST or CIFAR-10, real-world data is messy and evolving. However, data is the foundation of every machine learning-based application. With higher quality data or features, even fairly simple models may provide better and faster results. For deep learning, similar rules apply. In this section, we will introduce some common good practices that you can do to prepare your data.

Data cleaning

Before jumping into training, it's necessary to do some data cleaning, such as removing any corrupted samples. For example, we can remove short texts, highly distorted images, spurious output labels, features with lots of null values, and so on.

Data augmentation

Deep learning requires a large corpus of training data in order to effectively learn, but sometimes, collecting such data can be very expensive and unrealistic. One way to help is to do data augmentation, by artificially inflating the training set with label, preserving transformations. By increasing the sample amount, it can also help with overcoming the overfitting problem:

- Rule of thumb—such transformations or manipulations must be carefully designed, implemented, and tested. Working techniques can be domain-specific and may not be used generally.
- For image data, some simple techniques include re-scaling, random cropping, rotating, horizontal flipping, color jittering, and adding noise. By adding noise, a deep learning network can be taught to handle noise information at training time. For example, for image data, one can add salt-and-pepper noise. Some more advanced and complex techniques include augmenting images using contrast stretching, histogram equalization, and adaptive histogram equalization.
- Some open source tools provide data augmentation classes for easy use:
    - Keras (*ImageDataGenerator*) `https://keras.io/preprocessing/image/`
    - TensorFlow (TFLearn's *Data Augmentation*) `http://tflearn.org/data_augmentation/`
    - MXNet (Augmenter) `https://mxnet.incubator.apache.org/api/python/image.html#mxnet.image.Augmenter`

Data normalization

Another good practice is to normalize real-valued input data. We do it by subtracting the mean and dividing the standard deviation:

```
>> X -= np.mean(X, axis = 0) # zero-center
>>> X /= np.std(X, axis = 0) # normalize
```

Here, X is the input data. The reason why it helps is that each dimension of the input data may have a different range, and we use the same learning rate across all dimensions. Normalizing the data avoids the problem of over-compensating or under-compensating some dimensions.

Tricks in training

In this section, we will talk about a few techniques that can help to train a better network, including how to initialize weights, tips for optimization parameters, and how to reduce overfitting.

Weight initialization

Following techniques are involved in weight initialization:

- All-zero
- Random initialization
- ReLU initialization
- Xavier initialization

All-zero

First, do *NOT* use all-zero initialization. Given proper data normalization, it is expected that roughly half of the network weights will be positive and half will be negative. However, this does not mean that weights should be initialized in between, which is zero. Assuming all the weights are the same (no matter if they are zero or not), means that the backpropagation would produce the same result for different parts of the network, which cannot help much in learning.

Random initialization

Initialize the network according to a certain distribution, such as a normal distribution or a uniform distribution, with very small weights that are close to zero (called **symmetry breaking**). Different parts of the network will get distinct updates due to this randomness and thus grow diversely. For example, $W \sim \sigma \cdot \mathcal{N}(0,1)$, where $\mathcal{N}(0,1)$ is a zero mean, unit standard deviation is Gaussian, and σ is a small number, for example, 0.01 or 0.001. Or $W \sim \sigma \cdot \mathcal{U}(-1,1)$, where $\mathcal{U}(-1,1)$ is the uniform distribution between -1 and 1. There are two potential problems associated with the weights. One is that very small weights may lead to diminishing gradients as gradients are proportional to the value of weights, causing the gradient vanishing problem. The other problem is that large weights may cause the signal to be amplified too much in the backpropagation, which results in longer convergence time. Therefore, setting up a proper parameter σ is important.

A common way is to set it using the number of input nodes such that variance of the nodes does not grow with the number of inputs, for example $\sigma = 1/\sqrt{n_{in}}$, where n_{in} is the number of inputs, also called **fan-in**. This is trying to keep the network variance unity. Note that this does not consider the ReLU case.

For example, in one-line Python code, this can be as follows:

```
>>> w = np.random.randn(n_in) / sqrt(n_in)
```

ReLU initialization

For ReLU specifically, Kaiming He and others, in their paper, *Delving Deep into Rectifiers: Surpassing Human-Level Performance on ImageNet Classification* (https://arxiv.org/abs/1502.01852), designed a specific initialization for ReLUs as $\sigma = \sqrt{2.0/n_{in}}$.

For example, in one-line Python code, this can be as follows:

```
>>> w = np.random.randn(n_in) * sqrt(2.0/n_in)
```

How do we understand this? Intuitively, a rectifying linear unit is zero for half of its input, so we would need to double the size of weight variance to keep the signal's variance constant.

Xavier initialization

Xavier Glorot and Yoshua Bengio proposed another way of initialization called **Xavier** in their paper, *Understanding the difficulty of training deep feedforward neural networks* (http://proceedings.mlr.press/v9/glorot10a/glorot10a.pdf). Their major goal was to prevent gradient vanishing and too-large weight problems (as backpropagation grows proportionally to the value of the weights). In other words, the Xavier initialization tries to solve the following two problems at the same time:

- If the weights in a network start too small, then the signal shrinks as it passes through each layer until it's too tiny to be useful
- If the weights in a network start too large, then the signal grows as it passes through each layer until it's too massive to be useful

Glorot and Bengio proposed a more proper standard deviation value, $\sigma = \sqrt{2/(n_{in} + n_{out})}$, where n_{in} is the number of previous nodes/inputs (fan-in), and n_{out} is the number of outputs, also called **fan-out**.

Overall, the following table summarizes the initialization strategy:

Category	Formula for variance	Notes
Basic initializer	$1/n_{in}$	
He et al initializer	$2/n_{in}$	For ReLU
Xavier (or Glorot) initializer:	$2/(n_{in} + n_{out})$	

Optimization

Optimization is a critical part of learning. We use optimization to minimize the objective functions (the `error` function) to learn the correct network weights and structures.

While many advanced optimization algorithms have been developed, the most common optimization approach is still **Stochastic Gradient Descent (SGD)** and its variations, for example, momentum-based methods, AdaGrad, Adam, and RMSProp. We will mainly base our discussion in this section on SGD. Different from traditional gradient descent approaches in which the parameters are updated once by computing on all the training samples, SGD simply updates and computes the gradient of the parameters using only a single or a few training examples. It is often recommended to compute the gradient against more than one training sample (called a **mini-batch**) at each step, which is often more stable.

Learning rate

Learning rate is critical for fast convergence. Learning rate determines how much at each iteration-model parameter should be updated proportionally to the **Gradient of the loss function**:

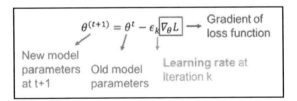

Choosing a proper learning rate can be difficult. A learning rate that is too small leads to very slow training and convergence, while a learning rate that is too large can lead to overshoot and bounce, and cause the loss function to fluctuate around the minimum or even to diverge.

There are a few ways of setting up learning rate:

- **Constant**: Learning rate remains the same for all epochs
- **Step decay**: Learning rate decays every *t* number of epochs
- **Inverse decay**: Learning rate decays as inverse of time, $\eta_t = \eta_0/(1 + \sigma t)$
- **Exponential decay**: Learning rate decays as natural exponential function, $\eta_t = \eta_0 e^{-\sigma t}$

Often, step decay is preferred as it is the simplest, most intuitive, and works well empirically. Also, there is only a single extra hyper-parameter, *t*, which needs to be set (*t* = 2, 10).

In practice, you can try using a smaller set of data with learning rate set as log-spaced values 10^{-1}, 10^{-2}, 10^{-3}, ... Then, narrow it down to the one with the lowest error and use it as a starting point. Or, setting the learning rate to 0.01 might be a safe bet. During learning, decrease the learning rate every *t* epochs (for example *t* = 10). Keep in mind that the proper learning rate highly depends on your data and your problem.

In addition to the previously mentioned traditional methods, which still require some manual decisions, fortunately there are many newly developed methods, such as momentum-based methods, which change the learning rate based on the curvature of the error function. Also, there has been a large number of studies on variations of SGD, which have adaptive learning rates that do not require manually setting, for example, AdaGrad, Adam (recommended), and RMSProp.

So which optimizer should be used in practice? Definitely the one that helps our model to learn properly and also converge quickly. A good practice is to start with step decay learning rate. For adaptive learning rate, Adam is often found to work well and outperform other adaptive techniques. If your input data is sparse, then methods such as SGD and momentum-based methods may perform poorly. Therefore, for sparse datasets one should use one of the adaptive learning rate methods.

Mini-batch

Note that in SGD, we often perform a weights update using mini-batch, which is usually between *32/64-256* samples. Compare this to batch gradient descent, which computes the gradient over the entire training data. SGD takes less memory and is not very prone to landing on a really bad spot (saddle point), as the noise carried by the small sample set helps the escape of the local minima. Compared to pure SGD, which updates parameters by the gradient computed on a single instance of the dataset, mini-batch SGD is also more stable and more efficient (with a relatively fast convergence) than looping over the entire dataset one sample each time.

Clip gradients

In very deep networks, such as recurrent networks (and possibly recursive ones), the gradient can become very small or very large quickly, and the locality assumption of gradient descent breaks down. The solution, first introduced by Mikolov, is to clip gradients to a maximum value, which makes a big difference in RNNs.

Choosing the loss function

The `loss` function is used to measure the inconsistency between predicted value ($\hat{y}$) and actual label (y) and guide the training process. Basically, the `loss` function determines where we want the network to go.

Multi-class classification

For classification problems (each sample only contains or relates to one class), mean squared error (MES/L2 loss) and cross-entropy loss are widely used. Also, softmax is often used for the last layer, and when numbers of classes are very large, one can choose hierarchical softmax. Hinge loss and squared hinge loss are also fine for this case. A side note is that, one should remember that softmax works as a squash function to assign probabilities (sum to one) to each of the classes, so the output value/probability of one class is not independent from other class probabilities.

Multi-class multi-label classification

For multi-label multi-class classification problems, that is, when each sample can have many correct answers, the sigmoid function is often used at the output layer of the neural network models (without applying softmax). With the probabilities of each class being independent from the other class probabilities, one can use the threshold for each class probability, so one sample may get multiple labels. Cross-entropy loss is still the most commonly used loss function in this case but would have a slightly different formula as compared to multi-class classification scenarios. In TensorFlow, one may choose `sigmoid_cross_entropy_with_logits` (https://www.tensorflow.org/api_docs/python/tf/nn/sigmoid_cross_entropy_with_logits) as the `loss` function.

Regression

For regression, traditional Euclidean loss and L1 loss are often used.

Others

For different problems, object functions can be different for the purpose of better determining the differences between the estimate versus the ground truth (note that ground truth may not just be a scale-like class label, for example, as in detection problems). For example, for object detection problems, there's a `loss` function named `focal loss`, which adds a factor to the standard cross-entropy criterion to help the learning focus on a sparse set of hard examples and prevent the vast number of easy negatives from overwhelming the detector during training.

Preventing overfitting

To prevent overfitting, the simplest method is to do the following:

- Reduce model size by lowering the number of units, layers, and other parameters
- Add a regularization term (L1 or L2) on the norm of the weights to the cost function

Additionally, in the following sections, there are several other techniques one can use during training.

Batch normalization

One of the popular techniques for preventing overfitting is batch normalization, which normalizes layers and allows us to train the normalization weights. During training, the distribution of each layer's inputs changes as the parameters of the previous layers change. This slows down the training by requiring lower learning rates and careful parameter initialization (remember the discussion in the weight initialization part in this chapter). Batch normalization tackles this problem (so-called **internal covariate shift**) by normalizing the input for every mini-batch. This allows us to use much higher learning rates and be less careful about initialization. It also acts as a regularizer, in some cases eliminating the need for Dropout. Batch normalization can be applied to any layer within the net and is often seen to be very effective, even when used in generative adversarial networks, such as CycleGAN.

Dropout

Dropout works by probabilistically removing a neuron from designated layers during training, or by dropping a certain connection. At training time, neurons are sampled at random from a Bernoulli distribution with $p = 0.5$ (note that at testing time all neurons are used, but the value of weights are halved). This helps to reduce co-adaptations (a feature cannot only be useful in the presence of particular other features) between neurons. Each neuron becomes more robust, and improves the training speed significantly. The following figure illustrates the network structure with Dropout at two epochs, from which we can see that essentially, with Dropout, we have formed distinct network architectures at each epoch and, jointly, this process can be thought of as a form of model bagging:

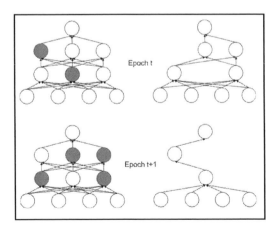

Early stopping

Early stopping refers to the way that we train the network by monitoring performance on a separate validation set and stopping the training when the validation error starts increasing or does not improve enough. This is referred to as a *beautiful free lunch* by Geoff Hinton.

Fine-tuning

Transfer learning is a technique in which we leverage a pre-trained neural network that is trained on similar but more comprehensive data, and fine-tune certain parts of the model to best solve a current problem in a similar domain. For more details on fine-tuning, please see the *Fine-tuning* section of this chapter.

Fine-tuning

In many common practices, data is limited. Training a deep neural network such as ConvNet, which has millions of parameters on a small set of data, can lead to overfitting. To avoid such issues, a common practice is to leverage an existing deep neural network that was trained on a much larger dataset, such as ImageNet (1.2 million labeled images), and fine-tune it on the smaller dataset at hand, which is not drastically different; that is, to continue to train the existing network using this new and smaller dataset. As we have discussed, one of the advantages of deep learning networks is that the first few layers often represent more general patterns mined from the data. Fine-tuning essentially leverages the common knowledge learned from a large pool of data and applies it to a specific area/application. For example, the first few layers in ConvNet may capture universal features such as curves and edges, which are relevant and useful to most image-related problems.

When to use fine-tuning

There are two major factors when considering whether to use fine-tuning—the size of the new dataset, and its similarity to the original dataset. Following are two cases where you can utilize fine-tuning:

- When the new data/domain is similar to the one used for training the existing model and your new dataset is small

- When your new dataset is quite different from the data used in the pre-trained model, but with enough samples, you may fine-tune the model even for a large number of layers but with a small learning rate

When not to use fine-tuning

There are a few cases where you may want to resort to other techniques rather than fine-tuning:

- When the new data/domain is drastically different from the one used for training the existing model. In such cases, training the model from scratch could be a better solution, given there are enough data volumes.
- When the new dataset is very small, for example, less than 2 thousands of samples. In such cases, continuing to train with such a small dataset may still lead to overfitting. However, one could use the existing network as a feature learner to extract a feature from the early layers and feed into traditional machine learning models, such as SVM. For example, one could take the output of the intermediate layer prior to the fully connected layers in ConvNet as features and train a linear SVM for classification purposes.

Tricks and techniques

Following are some general guidelines for fine-tuning:

- Replace the last fully connected layer. A common practice of fine tuning is to replace the last one or two fully connected layers (softmax) with a new structure of layers (softmax) that are specific to your own problem. For example, in AlexNet and ConvNet, the output has 1000 classes. One can replace the last layer, which has 1000 nodes, with the the number of desired classes.
- Use a smaller learning rate. As most parameters of the network have been trained and we are assuming these layers contain useful, universal pattern information from the data, the goal is not to over-tune these layers but rather train the layers—for example, the new, last few layers to accommodate our own problem. Therefore, we should use a smaller training rate such that the disturbances are not too great or too quick. A good practice is to set the initial learning rate to 10 times smaller than the one used for training from scratch. You can test on this parameter for best results.

- As we mentioned in the previous item, we are expecting that the existing network, especially the first few layers, contains useful, universal features. Therefore, sometimes we could freeze the weights of the first few layers of the pre-trained network to keep them intact. This also helps to avoid overfitting during the fine-tuning.

List of pre-trained models

The table here lists some online resources where you can find existing models using Caffe, TensorFlow, and so on. GitHub and Google are good places to find many state-of-the-art models or models that fit your own problems:

Platform	Bundle of existing popular models	Link
Caffe	Model Zoo: A platform for third-party contributors to share pre-trained Caffe models.	`https://github.com/BVLC/caffe/wiki/Model-Zoo`
TensorFlow	TensorFlow models contains a number of different models implemented in TensorFlow, including official models and research models. The research models part contains many models trained on various domains, such as image classification, object detection, and im2txt. Convert Caffe models to TensorFlow.	`https://github.com/tensorflow/models` and `https://github.com/ethereon/caffe-tensorflow`
Torch	LoadCaffe is a tool for porting the existing Caffe models to Torch7. OverFeat for torch—load existing OverFeat model (ConvNet from NYU).	`https://github.com/szagoruyko/loadcaffe` and `https://github.com/jhjin/overfeat-torch`
Keras	Keras contains some of the most popular state-of-the-art Convnet models, such as VGG16/19, Xception, ResNet50, and InceptionV3	`https://keras.io/applications/`
MxNet	**mxnet Model Gallery** maintains pre-trained Inception-BN (V2) and Inception V3.	`https://github.com/dmlc/mxnet-model-gallery`

Model compression

Deep learning network is known for its deep and complex structure, parameters can be millions, and so does the model size. However, for this mobile era, everything needs to be light and and instant even with the fast improvement in terms of hardware and CPU/GPU capability. Customers expect advanced applications happen on the go, and on the device without any personal information been uploaded to some server or cloud.

The most important characteristics of deep learning has unfortunately became the hurdle for fast, online, mobile applications. There are many real-time applications, mobile applications, wearable applications urging for the progress of portable deep learning, i.e. a advanced system with limited resources, for example memory, CPU, energy and bandwidth.

Deep compression significantly reduces the computation and storage required by neural networks. The goal and benefit of compression often include the following:

- Smaller Size: compare size by 30x-50x to fit in mobile app requirement
- Accuracy: no or acceptable loss of accuracy
- Speedup: faster inference or real time
- Offline: No dependency on network connection and protect user privacy
- Low Power: energy efficiency

There are generally two categories of approach of model comparison, one way is to design smartly to have a more concise network but with similar performance, for example: Transferred/compact convolutional filters, Knowledge distillation. Another way is to compress the model, i.e. taking the existing deep learning model and compress it by pruning unnecessary parts (neurons, connections) that don't matter too much in the final results or transforming such as applying low-rank factorization to eliminate the informative parameters.

Yu Cheng and others in their new survey *A Survey of Model Compression and Acceleration for Deep Neural Networks* (2017) summarize different approaches of model compression as follows:

Theme Name	Description	Applications	More details
Parameter pruning and sharing	Reducing redundant parameters which are not sensitive to the performance	Convolutional layer and fully connected layer	Robust to various settings, can achieve good performance, can support both train from scratch and pre-trained model
Low-rank factorization	Using matrix/tensor decomposition to estimate the informative parameters	Convolutional layer and fully connected layer	Standardized pipeline, easily to be implemented, can support both train from scratch and pre-trained model
Transfered/compact convolutional filters	Designing special structural convolutional filters to save parameters	Only for convolutional layer	Algorithms are dependent on applications, usually achieve good performance only support train from scratch
Knowledge distillation	Training a compact neural network with distilled knowledge of a large model	Convolutional layer and fully connected layer	Model performances are sensitive to applications and network structure only support train from scratch

Summarization table of different approaches of model compression from Yu Cheng and others' survey of A Survey of Model Compression and Acceleration for Deep Neural Networks(2017)

Some good results have been achieved for example, in Li and other's work *pruning filters for efficient convnets*, the authors were able to reduce the inference time of VGG-16 by up to 34% and ResNet-110 by up to 38%. In Han and other's work of *Deep Compression: Compressing Deep Neural Networks with Pruning, Trained Quantization and Huffman Coding* (2016), the authors were able to reduce the storage required by AlexNet(60 M parameters) by 35x on ImageNet dataset, that is, from 240 MB to 6.9 MB, without loss of accuracy. For VGG-16 model (130 M parameters,), their method is able to reduce the size of model by 49x from 552 MB to 11.3 MB, again with no loss of accuracy. This allows fitting the model into on-chip SRAM (Static random-access memory) cache rather than off-chip **Dynamic random-access memory (DRAM)**. This paper won best paper award in ICLR 2016. This approach include three parts: network pruning, weight sharing and Huffman Coding. Pruning reduces the number of weights by 10x, while quantization further improves the compression rate: between 27x and 31x. Huffman coding gives more compression: between 35x and 49x. The compression rate already included the meta-data for sparse representation. The compression scheme doesn't incur any accuracy loss. The following figure shows the three stages of comparison:

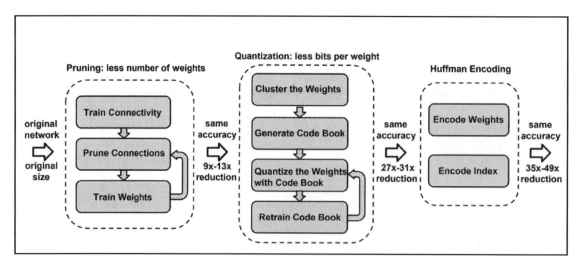

The three stage compression pipeline from Han's paper Deep Compression: Compressing Deep Neural Networks with Pruning, Trained Quantization and Huffman Coding (ICLR, 2016): pruning, quantization and Huffman coding

The first step is *network pruning*, in this step, connections with small weights below a certain threshold are removed from the network. Because of this removal, performance may be impacted, therefore, the pruned network is retrained to learn the final weights in the new sparse setting.

The second step is *weight quantization and sharing*. The flow is illustrated in the following figure:

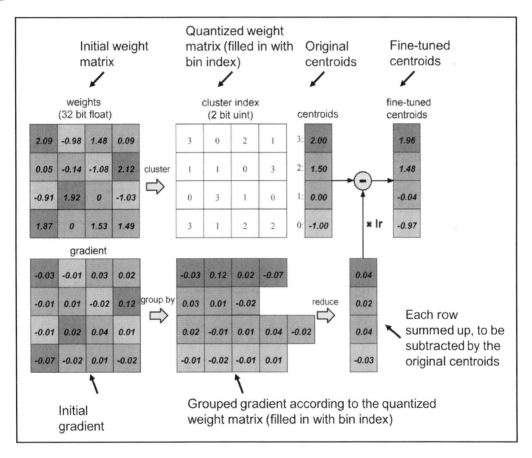

Illustration of Weight quantization and sharing from Song Han's PhD thesis Efficient Methods and Hardware for Deep Learning, 2017 (url: https://purl.stanford.edu/qf934gh3708)

Suppose the layer has 4 inputs and 4 outputs, the weight matrix is of size 4 x 4 (left top). Entries in this weight matrix are first grouped/clustered into 4 centroids (represented with 4 colors) with bin index 0-3 and centroids value of (-1.00, 0.00, 1.50 and 2.00). Then we can quantize the weight matrix by their bin index. During training, to update the current network weights, gradients are grouped by the marked weight bin index/color. Gradients fall into the same bin are first aggregated by sum as the finetune value for the centroids. The centroids value subtract the fine-tune value to obtain the fine-tuned centroids. Weights from the same layer if fall into the same cluster will share the same weight. Weights are not shared across layers.

At the third step, Huffman coding was applied to the weight values which saves 20% to 30% of network storage.

Deep compression is still very young as compared to other areas of deep learning, but it's very important as the world now is living mostly on mobile. There are few practical suggestions regarding which approach should be used for compression:

- Pruning and sharing could give reasonable compression rate and not much performance loss, also results are more stable
- Both pruning and sharing or low rank factorization approaches need pretrained models
- If training from scratch, transferred compact filter (only for Conv layer) and distillation type of approach can be applied, or one can try the **Dense-Sparse-Dense (DSD)** proposed by Han in their paper of *DSD: Dense-Sparse-Dense Training for Deep Neural Networks* (2017)
- Different compression approaches can be jointly leveraged, meaning it's OK to combine two or more techniques to maximize the compression rate or inference speed
- Keep in mind that sometime a re-training is necessary after pruning or other types of transformation to keep the performance

There are several other good suggestions can be found in Yu Cheng and others' survey paper, *A Survey of Model Compression and Acceleration for Deep Neural Networks* (2017). Interested user can dive a bit deeper.

Summary

In this chapter, we talked about some important tips and tricks that can be used for preparing your data for deep learning, optimization/training, and leveraging existing pre-trained models. In practice, you may face complicated scenarios that may not be solved by these general/standard techniques directly. However, a rule of thumb is that you should always start with trying to understand your data and problem better, and at the same time dive into the learning process (for example, utilizing some visualization tool) to understand how information has been processed and learned by the network. Such understanding will be extremely valuable to you when debugging the model and improving the results.

In the next chapter, we will be going through various trends in deep learning.

10
Deep Learning Trends

We have covered a lot of deep learning material so far in this book. In this chapter, we will summarize some of the upcoming ideas in deep learning. Specifically, we will answer the following questions:

- What are some of the upcoming trends in newly developed algorithms?
- What are some of the new applications of deep learning?

Recent models for deep learning

A number of recent deep learning techniques have been proposed that extend the core ideas of deep learning to new applications and learning scenarios. In this section, we will cover two such models that have gained prominence recently.

Generative Adversarial Networks

Recently, one popular field of machine learning that has seen the use of deep learning techniques is generative learning. Generative learning can be defined as a technique for learning joint probability estimates, $P(x,y)$ from features and labels. It builds a probabilistic model of labels and can be robust to missing data and noisy data. Additionally, such models can also be used to generate samples, which can be further used to train advanced machine learning models. A discriminative model on the other hand learns a function that maps data x with label y, thereby learning a conditional probability distribution of $P(y|x)$. Though in recent years, discriminative models have shown promising results in machine learning tasks, generative models nevertheless have their own advantages over discriminative models. Most of this interest in generative models can be traced back to their ability to understand and explain the underlying structure of the data without any labels.

The **Generative Adversarial Network (GAN)** is a recent idea that attempts to combine ideas from both generative and discriminative learning. The core idea behind GAN is to have two adversarial or competing models. The first model acts as a generative model and tries to generate real-looking data samples based on an inherent probability distribution. Typically, this is done by adding some noise to a latent space of data samples. The second model, which is a discriminator, receives a generated sample from the generative model as well as a real-world sample from the training dataset, and is asked to distinguish between the two sources. The result from the discriminator is fed back to the generator, which fine-tunes its data generation scheme to better fit real-world images from the training dataset.

These two adversarial networks play a continuous competing game, where the generator model learns to produce increasingly realistic data samples and the discriminator model gets better at discriminating real data from generated data. Eventually, once the training converges, the generated samples become indistinguishable from the real-world data. The following figure, *Overview of a Generative Adversarial Network*, illustrates this concept in more detail:

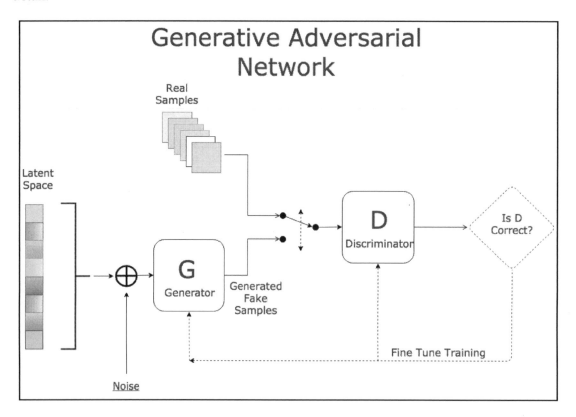

Overview of a Generative Adversarial Network (Source: https://www.linkedin.com/pulse/gans-one-hottest-topics-machine-learning-al-gharakhanian/)

Capsule networks

Capsule networks are one of the recent developments in deep learning. They are meant to address the existing limitations of the **Convolution Neural Network (CNN)**. CNNs have shown a remarkable ability to learn image features that are invariant to orientation and spatial changes. However, a core representation of an object in CNN is simply an unordered pooling of such invariant features. It has no understanding of the relative spatial relationship among these features. For example, a CNN trained on recognizing human faces will still detect a synthetic image of a distorted human face (facial features such as nose and eyes in wrong places) as long as the facial features are present in the image. It does so because all the trained CNN filters produce a strong activation for most of the facial features found in a normal human face. If we look through the filter interaction across layers more deeply, we will realize that a CNN effectively pools activation of the preceding layer to reduce the size of the data input to the next layer. This is usually done through the max pooling operation. Since the max function does not preserve order and only yields the maximum value of the set, the relative spatial ordering of filter actions in the preceding layers are lost.

The key idea behind the capsule network is to address this limitation of pooling by using ideas from computer graphics. In computer graphics, there is a technique called **rendering maps**, an internal representation of a physical object into a real-world image. This internal representation of a physical object is a hierarchical representation that also takes into account relative positions of objects. This is also referred to as pose, which is simply a combination of translation and rotation parameters of an object. The central idea in a capsule network is to preserve the hierarchical pose relationship between object parts. Another advantage of such an approach is that it requires a minimal amount of training data to learn a human-like model. This is a great improvement over existing models, such as CNNs, that require a large amount of training data to achieve optimal performance. Current implementations of capsule networks are slower than modern deep learning techniques. However, it remains to be seen if more innovation will lead to faster training of capsule networks in years to come.

Novel applications

So far in this book, we have seen numerous applications of deep learning in areas of text mining, computer vision, and multi-model learning. However, the ability to learn powerful, generalized representations of data has led to a recent surge in the number of new application domains for deep learning. These application areas range from healthcare, to software engineering, to computer systems organizations. In this section, we will look at some of the interesting novel applications of deep learning in these domains.

Genomics

One of the interesting application areas of deep learning is genomics, where advanced CNN models are used to learn structure from large and high-dimensional DNA datasets. One of the earliest applications in this space was using handcrafted features with the full connected feed forward neural network for predicting the splicing activity of an exon. Recently, a new technique has been proposed in the form of an open source implementation called *Basset: Learning the regulatory code of the accessible genome with deep convolutional neural networks* (http://genome.cshlp.org/content/early/2016/05/03/gr.200535.115.abstract), which predicts gene accessibility (DNase I hypersensitivity) across 164 cell types. To solve this problem, Basset uses a deep CNN. To formulate the problem of gene accessibility prediction into a ConvNet-based classification problem, Basset first encodes the input gene sequence into a one hot code sequence as shown in the following figure, *Overview of a Basset gene accessibility prediction workflow*. This is typically achieved by converting an input gene sequence into a one-hot sequence matrix with four rows (one row for each of the nucleotide bases of DNA strand ACGT, representing adenine, citosine, guanine and thymine). This representation has a close representation to an input image, which has a similar matrix representation. This one-hot-coded sequence is now fed to the first convolution layer, which uses a set of predefined position, weighted matrices (filters) and convolves them to generate a filter response. This response is passed through a rectified linear unit through which a max pooling operation is performed. This process is repeated over subsequent convolution layers. Finally, two fully connected layers map these convolution outputs to a 164-dimensional probability distribution indicating the likelihood of gene accessibility for each of the 164 cell types in question. The following figure, *Overview of a Basset gene accessibility prediction workflow*, illustrates this process in more detail:

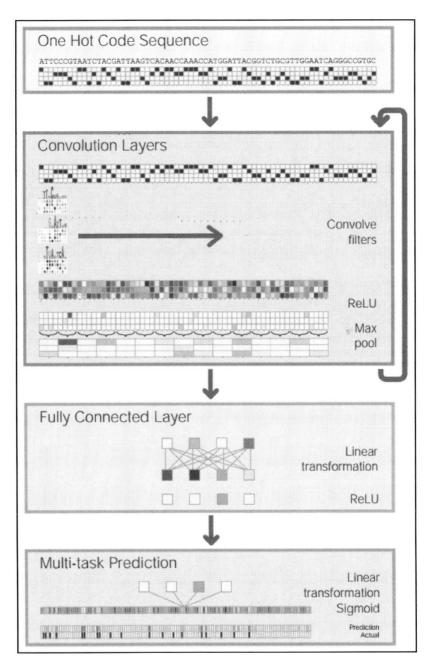

Overview of a Basset gene accessibility prediction workflow (Source: http://genome.cshlp.org/content/early/2016/05/03/gr.200535.115.full.pdf+html)

One of the additional advantages of using CNNs for gene accessibility prediction is that you can visualize the learned filters and correlate them with well-known sequence motives. The following figure, *Alignment of learned motifs from CNN with known CIS-BP Motifs*, shows two such examples. The first motive on the left is a critical CTCF gene motive, which is learned by the network using a set of 12 filters. Some of these filters are shown as follows and illustrate the alignment of learned filters with the known motive form. Similar learning is shown for gene **NR1H2**, where the model learns two distinct sets of filters that represent two distinct regions of the known **NR1H2** motive:

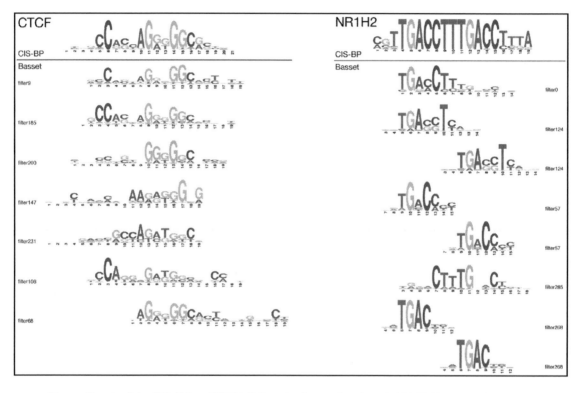

Alignment of learned motifs from CNN with known CIS-BP Motifs (Source: http://genome.cshlp.org/content/early/2016/05/03/gr.200535.115.full.pdf+html)

The following figure, *Deep Convolution Neural Network Architecture in Basset,* details the outline of the network architectures and shows three convolution layers followed by two fully connected layers with Dropout regularization:

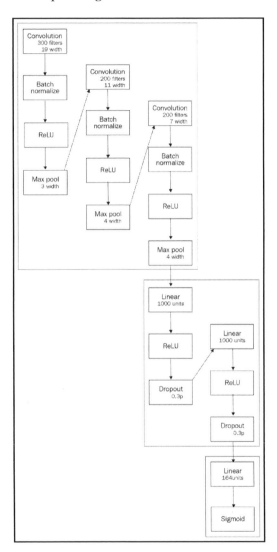

Deep Convolution Neural Network Architecture in Basset (Source: http://genome.cshlp.org/content/early/2016/05/03/gr.200535.115.full.pdf+html)

Predictive medicine

One of the other interesting applications of deep learning is predictive medicine, where the goal is to model patient illness and diagnostic processes that typically have long-range temporal dependencies. *DeepCare: A Deep Dynamic Memory Model for Predictive Medicine* (https://arxiv.org/pdf/1602.00357.pdf) is a recently introduced deep dynamic neural network that attempts to solve this problem. It creates a map of a patient's medical history using information from their electronic medical record, infers current illness state from the patient's current hospitalization, and predicts future medical outcome. DeepCare is built upon **Long Short-Term Memory (LSTM)**, which is slightly modified to capture irregular hospitalization timing and intervention. The following figure, *DeepCare: Admission embedding and modified LSTM as a carrier of illness*, illustrates DeepCare in action. For any given admission at time, **t**, a patient receives diagnosis as well as a medical procedure. Information coming from both these fields is categorical in nature and needs to be converted into a continuous feature space. DeepCare uses commonly used word-embedding models to convert both diagnoses and medical features into a real-valued feature vector. This feature vector is now input for the LSTM for further modeling:

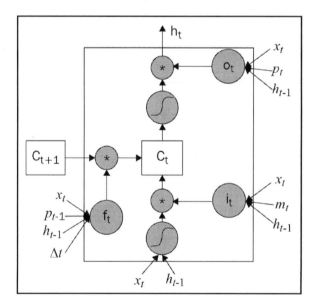

DeepCare: Admission embedding and modified LSTM as a carrier of illness

The following figure, *DeepCare LSTM architecture overview*, describes the DeepCare LSTM architecture in more detail. As shown, the bottom layers receive a transformed feature vector, which is passed through LSTM to compute a corresponding sequence of latent illness states $h_0, h_1 \ldots h_n$. To account for varying lengths of hospitalization span, a multi-scale weighted pooling is applied on top of the illness state to yield a concatenated latent illness space representation. Finally, this latent illness representation is fed to an output classifier for the eventual classification of medical intervention:

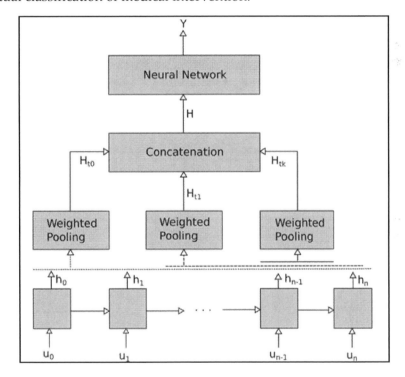

DeepCare LSTM architecture overview

Clinical imaging

Following the success of deep learning models in computer vision, one of the earliest applications of deep learning on clinical data was clinical imaging. More specifically, predicting the onset of Alzheimer's disease using the analysis of brain magnetic resonance imaging scans received widespread attention. CNNs have become popular for performing these tasks.

Recently, Payan and their co-authors (https://arxiv.org/pdf/1502.02506.pdf) have proposed a neuroimaging study for 3D CNNs for predicting Alzheimer's disease. This work differs from its predecessor as it uses two deep learning models to achieve its goal, namely spare autoencoder and 3D convolution network. The following figure, *Alzheimer prediction deep learning network*, outlines the architecture of this deep learning model. As shown, the input, **MRI scan** is first passed through a **sparse autoencoder**, which learns a low-dimensional embedding of the high-dimensional input scan. This low-dimensional is used to initialize the filters across different layers of the 3D convolution network. Having pre-trained the network, a simple fine-tuning of the convolution network is performed by using the original scan as the raw input. The output of the convolution network is mapped to a three node output layer. The three-nodes in the output layer represent the three stages of the disease, namely **Alzheimer's Disease (AD)**, **mild cognitive impairment (MCI)**, and **healthy cognition (HC)**:

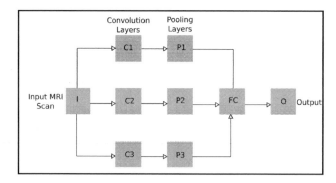

Alzheimer prediction deep learning network

Lip reading

Another interesting application of deep learning is lip reading sentences in the wild. Chung and their co-authors (https://arxiv.org/pdf/1611.05358v1.pdf) in their recent work proposed a method to recognize spoken words by a talking face, with or without audio. The core idea behind the model is a watch-listen-attend-spell network. This network models each output character, y_i as a conditional distribution of all previous characters, $y<i$, input visual sequence of lip images, x^v, and input audio sequence, x^a, as:

$$P(y|x^v, x^a) = \prod_i P(y_i|y_{<i}, x^v, x^a)$$

The following figure, *Overview of a lip reading application using Watch, Listen, Attend, and Spell architecture*, summarizes the proposed model, which consists of three components as follows:

- **Watch network**: This module takes the input lip image and passes it through a CNN and subsequently to a LSTM based recurrent network.
- **Listen network**: This network is an LSTM encoder which takes features from raw audio. In this network, 13-dimensional **Mel-Frequency Cepstral Coefficient (MFCC)** features are used.
- **Spell network**: This network is based on an LSTM transducer with an added dual-attention mechanism. At each time step, this network produces a character as well as two attention vectors. These attention vectors correspond to output states from watch and listen networks and are used to select an appropriate image and audio sample from them:

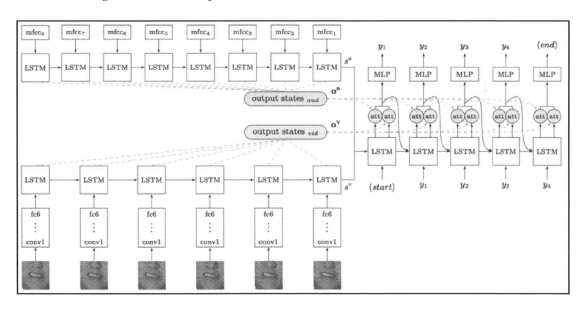

Overview of a lip reading application using Watch, Listen, Attend, and Spell architecture (Source: https://arxiv.org/pdf/1611.05358v1.pdf)

Visual reasoning

Critical reasoning is often touted as one of the hardest problems for an **artificial intelligence (AI)** agent to solve. Visual reasoning is a special form of critical reasoning task, where the goal is to answer a question using an image. The following figure, *Example of a visual reasoning problem*, shows an example of a visual reasoning problem. Given the original image, two kinds of question could be posed:

- **Non-relational questions**: These are the questions that cater to one specific object in the image
- **Relational questions**: These are the questions that necessitate the knowledge of multiple objects in the image, as well as their relationship in the image:

Original Image:

Non-relational question:

What is the size of the brown sphere?

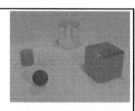

Relational question:

Are there any rubber things that have the same size as the yellow metallic cylinder?

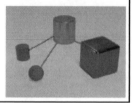

Example of a visual reasoning problem (Source: https://arxiv.org/pdf/1706.01427.pdf)

Santoro and their co-authors (`https://arxiv.org/pdf/1706.01427.pdf`) have recently proposed a **Relation Network (RN)**, which attempts to solve the visual reasoning problem described previously. This network uses multiple deep learning models to perform its task. As shown in the following figure, *Visual reasoning network*, the reasoning network takes a question and image pair as its input and produces a text response. The input question is fed to an LSTM network that computes an embedding of question vectors. The input images on the other hand are fed to a 4-layered CNN, which computes multiple feature maps characterizing the image. A coordinate wise slicing of feature maps is performed, which yields a set of objects. All pairwise combinations of objects are generated and are combined with question vectors to generate a triplet. This triplet is now passed through a multi-layered perceptron. The output of this perceptron is summed and fed to another softmax classifier to generate a probabilistic distribution of all the candidate answers:

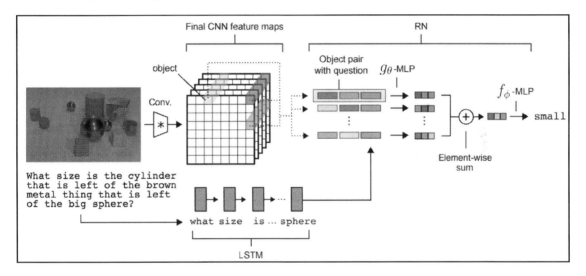

Visual reasoning network (Source: https://arxiv.org/pdf/1706.01427.pdf)

Code synthesis

One of the grand visions of AI is the ability to write a computer program from a textual description. This problem is often referred to as code synthesis. Beltramelli and their co-authors (`https://arxiv.org/pdf/1705.07962.pdf`) recently proposed a system called **pix2code**, which attempts to solve this problem in some capacity. The goal for this system is to take a **Graphical User Interface (GUI)** screenshot as its input and generate **Domain Specific Language (DSL)** code, which can be further compiled as a source code. The following figure, *A pix2code Example: A GUI Snapshot on the left is transformed to a simple DSL on the right*, shows an example of such an input screenshot on the left and corresponding DSL on the right:

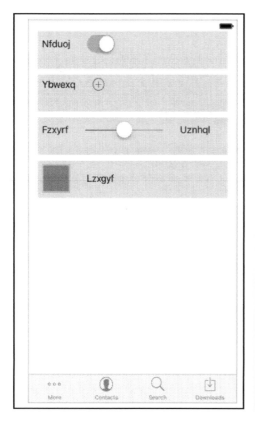

```
stack {
    row {
        label, switch
    }
    row {
        label, btn-add
    }
    row {
        label, slider, label
    }
    row {
        img, label
    }
}
footer {
    btn-more, btn-contact, btn-search, btn-download
}
```

A pix2code Example: A GUI Snapshot on the left is transformed to a simple DSL on the right (Source: https://arxiv.org/pdf/1705.07962.pdf)

A pix2code system has two modules: training and decoding. The training module takes the GUI screenshot as its input along with the sequence of DSL tokens. The GUI screenshot is fed to a CNN, which converts this into a feature vector. The sequence of DSL tokens is fed to an LSTM that maps it to an output vector. Finally, the LSTM and CNN outputs are combined and passed through a second LSTM, which generates the next DSL token. The following figure, *The pix2code training architecture overview*, illustrates this training process:

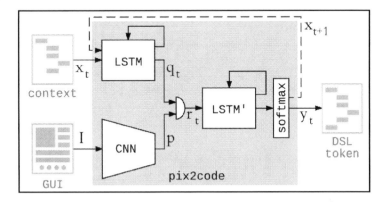

The pix2code training architecture overview (Source: https://arxiv.org/pdf/1705.07962.pdf)

Once the pix2code model is trained, it is applied to a new GUI screenshot. This is achieved by a decoding module, which takes a GUI and a context of previously predicted DSL tokens and emits the most likely DSL token. The input context to decode is now updated with this predicted token, and this process is repeated till an end-delimiter token is generated by the decoder. The sequence of all predicted tokens is now compiled into a target code block. The following figure, *A pix2code decoding architecture overview*, outlines this decoding process:

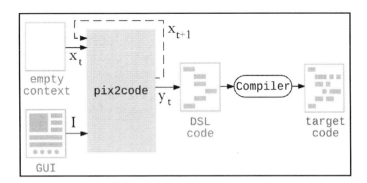

A pix2code decoding architecture overview (Source: https://arxiv.org/pdf/1705.07962.pdf)

The pix2code shows some promising results, with an accuracy rate of 77% in generating the correct DSL tokens. The following figure, *Pix2code results: Ground truth on the left, generated UI on the right*, shows a qualitative example of pix2code, where the ground truth UI is shown on the left and the system generated UI is shown on the right. As can be seen, pix2code is able to reliably generate all the GUI elements except two:

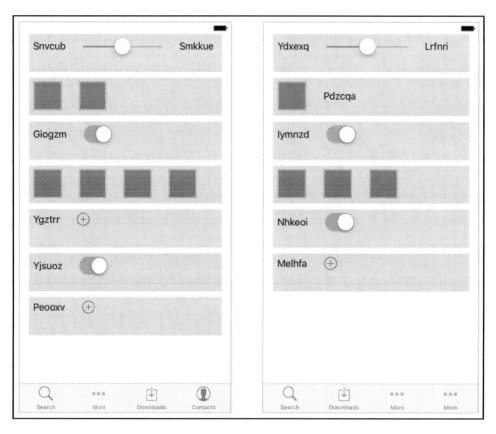

Pix2code results: Ground truth on the left, generated UI on the right (Source: https://arxiv.org/pdf/1705.07962.pdf)

Summary

In this chapter, we outlined some new directions for deep learning research. We introduced core concepts behind popular deep learning-based generative modeling techniques, such as the Generative Adversarial Network.

We also discussed the key ideas behind capsule networks and what problems they aim to solve. Finally, we covered a number of novel application domains where deep learning is being applied today. We described these applications in detail and also showed how deep learning models are being used to achieve superior performance in these domains.

In this book, we have attempted to bring together key ideas in deep learning from a practitioner's perspective. We sincerely hope you like this book and provide us with feedback to improve future editions.

Other Books You May Enjoy

If you enjoyed this book, you may be interested in these other books by Packt:

Deep Learning with Keras
Antonio Gulli, Sujit Pal

ISBN: 978-1-78712-842-2

- Optimize step-by-step functions on a large neural network using the Backpropagation Algorithm
- Fine-tune a neural network to improve the quality of results
- Use deep learning for image and audio processing
- Use Recursive Neural Tensor Networks (RNTNs) to outperform standard word embedding in special cases
- Identify problems for which Recurrent Neural Network (RNN) solutions are suitable
- Explore the process required to implement Autoencoders
- Evolve a deep neural network using reinforcement learning

Artificial Intelligence with Python
Prateek Joshi

ISBN: 978-1-78646-439-2

- Realize different classification and regression techniques
- Understand the concept of clustering and how to use it to automatically segment data
- See how to build an intelligent recommender system
- Understand logic programming and how to use it
- Build automatic speech recognition systems
- Understand the basics of heuristic search and genetic programming
- Develop games using Artificial Intelligence
- Learn how reinforcement learning works
- Discover how to build intelligent applications centered on images, text, and time series data
- See how to use deep learning algorithms and build applications based on it

Leave a review – let other readers know what you think

Please share your thoughts on this book with others by leaving a review on the site that you bought it from. If you purchased the book from Amazon, please leave us an honest review on this book's Amazon page. This is vital so that other potential readers can see and use your unbiased opinion to make purchasing decisions, we can understand what our customers think about our products, and our authors can see your feedback on the title that they have worked with Packt to create. It will only take a few minutes of your time, but is valuable to other potential customers, our authors, and Packt. Thank you!

Index

73826951R00160

Made in the USA
San Bernardino, CA
10 April 2018